STARSHIP TROOPERS™

INTRODUCTION

What you have in your hand is a high-quality collection of the comic-book series that includes those based on my screenplay adaptation for the movie version of Robert Heinlein's science-fiction classic, *Starship Troopers*. This is not intended as a substitute for reading Heinlein's book, and if you have to pass a test on the content of it and all you do is read this, you'll fail. However, if you are stuck and the test begins in five minutes or so, I'll devote the space Dark Horse has graciously provided to a rambling discussion of the novel and talk as little about the movie and this collection as possible.

Starship Troopers is a powerful, perhaps even dangerous, book that taps straight into the heart of that part of the human spirit that relishes the glory of war. The book is the sort of heroic depiction of war that makes the horrors of battle look like a helluva lot of fun, even as you are losing friends and father figures to an insect enemy. You can say this of the movie, too, and in many ways, I think the movie is a sardonic mirror image of Heinlein's serious polemic.

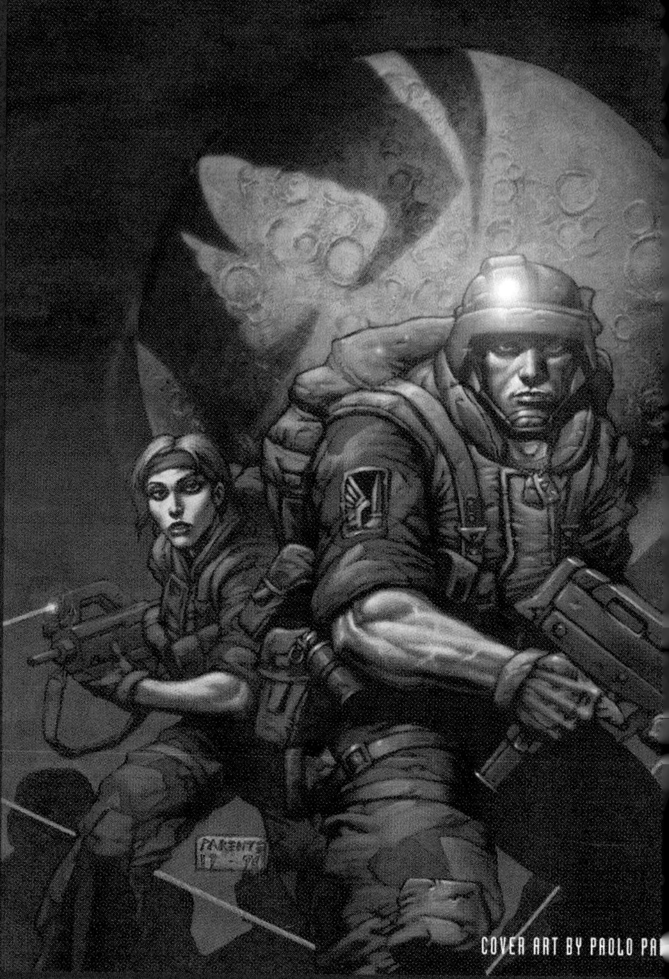
COVER ART BY PAOLO PA

INSECT TOUCH

I read the book three times the summer I was 12. It was a fascinating adventure about guys (not that much older than me) in the future, jumping out of spaceships and fighting alien bugs. I believe I began to think about this as a movie myself, and I hoped one day that I could make movies in Hollywood.

As fate would have it, the next time I read the book I was under contract to write a movie based on it for TriStar Pictures. Imagine my surprise when I discovered that many of my boyhood memories of bugs and combat were in fact my own imaginings! The book contained very little actual description of battles and very little plot. In fact, twenty years later, *Starship Troopers* read like a biting attack on humanists, social scientists, an people who consider themselves liberal.

Anyone who's read the book kno Heinlein has no truck with any of those s ideas. People respond best to military-st justice and corporal punishment, asserts Heinlein. This is a simple lesson every bo who's ever raised a dog learns. A dog ne a smart rap on the nose to keep from soi the carpet. The universe works on a Darwir paradigm, says Heinlein, and so does lif It's all biology in one form or another, fr the housebreaking of a boy's puppy to th explanation of why war must occur betw species and why species must compete fo dominance or die.

What a nightmare idea for our politically correct times: Conflict between

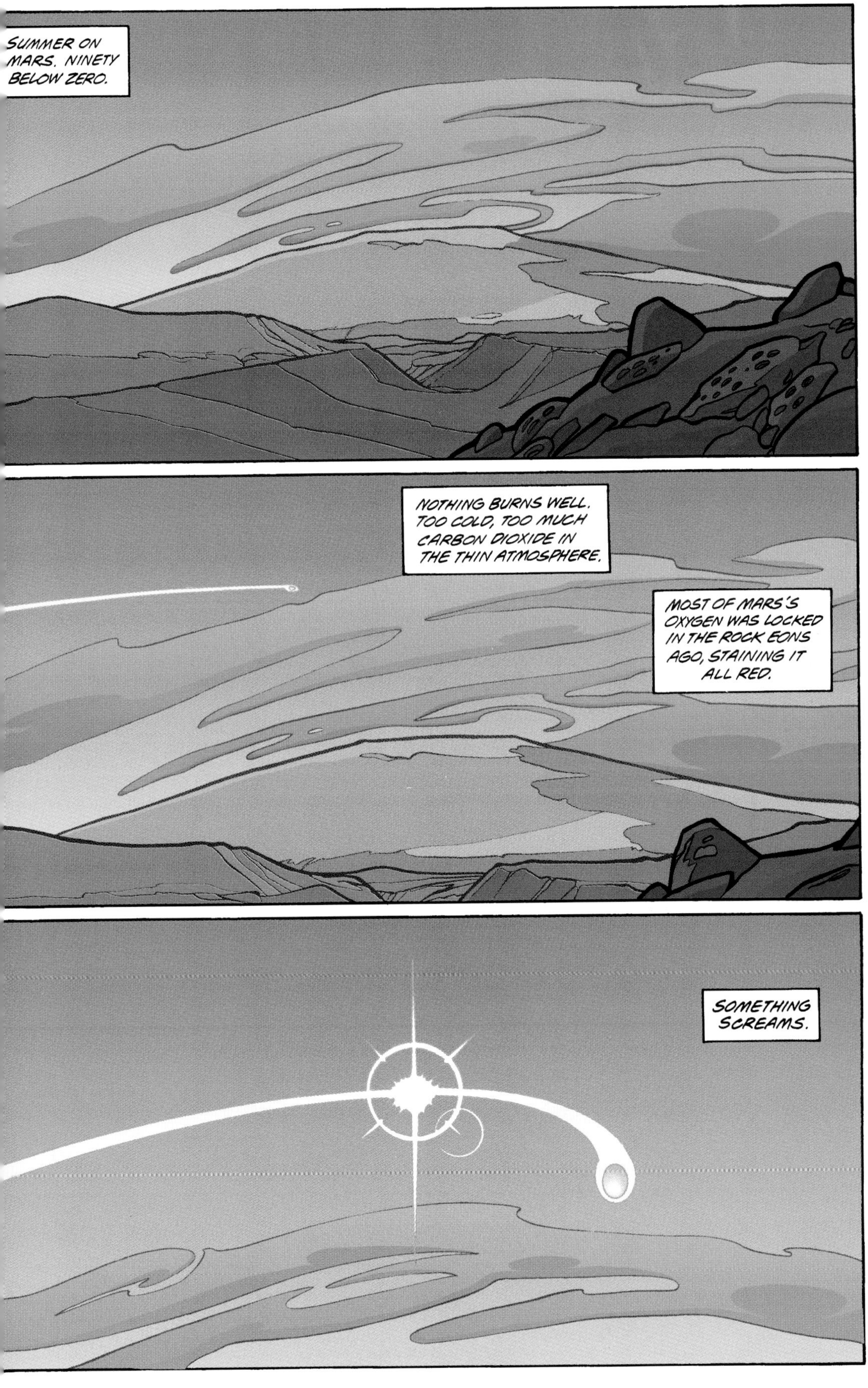
SUMMER ON MARS. NINETY BELOW ZERO.
NOTHING BURNS WELL. TOO COLD, TOO MUCH CARBON DIOXIDE IN THE THIN ATMOSPHERE.
MOST OF MARS'S OXYGEN WAS LOCKED IN THE ROCK EONS AGO, STAINING IT ALL RED.
SOMETHING SCREAMS.

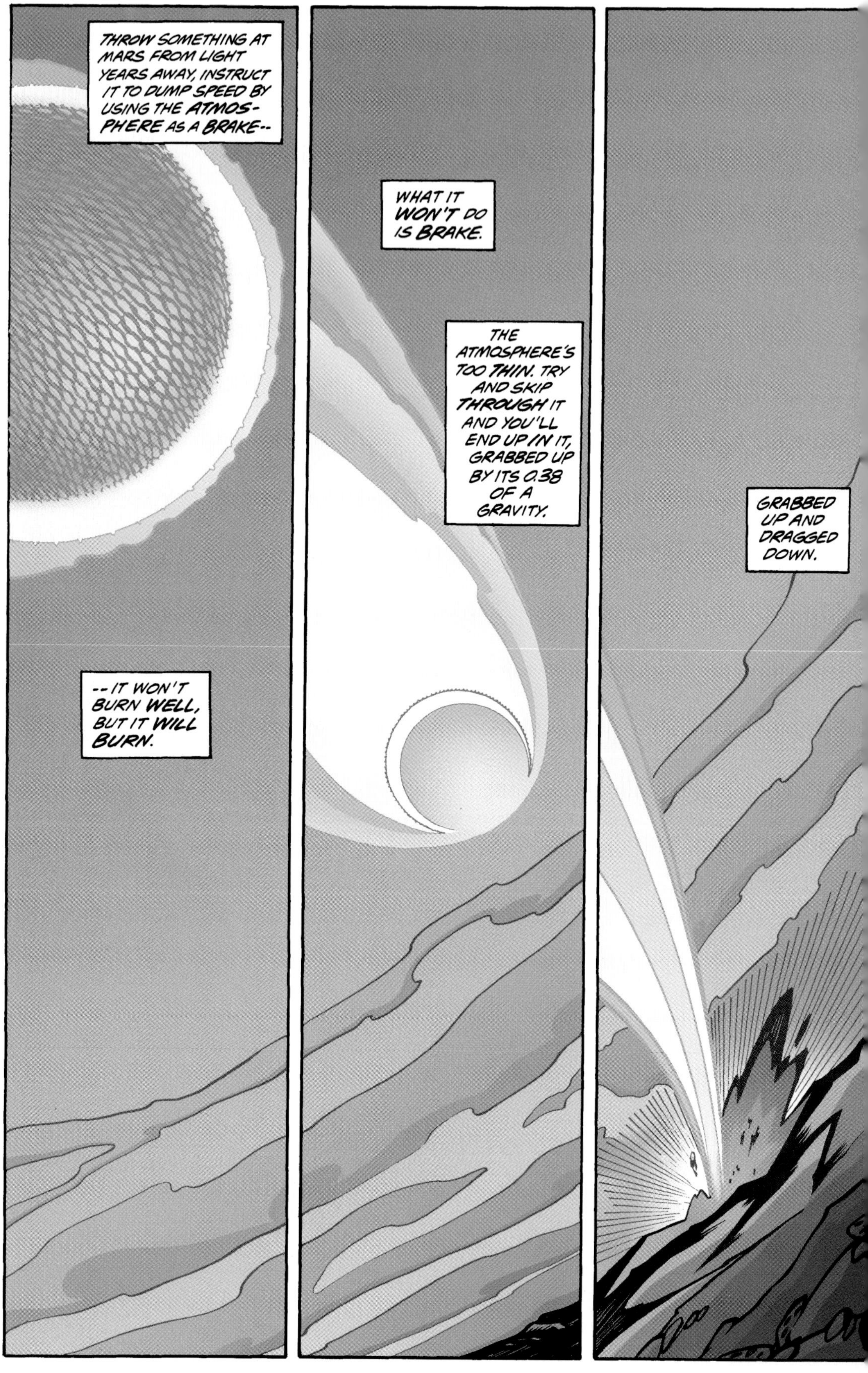
THROW SOMETHING AT MARS FROM LIGHT YEARS AWAY, INSTRUCT IT TO DUMP SPEED BY USING THE ATMOSPHERE AS A BRAKE--
--IT WON'T BURN WELL, BUT IT WILL BURN.
WHAT IT WON'T DO IS BRAKE.
THE ATMOSPHERE'S TOO THIN. TRY AND SKIP THROUGH IT AND YOU'LL END UP IN IT, GRABBED UP BY ITS 0.38 OF A GRAVITY.
GRABBED UP AND DRAGGED DOWN.

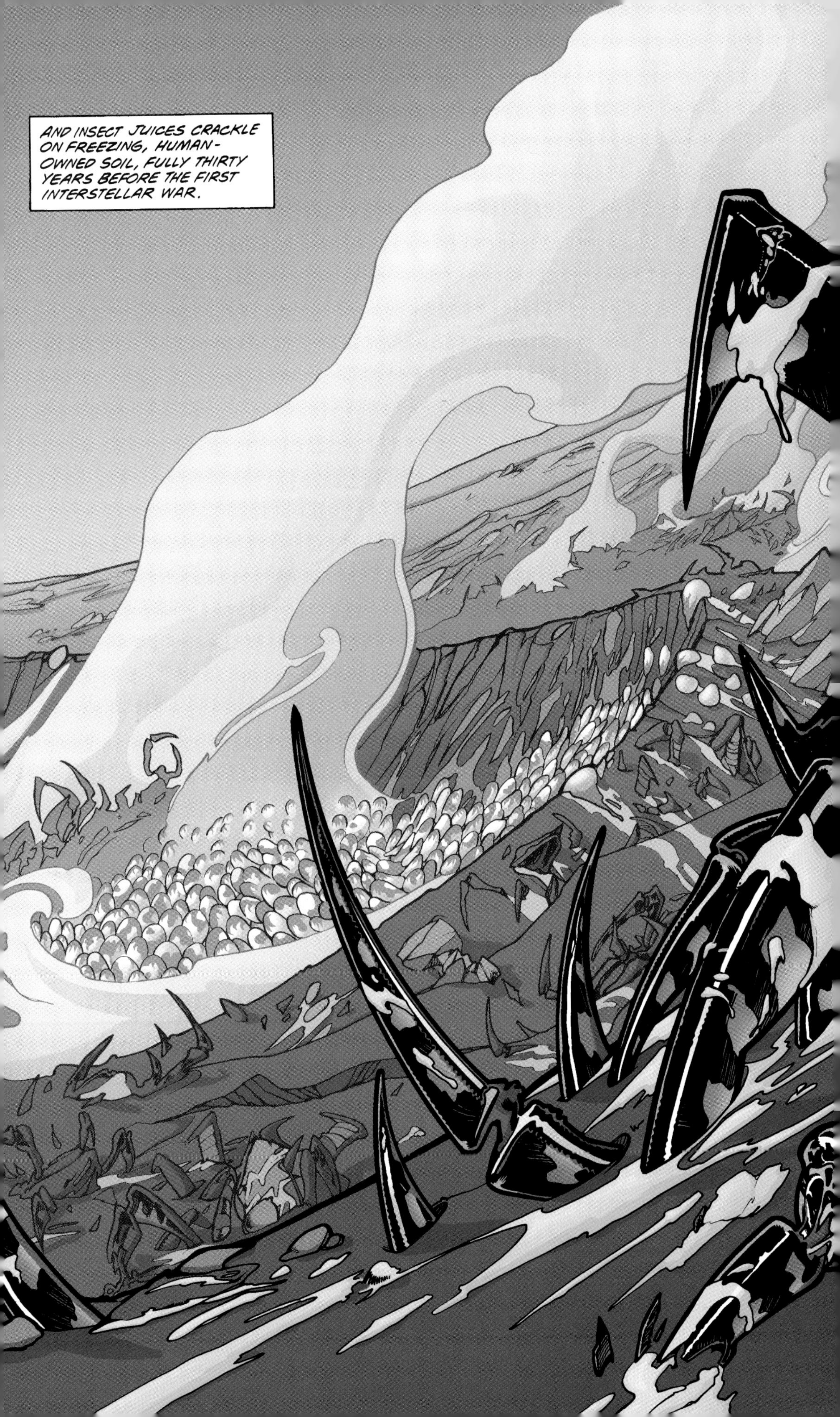
AND INSECT JUICES CRACKLE ON FREEZING, HUMAN-OWNED SOIL, FULLY THIRTY YEARS BEFORE THE FIRST INTERSTELLAR WAR.

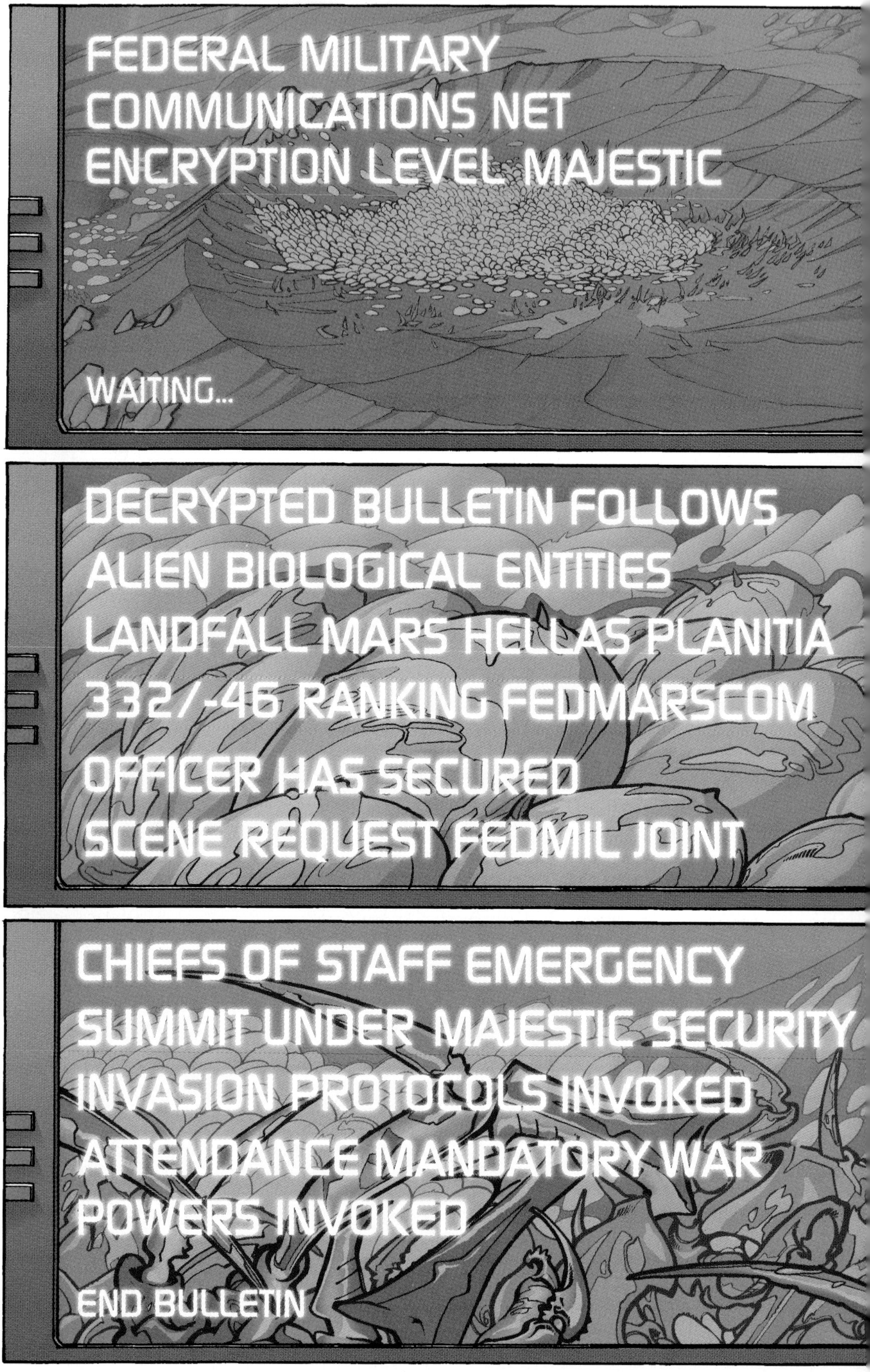
FEDERAL MILITARY COMMUNICATIONS NET ENCRYPTION LEVEL MAJESTIC
WAITING...
DECRYPTED BULLETIN FOLLOWS ALIEN BIOLOGICAL ENTITIES LANDFALL MARS HELLAS PLANITIA 332/-46 RANKING FEDMARSCOM OFFICER HAS SECURED SCENE REQUEST FEDMIL JOINT
CHIEFS OF STAFF EMERGENCY SUMMIT UNDER MAJESTIC SECURITY INVASION PROTOCOLS INVOKED ATTENDANCE MANDATORY WAR POWERS INVOKED
END BULLETIN

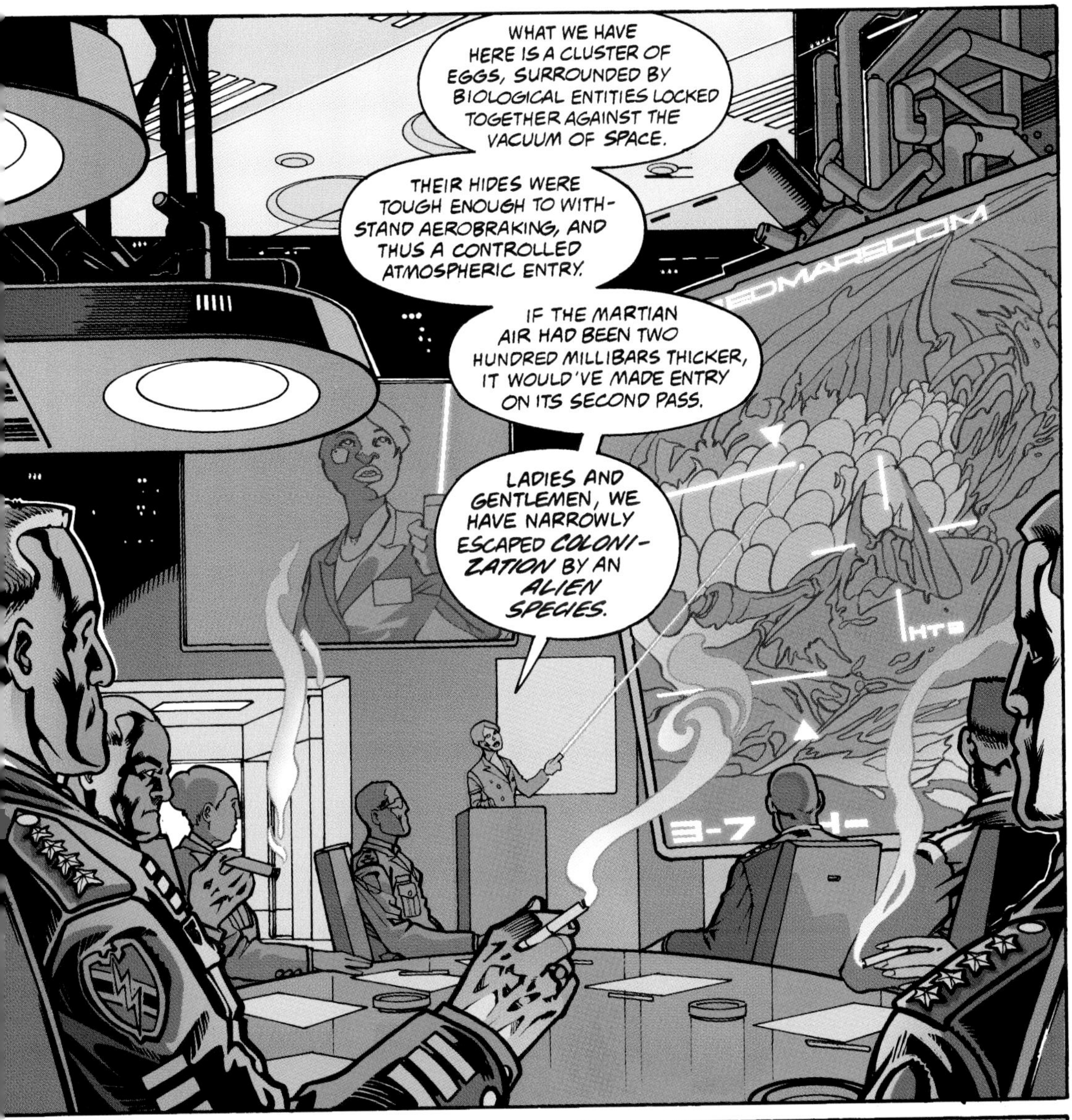
WHAT WE HAVE HERE IS A CLUSTER OF EGGS, SURROUNDED BY BIOLOGICAL ENTITIES LOCKED TOGETHER AGAINST THE VACUUM OF SPACE.
THEIR HIDES WERE TOUGH ENOUGH TO WITH-STAND AEROBRAKING, AND THUS A CONTROLLED ATMOSPHERIC ENTRY.
IF THE MARTIAN AIR HAD BEEN TWO HUNDRED MILLIBARS THICKER, IT WOULD'VE MADE ENTRY ON ITS SECOND PASS.
LADIES AND GENTLEMEN, WE HAVE NARROWLY ESCAPED *COLONI-ZATION* BY AN *ALIEN SPECIES.*

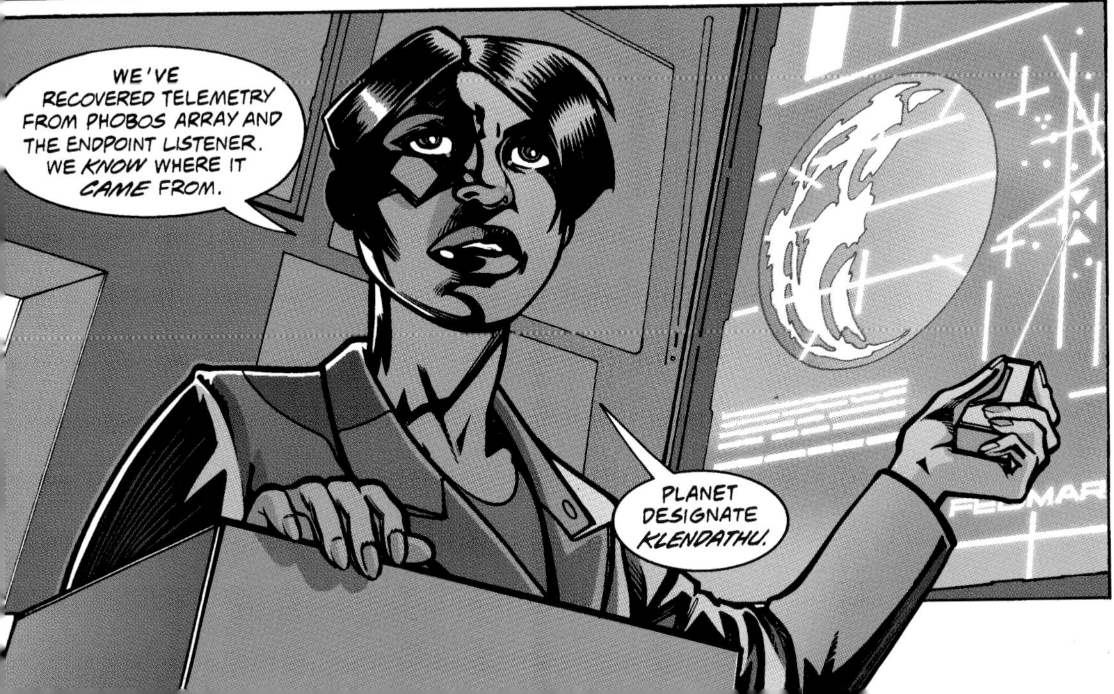
WE'VE RECOVERED TELEMETRY FROM PHOBOS ARRAY AND THE ENDPOINT LISTENER. WE *KNOW* WHERE IT *CAME* FROM.
PLANET DESIGNATE *KLENDATHU.*

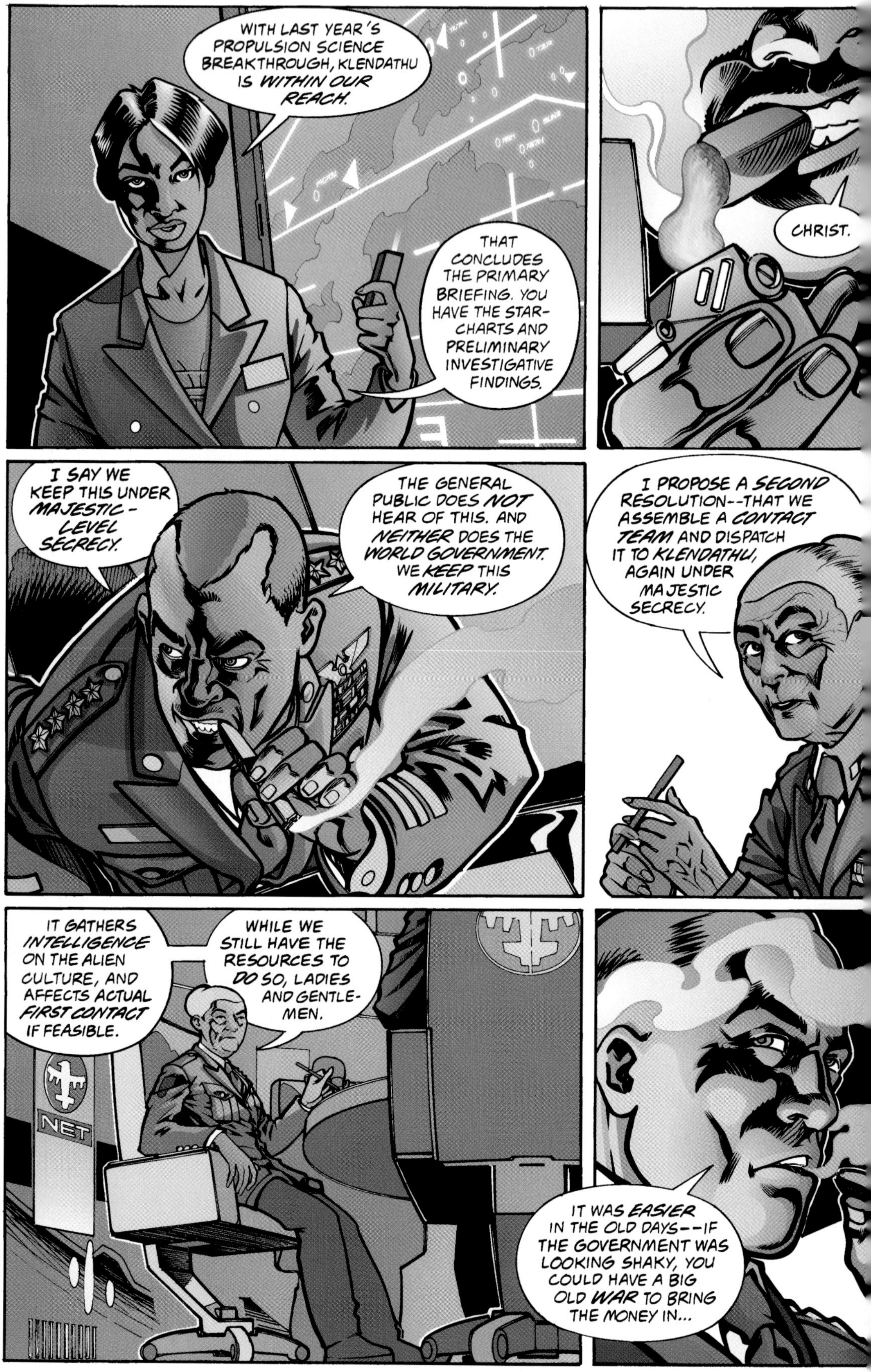
WITH LAST YEAR'S PROPULSION SCIENCE BREAKTHROUGH, KLENDATHU IS WITHIN OUR REACH.
THAT CONCLUDES THE PRIMARY BRIEFING. YOU HAVE THE STAR-CHARTS AND PRELIMINARY INVESTIGATIVE FINDINGS.
CHRIST.
I SAY WE KEEP THIS UNDER MAJESTIC-LEVEL SECRECY.
THE GENERAL PUBLIC DOES NOT HEAR OF THIS. AND NEITHER DOES THE WORLD GOVERNMENT. WE KEEP THIS MILITARY.
I PROPOSE A SECOND RESOLUTION--THAT WE ASSEMBLE A CONTACT TEAM AND DISPATCH IT TO KLENDATHU, AGAIN UNDER MAJESTIC SECRECY.
IT GATHERS INTELLIGENCE ON THE ALIEN CULTURE, AND AFFECTS ACTUAL FIRST CONTACT IF FEASIBLE.
WHILE WE STILL HAVE THE RESOURCES TO DO SO, LADIES AND GENTLE-MEN.
NET
IT WAS EASIER IN THE OLD DAYS--IF THE GOVERNMENT WAS LOOKING SHAKY, YOU COULD HAVE A BIG OLD WAR TO BRING THE MONEY IN...

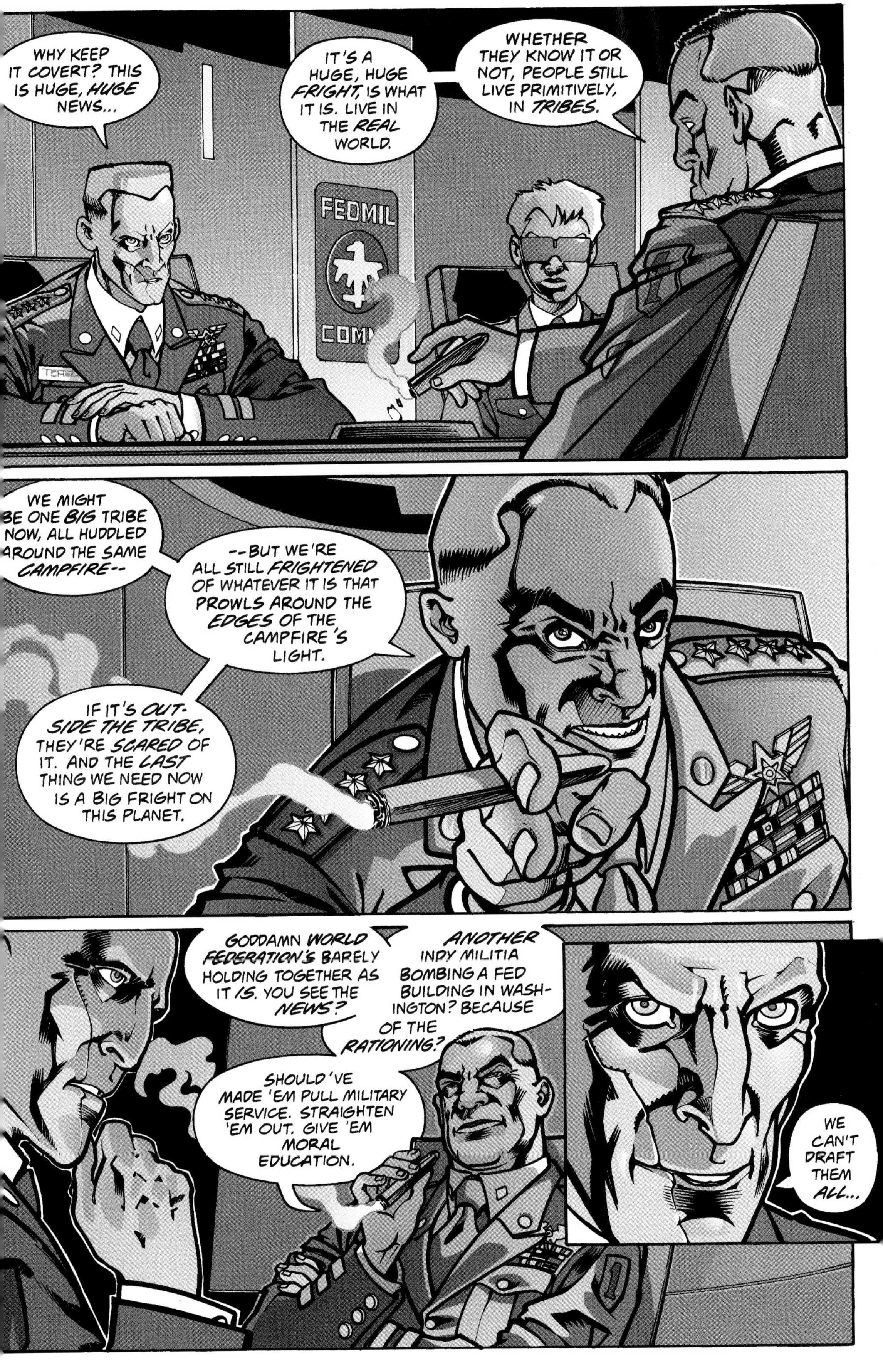
WHY KEEP IT COVERT? THIS IS HUGE, HUGE NEWS...
IT'S A HUGE, HUGE FRIGHT, IS WHAT IT IS. LIVE IN THE REAL WORLD.
WHETHER THEY KNOW IT OR NOT, PEOPLE STILL LIVE PRIMITIVELY, IN TRIBES.
FEDMIL
COM
WE MIGHT BE ONE BIG TRIBE NOW, ALL HUDDLED AROUND THE SAME CAMPFIRE--
--BUT WE'RE ALL STILL FRIGHTENED OF WHATEVER IT IS THAT PROWLS AROUND THE EDGES OF THE CAMPFIRE'S LIGHT.
IF IT'S OUTSIDE THE TRIBE, THEY'RE SCARED OF IT. AND THE LAST THING WE NEED NOW IS A BIG FRIGHT ON THIS PLANET.
GODDAMN WORLD FEDERATION'S BARELY HOLDING TOGETHER AS IT IS. YOU SEE THE NEWS?
ANOTHER INDY MILITIA BOMBING A FED BUILDING IN WASHINGTON? BECAUSE OF THE RATIONING?
SHOULD'VE MADE 'EM PULL MILITARY SERVICE. STRAIGHTEN 'EM OUT. GIVE 'EM MORAL EDUCATION.
WE CAN'T DRAFT THEM ALL...

ONE YEAR LATER.

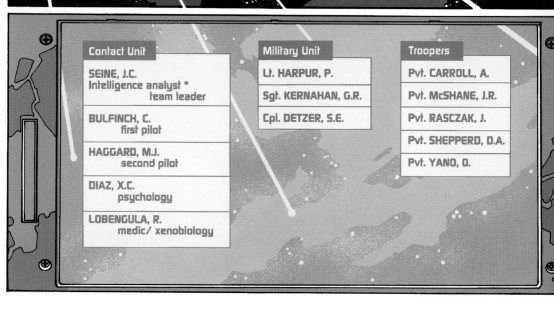

Contact Unit	Military Unit	Troopers
SEINE, J.C. Intelligence analyst * team leader	**Lt. HARPUR, P.**	**Pvt. CARROLL, A.**
BULFINCH, C. first pilot	**Sgt. KERNAHAN, G.R.**	**Pvt. McSHANE, J.R.**
HAGGARD, M.J. second pilot	**Cpl. DETZER, S.E.**	**Pvt. RASCZAK, J.**
DIAZ, X.C. psychology		**Pvt. SHEPPERD, D.A.**
LOBENGULA, R. medic/ xenobiology		**Pvt. YANO, O.**

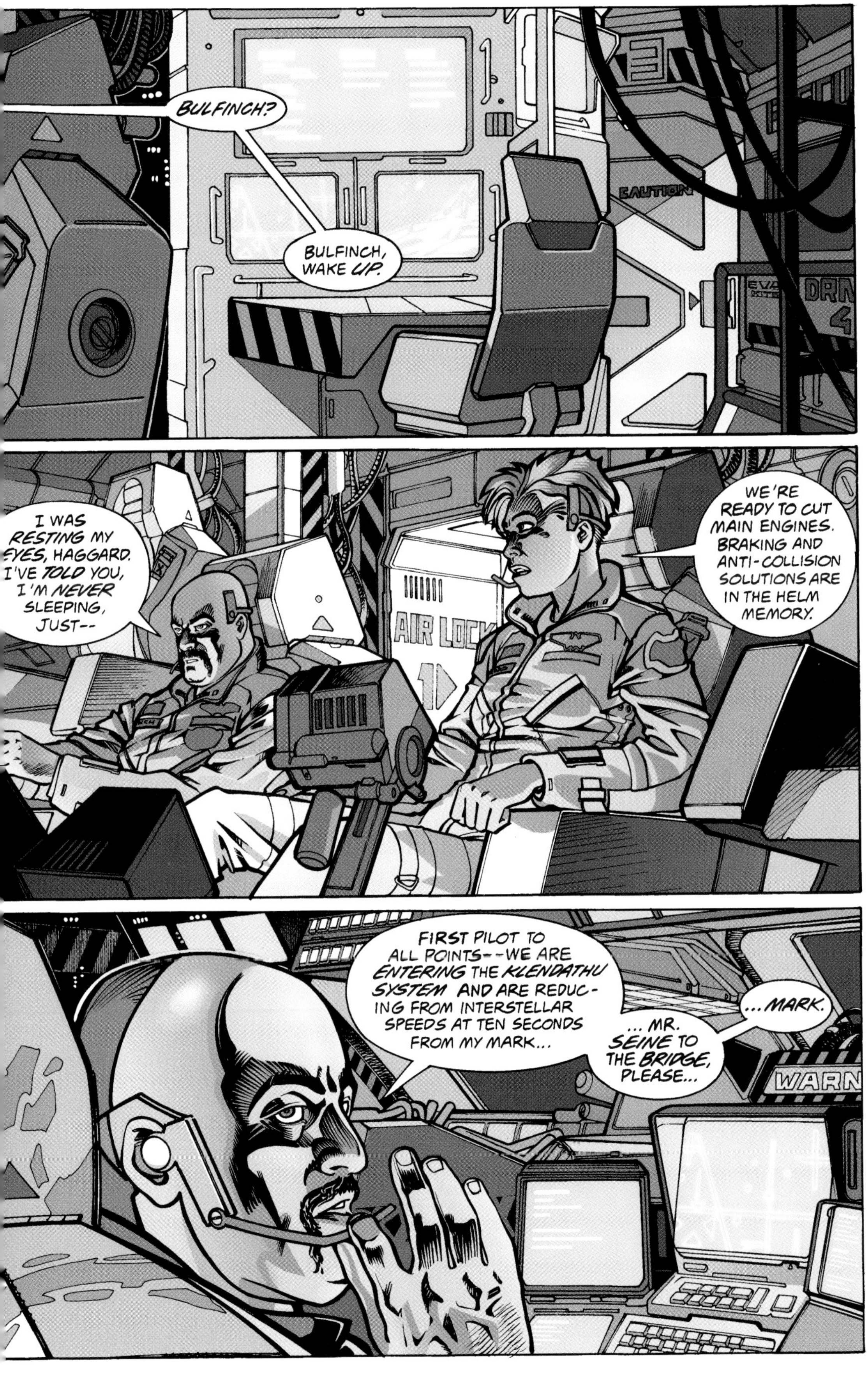
BULFINCH?
BULFINCH, WAKE UP.
CAUTION
EVA KIT
DRN 4
I WAS RESTING MY EYES, HAGGARD. I'VE TOLD YOU, I'M NEVER SLEEPING, JUST--
WE'RE READY TO CUT MAIN ENGINES. BRAKING AND ANTI-COLLISION SOLUTIONS ARE IN THE HELM MEMORY.
AIR LOCK
FIRST PILOT TO ALL POINTS--WE ARE ENTERING THE KLENDATHU SYSTEM AND ARE REDUCING FROM INTERSTELLAR SPEEDS AT TEN SECONDS FROM MY MARK...
... MR. SEINE TO THE BRIDGE, PLEASE...
...MARK.
WARN

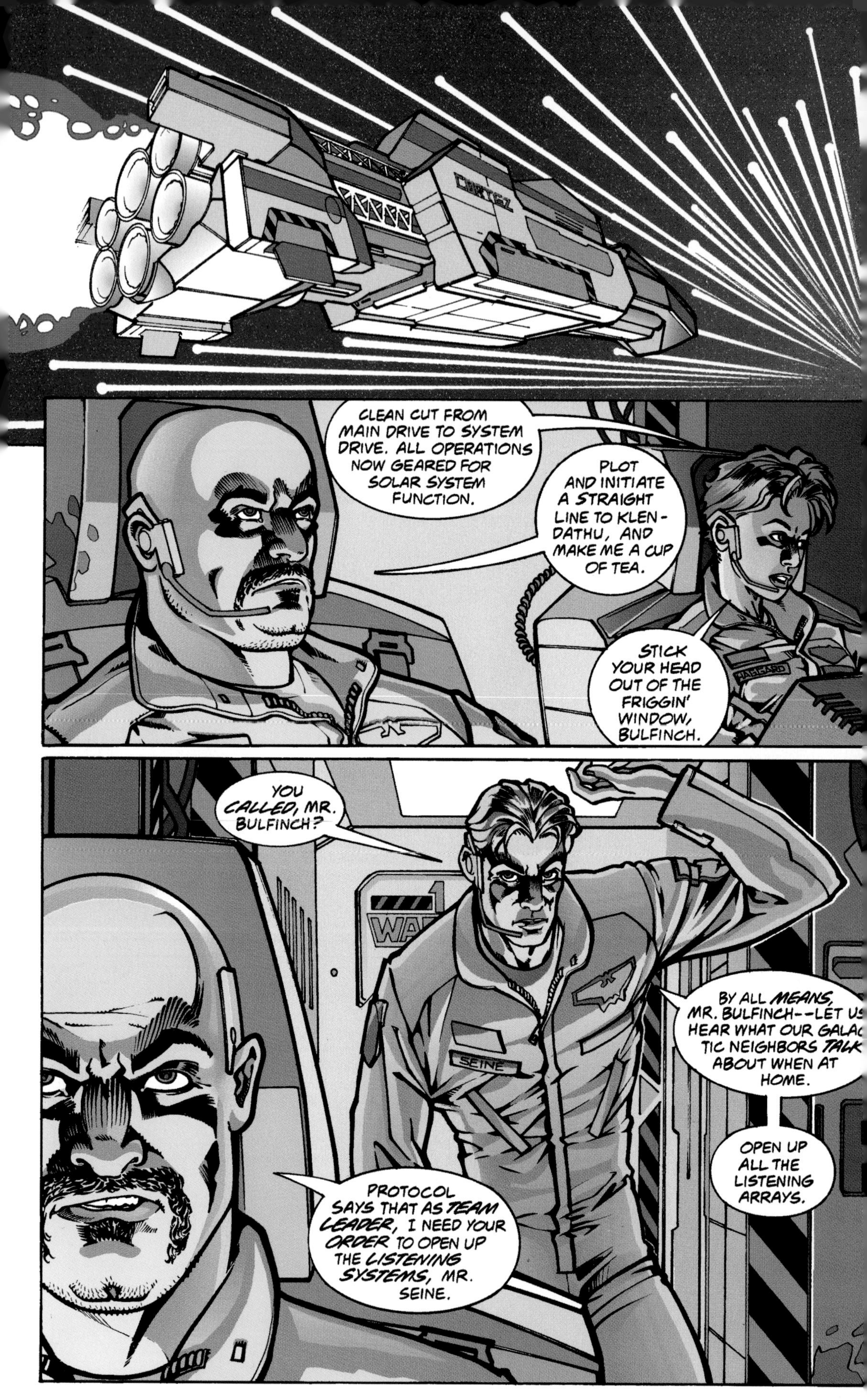

CLEAN CUT FROM MAIN DRIVE TO SYSTEM DRIVE. ALL OPERATIONS NOW GEARED FOR SOLAR SYSTEM FUNCTION.
PLOT AND INITIATE A *STRAIGHT* LINE TO KLEN-DATHU, AND MAKE ME A CUP OF TEA.
STICK YOUR HEAD OUT OF THE FRIGGIN' WINDOW, BULFINCH.
HAGGARD
YOU *CALLED*, MR. BULFINCH?
SEINE
PROTOCOL SAYS THAT AS *TEAM LEADER*, I NEED YOUR *ORDER* TO OPEN UP THE *LISTENING SYSTEMS*, MR. SEINE.
BY ALL *MEANS*, MR. BULFINCH--LET US HEAR WHAT OUR GALAC TIC NEIGHBORS *TALK* ABOUT WHEN AT HOME.
OPEN UP ALL THE LISTENING ARRAYS.

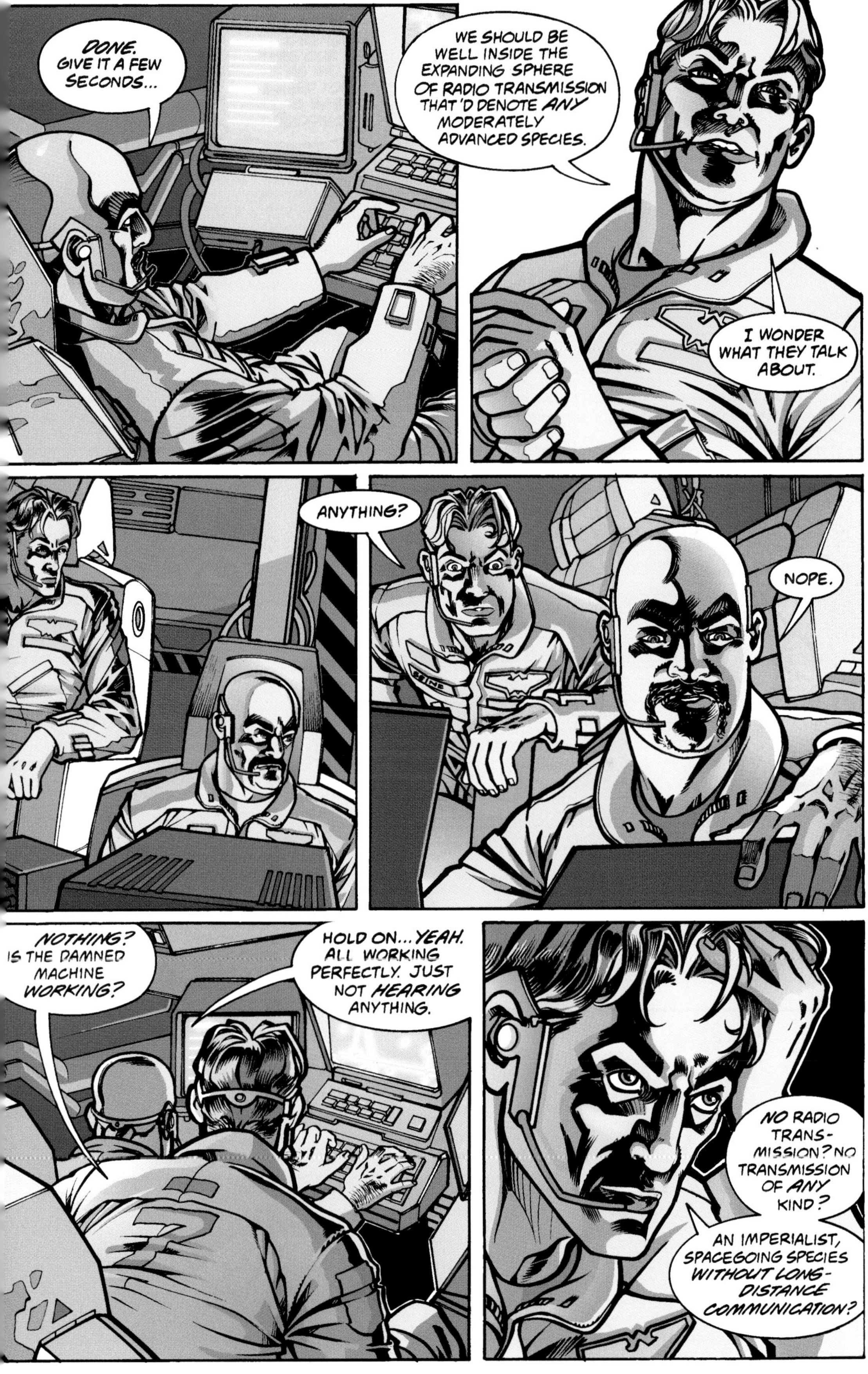
DONE. GIVE IT A FEW SECONDS...
WE SHOULD BE WELL INSIDE THE EXPANDING SPHERE OF RADIO TRANSMISSION THAT'D DENOTE ANY MODERATELY ADVANCED SPECIES.
I WONDER WHAT THEY TALK ABOUT.
ANYTHING?
NOPE.
NOTHING? IS THE DAMNED MACHINE WORKING?
HOLD ON... YEAH. ALL WORKING PERFECTLY. JUST NOT HEARING ANYTHING.
NO RADIO TRANS-MISSION? NO TRANSMISSION OF ANY KIND?
AN IMPERIALIST, SPACEGOING SPECIES WITHOUT LONG-DISTANCE COMMUNICATION?

DIAZ? COME *IN* HERE.

TIME FOR YOUR FIRST *PSYCHOLOGICAL* PROFILE.

THE ALIEN HAVE NO LOT RANGE COM- MUNICATIO *THEORIE*

WHAT'S UP? DID HAGGARD FINALLY KILL BULFINCH? OR DID SHE ACTUALLY CRACK AND MAKE SOME TEA?

HM.

TWO POSSIBILITIES-- A CIVILIZATION *SO* STRICT AND INFLEXIBLE THAT COMMUNICATION, EXCEPT IN CLOSE RANGE, IS *DISALLOWED?*

SO, *WHAT?* THEY COLONIZE A WORLD AND NEVER SPEAK TO THEIR COLONISTS *AGAIN?*

I'M BRINGING UP THE *BUFFER* GENERATORS... DENSE SPACE AHEAD...

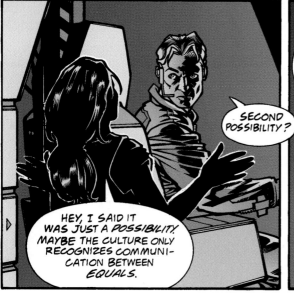

SECOND POSSIBILITY?

HEY, I SAID IT WAS JUST A *POSSIBILITY.* MAYBE THE CULTURE ONLY RECOGNIZES COMMUNI- CATION BETWEEN *EQUALS.*

THERE'S NOBODY *ON* KLENDATHU AND WE'VE COME A VERY LONG WAY FOR *NOTHING.*

HEY, YOU *ASKED.*

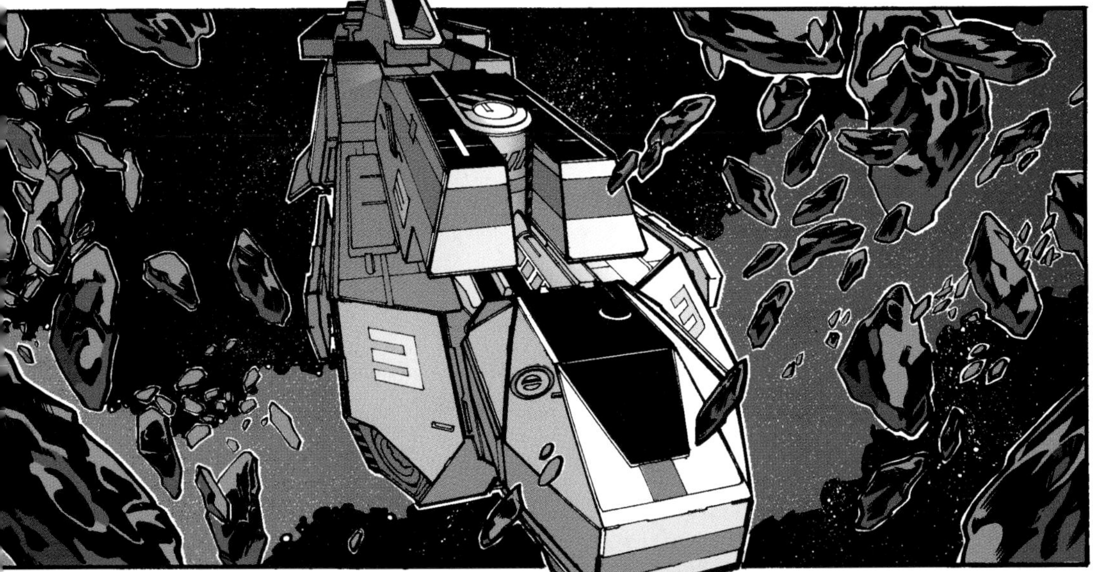

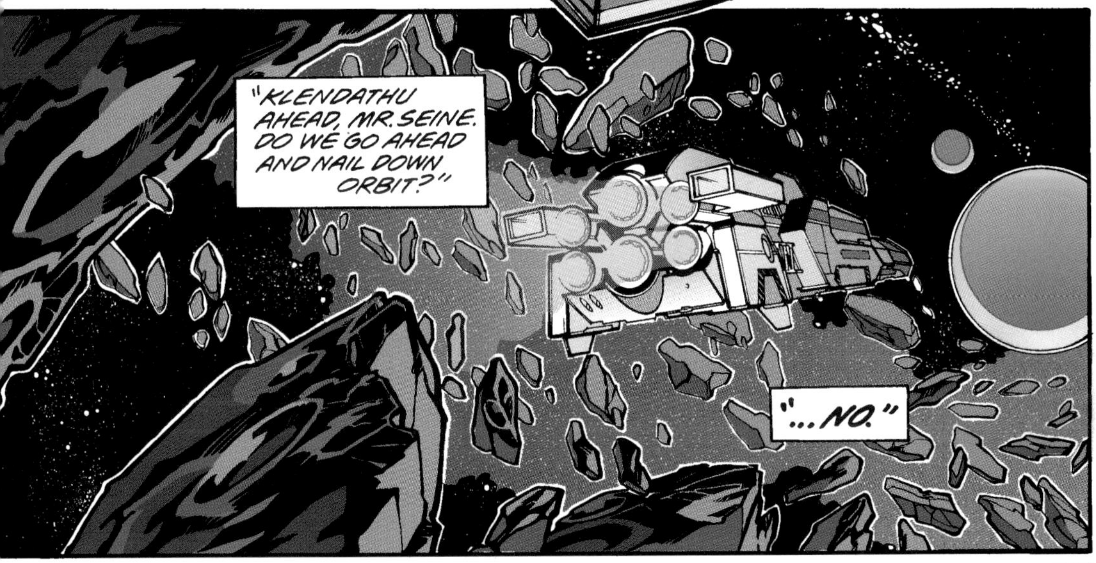
"KLENDATHU AHEAD, MR. SEINE. DO WE GO AHEAD AND NAIL DOWN ORBIT?"
"...NO."

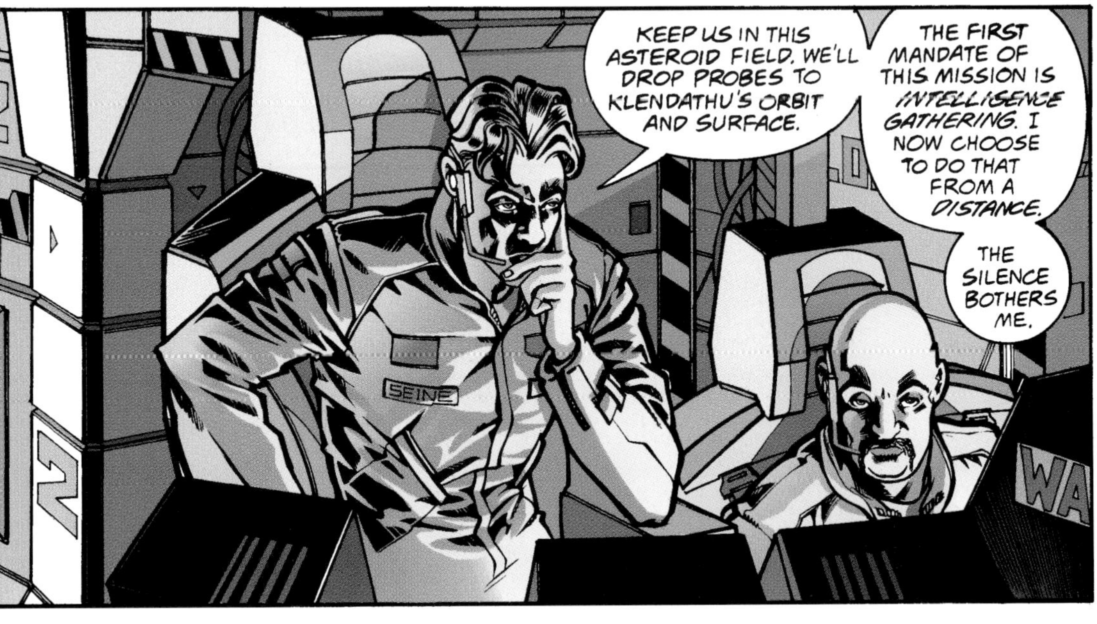
KEEP US IN THIS ASTEROID FIELD. WE'LL DROP PROBES TO KLENDATHU'S ORBIT AND SURFACE.
THE FIRST MANDATE OF THIS MISSION IS INTELLIGENCE GATHERING. I NOW CHOOSE TO DO THAT FROM A DISTANCE.
THE SILENCE BOTHERS ME.
SEINE

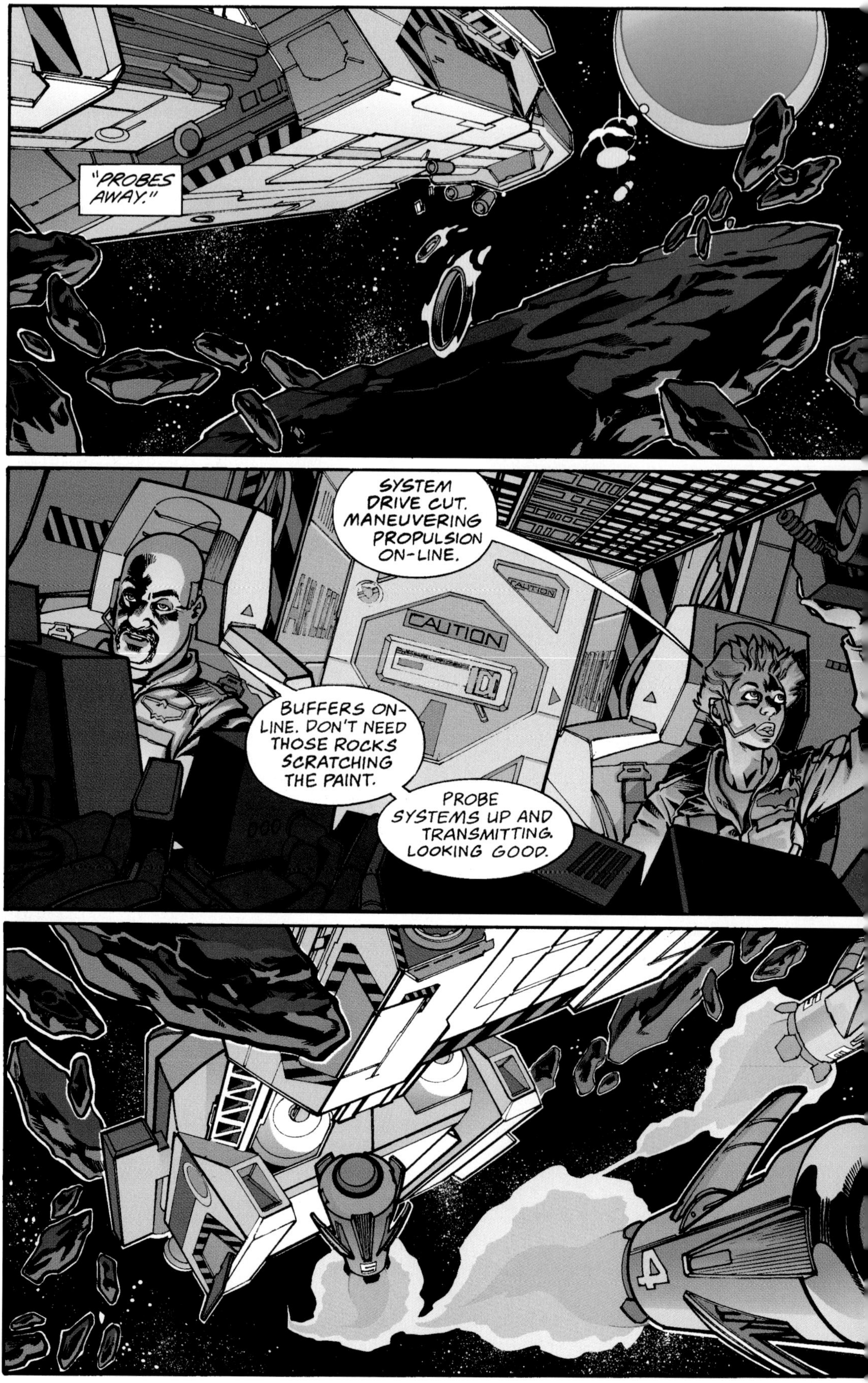
"PROBES AWAY."
SYSTEM DRIVE CUT. MANEUVERING PROPULSION ON-LINE.
CAUTION
CAUTION
BUFFERS ON-LINE. DON'T NEED THOSE ROCKS SCRATCHING THE PAINT.
PROBE SYSTEMS UP AND TRANSMITTING. LOOKING GOOD.

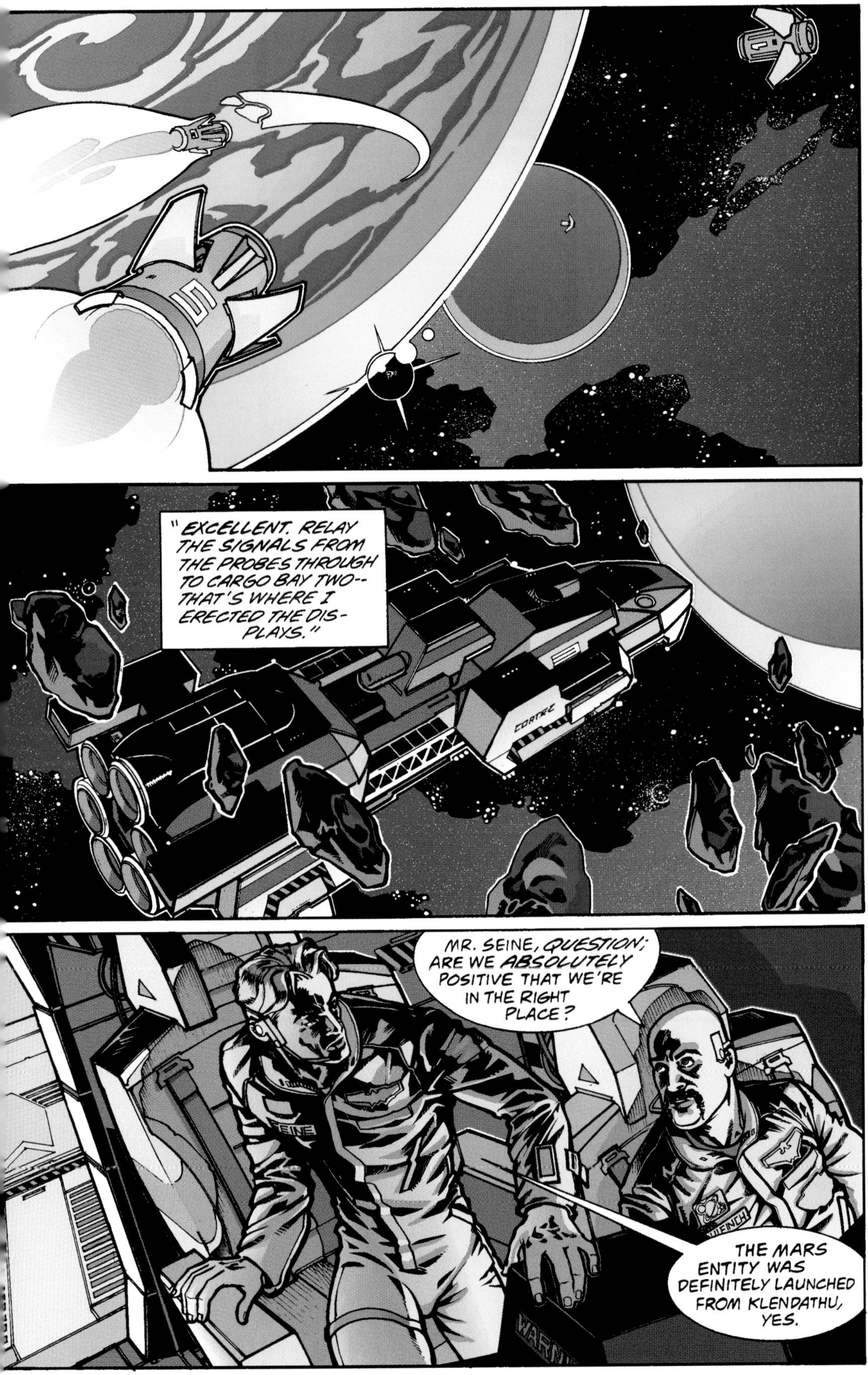
"EXCELLENT. RELAY THE SIGNALS FROM THE PROBES THROUGH TO CARGO BAY TWO-- THAT'S WHERE I ERECTED THE DIS-PLAYS."
CORTEZ
MR. SEINE, QUESTION; ARE WE ABSOLUTELY POSITIVE THAT WE'RE IN THE RIGHT PLACE?
SEINE
THE MARS ENTITY WAS DEFINITELY LAUNCHED FROM KLENDATHU, YES.

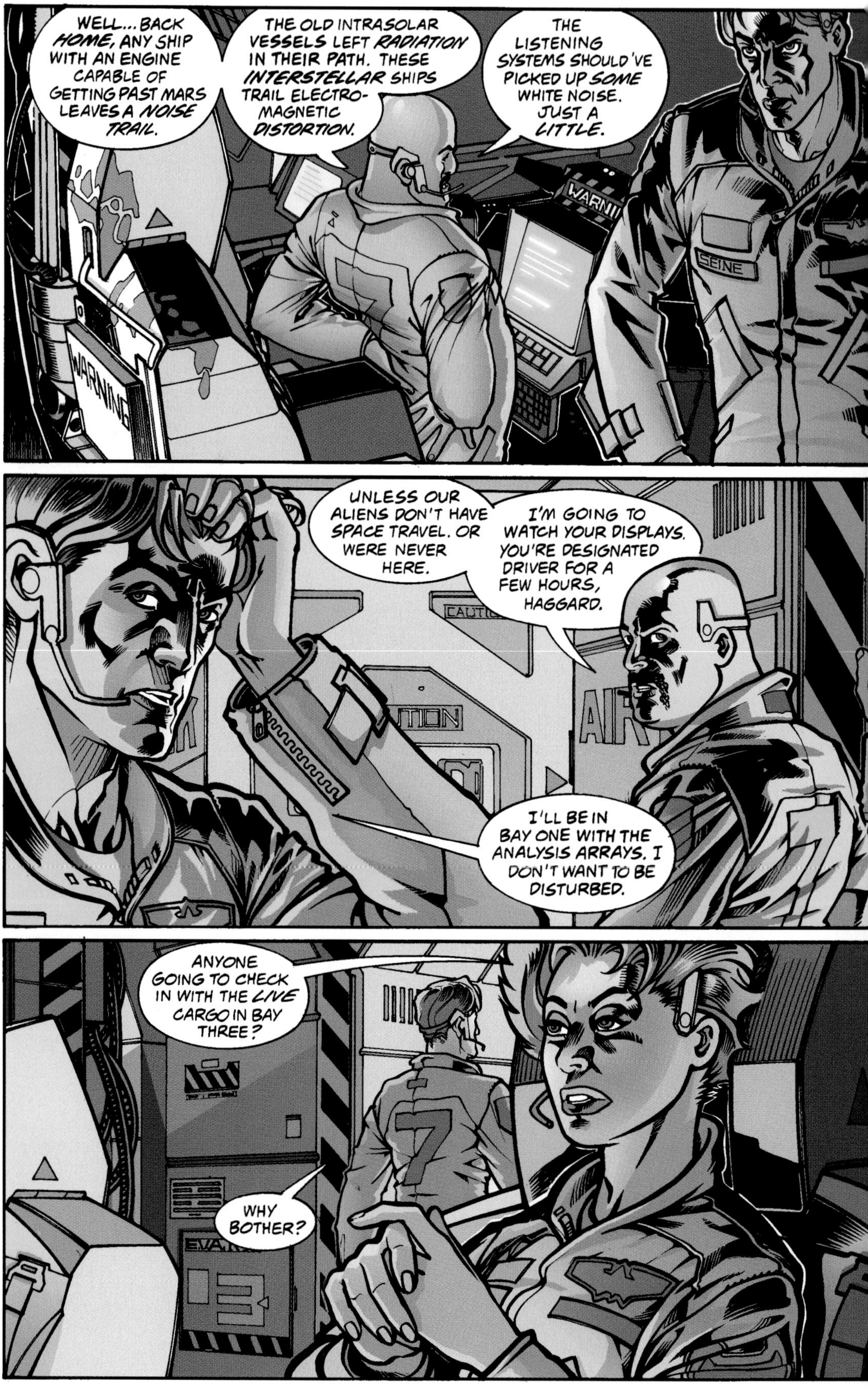
WELL... BACK HOME, ANY SHIP WITH AN ENGINE CAPABLE OF GETTING PAST MARS LEAVES A NOISE TRAIL.
THE OLD INTRASOLAR VESSELS LEFT RADIATION IN THEIR PATH. THESE INTERSTELLAR SHIPS TRAIL ELECTRO-MAGNETIC DISTORTION.
THE LISTENING SYSTEMS SHOULD'VE PICKED UP SOME WHITE NOISE. JUST A LITTLE.
WARNING
SEINE
UNLESS OUR ALIENS DON'T HAVE SPACE TRAVEL. OR WERE NEVER HERE.
I'M GOING TO WATCH YOUR DISPLAYS. YOU'RE DESIGNATED DRIVER FOR A FEW HOURS, HAGGARD.
I'LL BE IN BAY ONE WITH THE ANALYSIS ARRAYS. I DON'T WANT TO BE DISTURBED.
ANYONE GOING TO CHECK IN WITH THE LIVE CARGO IN BAY THREE?
WHY BOTHER?

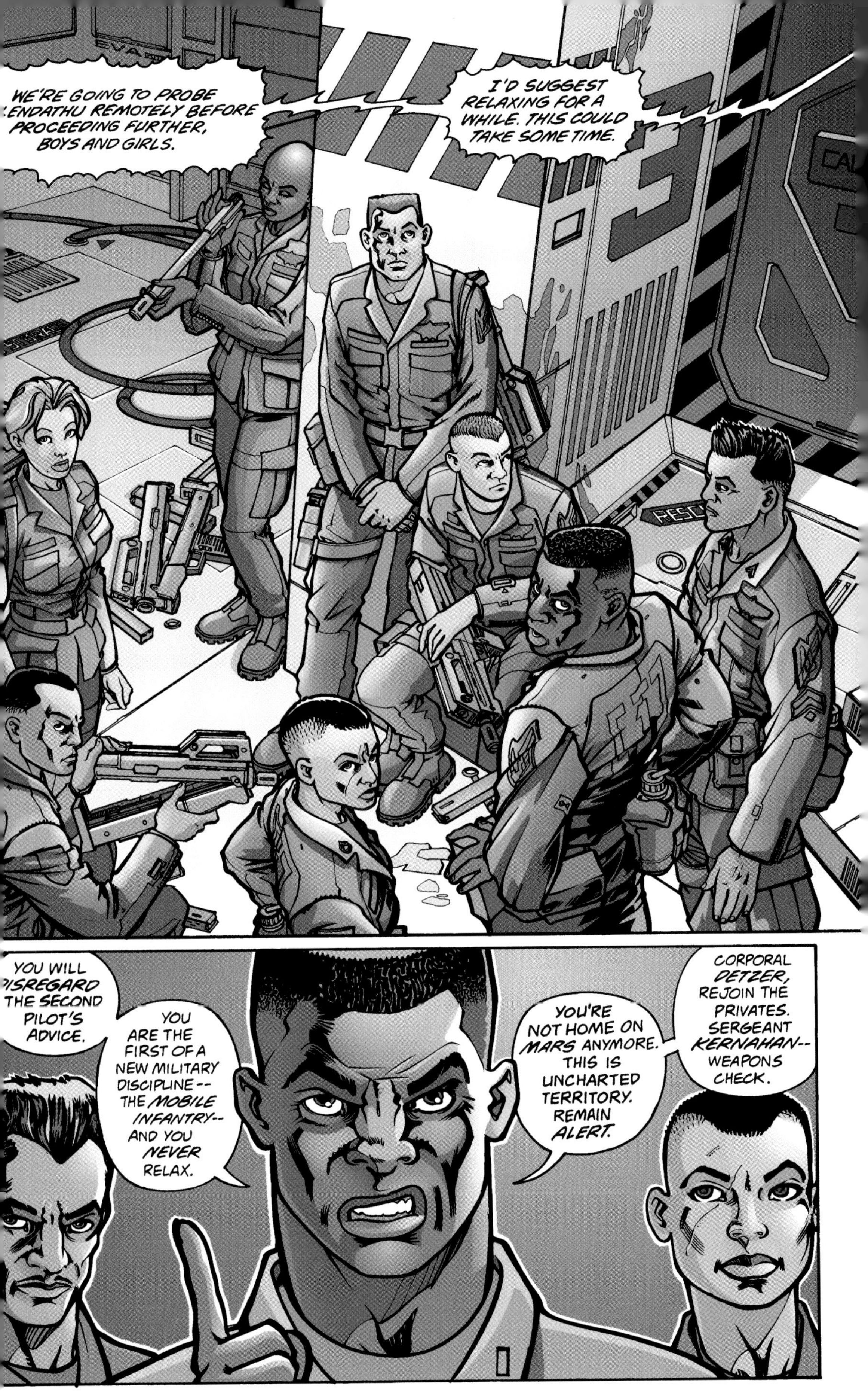
WE'RE GOING TO PROBE KENDATHU REMOTELY BEFORE PROCEEDING FURTHER, BOYS AND GIRLS.
I'D SUGGEST RELAXING FOR A WHILE. THIS COULD TAKE SOME TIME.
YOU WILL DISREGARD THE SECOND PILOT'S ADVICE.
YOU ARE THE FIRST OF A NEW MILITARY DISCIPLINE -- THE MOBILE INFANTRY -- AND YOU NEVER RELAX.
YOU'RE NOT HOME ON MARS ANYMORE. THIS IS UNCHARTED TERRITORY. REMAIN ALERT.
CORPORAL DETZER, REJOIN THE PRIVATES. SERGEANT KERNAHAN -- WEAPONS CHECK.

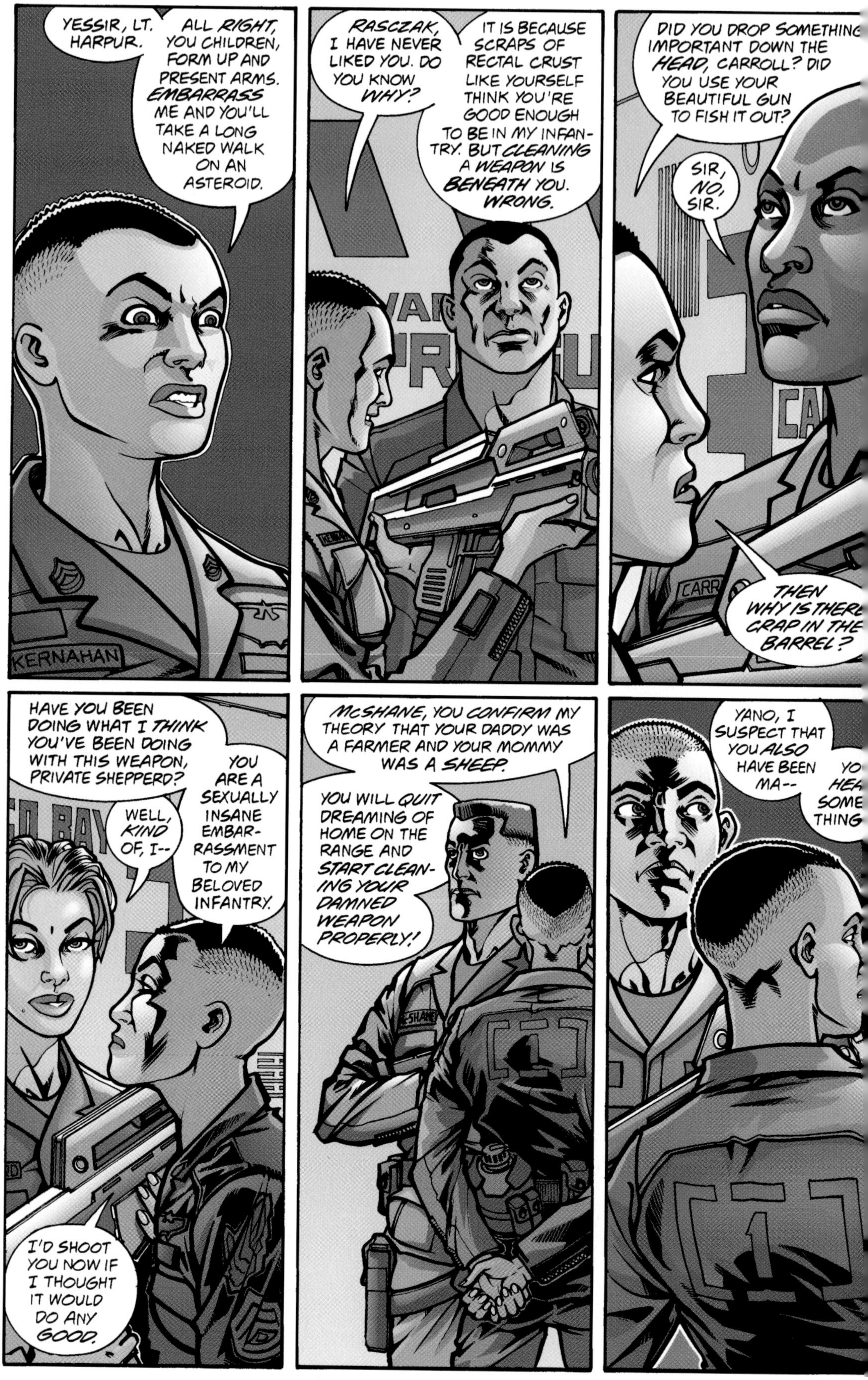
YESSIR, LT. HARPUR.
ALL RIGHT, YOU CHILDREN, FORM UP AND PRESENT ARMS. EMBARRASS ME AND YOU'LL TAKE A LONG NAKED WALK ON AN ASTEROID.
KERNAHAN
RASCZAK, I HAVE NEVER LIKED YOU. DO YOU KNOW WHY?
IT IS BECAUSE SCRAPS OF RECTAL CRUST LIKE YOURSELF THINK YOU'RE GOOD ENOUGH TO BE IN MY INFANTRY. BUT CLEANING A WEAPON IS BENEATH YOU. WRONG.
DID YOU DROP SOMETHING IMPORTANT DOWN THE HEAD, CARROLL? DID YOU USE YOUR BEAUTIFUL GUN TO FISH IT OUT?
SIR, NO, SIR.
THEN WHY IS THERE CRAP IN THE BARREL?
HAVE YOU BEEN DOING WHAT I THINK YOU'VE BEEN DOING WITH THIS WEAPON, PRIVATE SHEPPERD?
WELL, KIND OF, I--
YOU ARE A SEXUALLY INSANE EMBARRASSMENT TO MY BELOVED INFANTRY.
I'D SHOOT YOU NOW IF I THOUGHT IT WOULD DO ANY GOOD.
McSHANE, YOU CONFIRM MY THEORY THAT YOUR DADDY WAS A FARMER AND YOUR MOMMY WAS A SHEEP.
YOU WILL QUIT DREAMING OF HOME ON THE RANGE AND START CLEANING YOUR DAMNED WEAPON PROPERLY!
YANO, I SUSPECT THAT YOU ALSO HAVE BEEN MA--

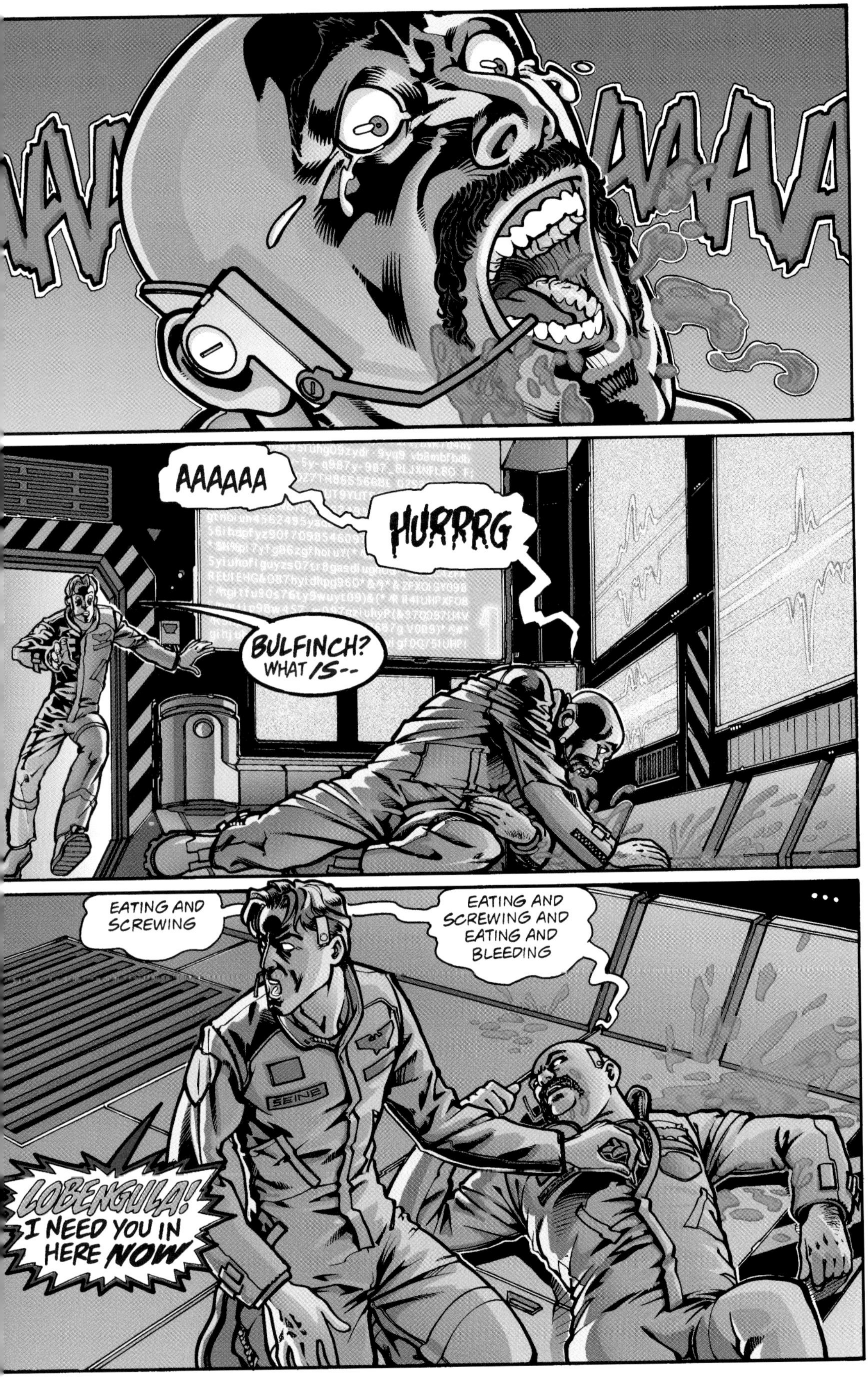
AAAAAAAAA
AAAAAA
HURRRG
BULFINCH? WHAT IS--
EATING AND SCREWING
EATING AND SCREWING AND EATING AND BLEEDING
LOBENGULA! I NEED YOU IN HERE NOW

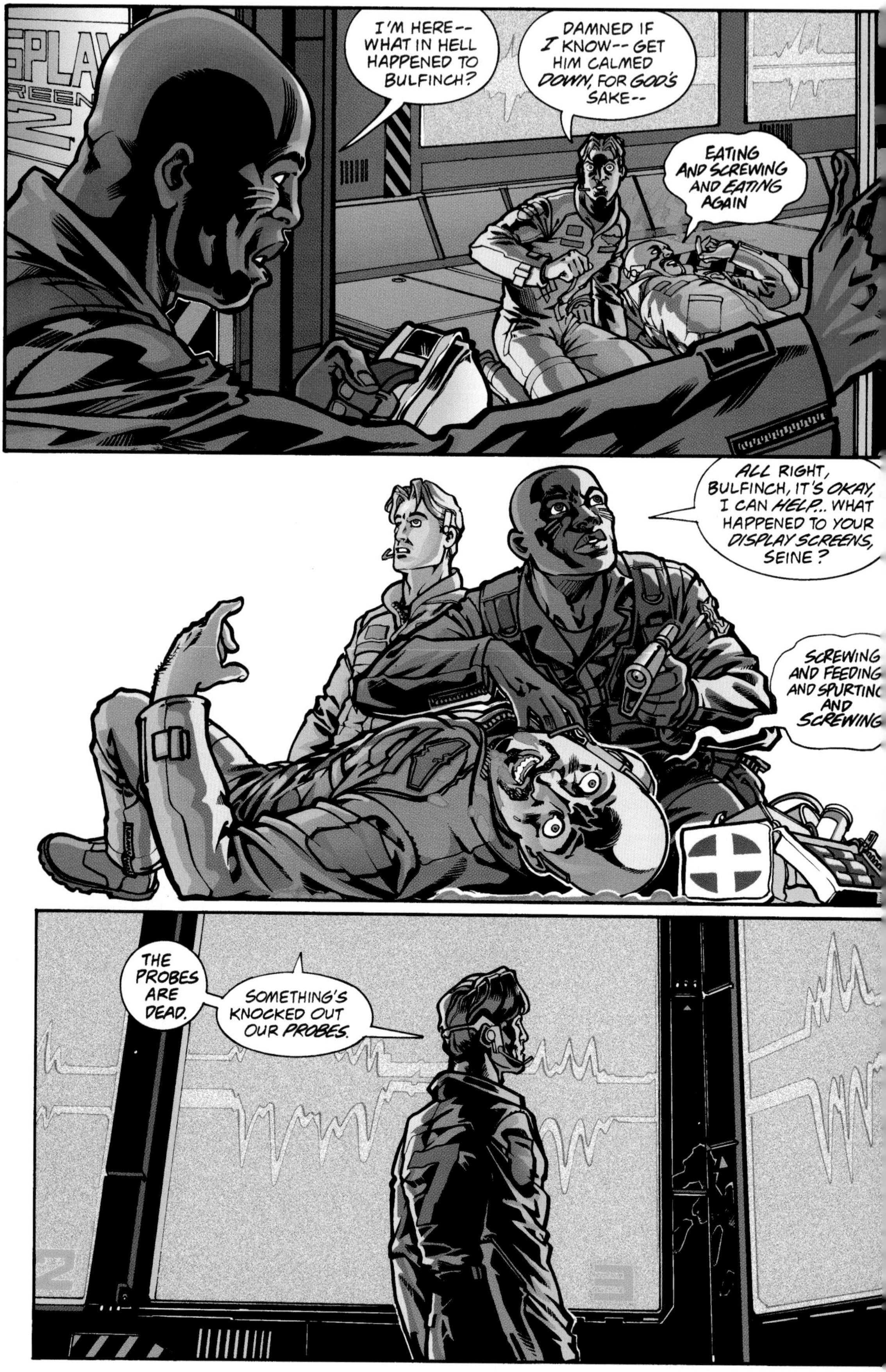
I'M HERE-- WHAT IN HELL HAPPENED TO BULFINCH?
DAMNED IF I KNOW-- GET HIM CALMED DOWN, FOR GOD'S SAKE--
EATING AND SCREWING AND EATING AGAIN
ALL RIGHT, BULFINCH, IT'S OKAY, I CAN HELP... WHAT HAPPENED TO YOUR DISPLAY SCREENS, SEINE?
SCREWING AND FEEDING AND SPURTIN AND SCREWING
THE PROBES ARE DEAD.
SOMETHING'S KNOCKED OUT OUR PROBES.

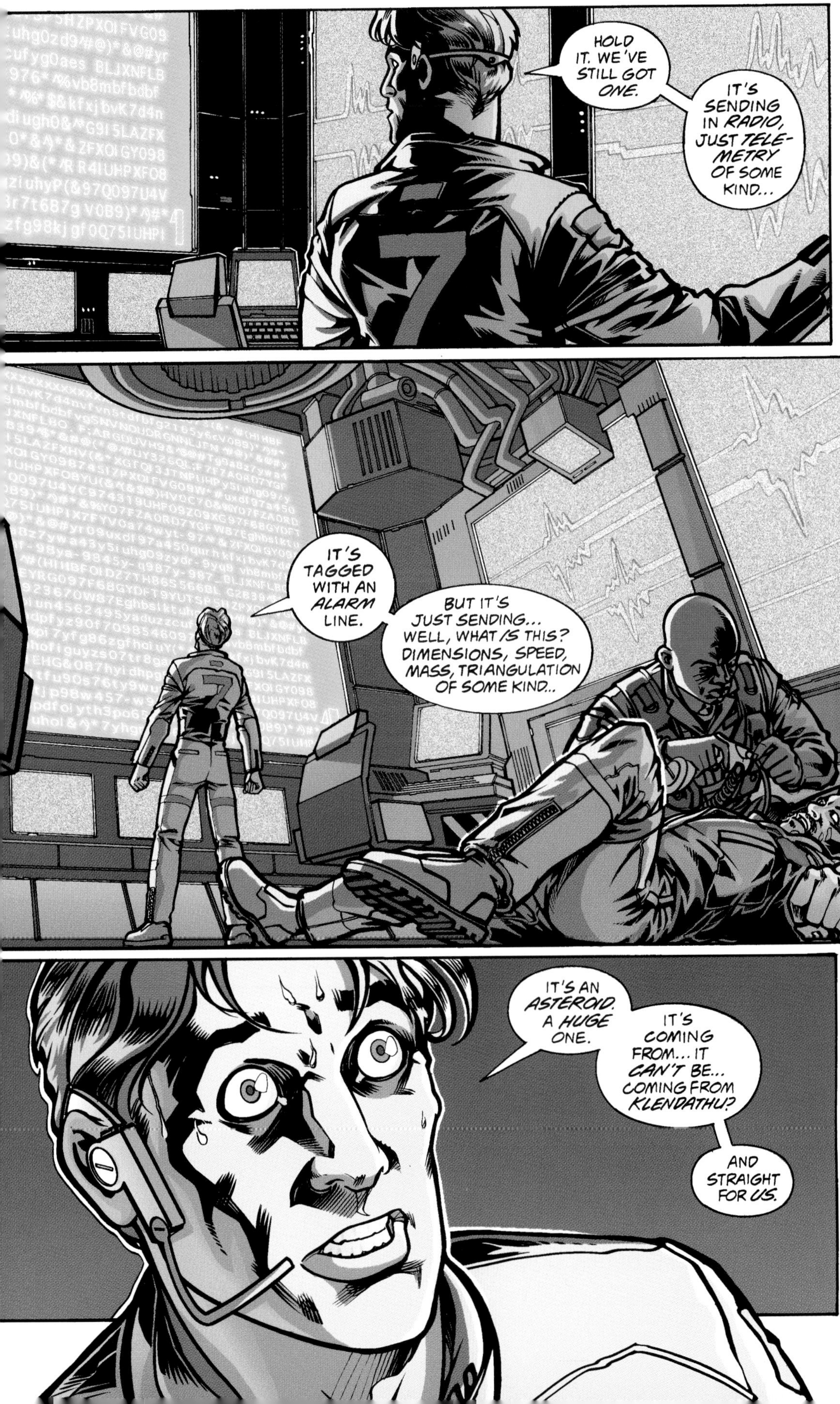
HOLD IT. WE'VE STILL GOT ONE.
IT'S SENDING IN RADIO, JUST TELEMETRY OF SOME KIND...
IT'S TAGGED WITH AN ALARM LINE.
BUT IT'S JUST SENDING... WELL, WHAT IS THIS? DIMENSIONS, SPEED, MASS, TRIANGULATION OF SOME KIND...
IT'S AN ASTEROID. A HUGE ONE.
IT'S COMING FROM... IT CAN'T BE... COMING FROM KLENDATHU?
AND STRAIGHT FOR US.

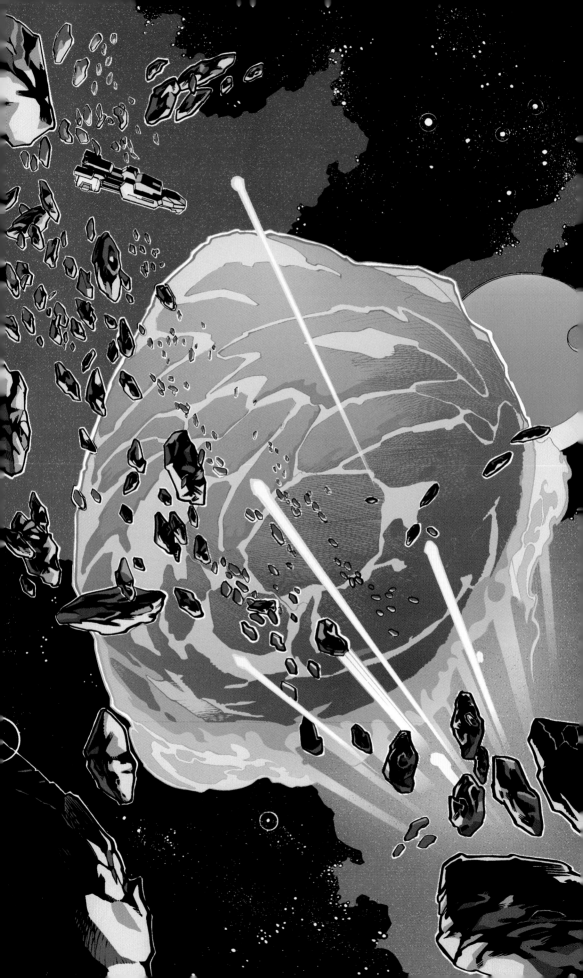

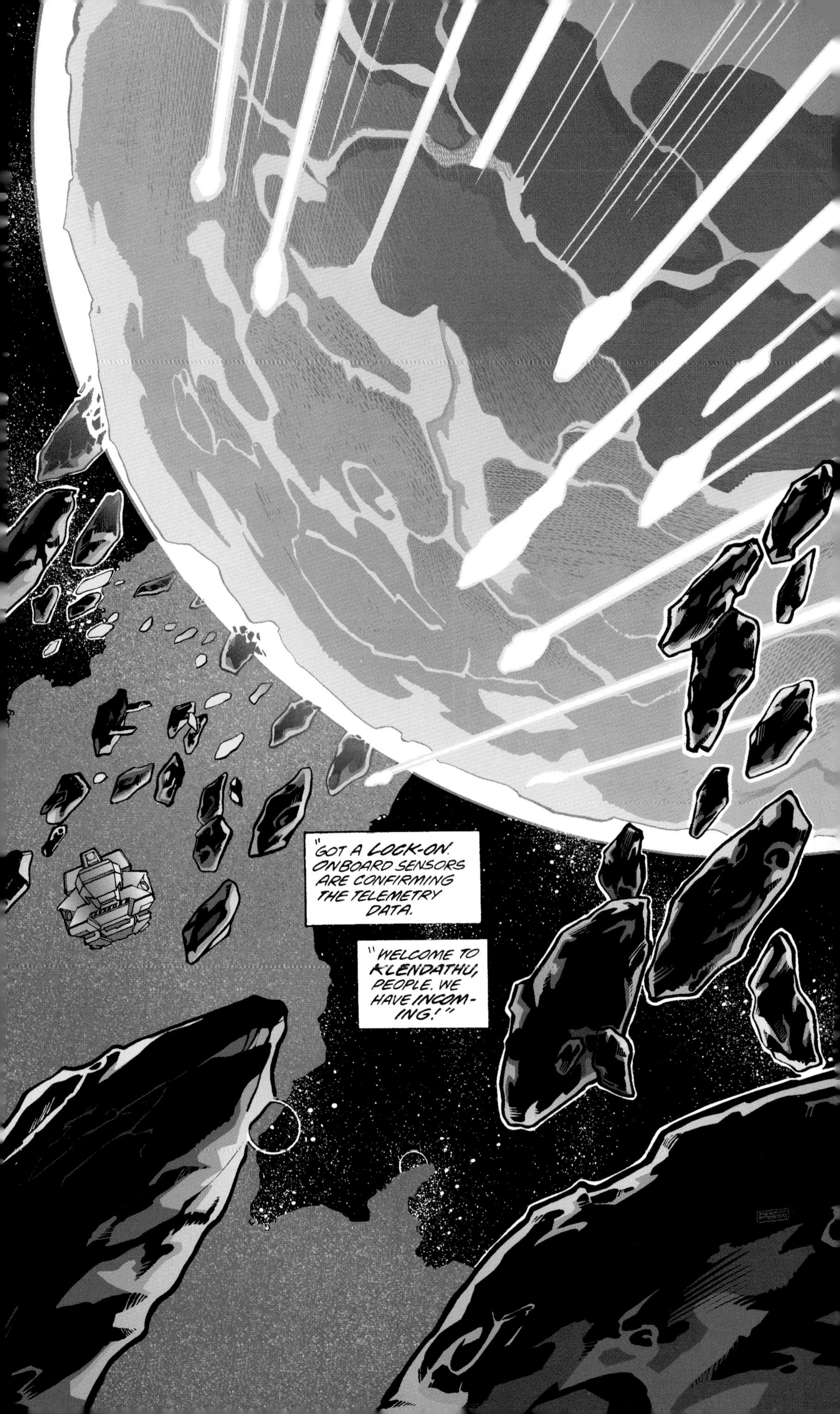
"GOT A LOCK-ON. ONBOARD SENSORS ARE CONFIRMING THE TELEMETRY DATA.
"WELCOME TO KLENDATHU, PEOPLE. WE HAVE INCOMING!"

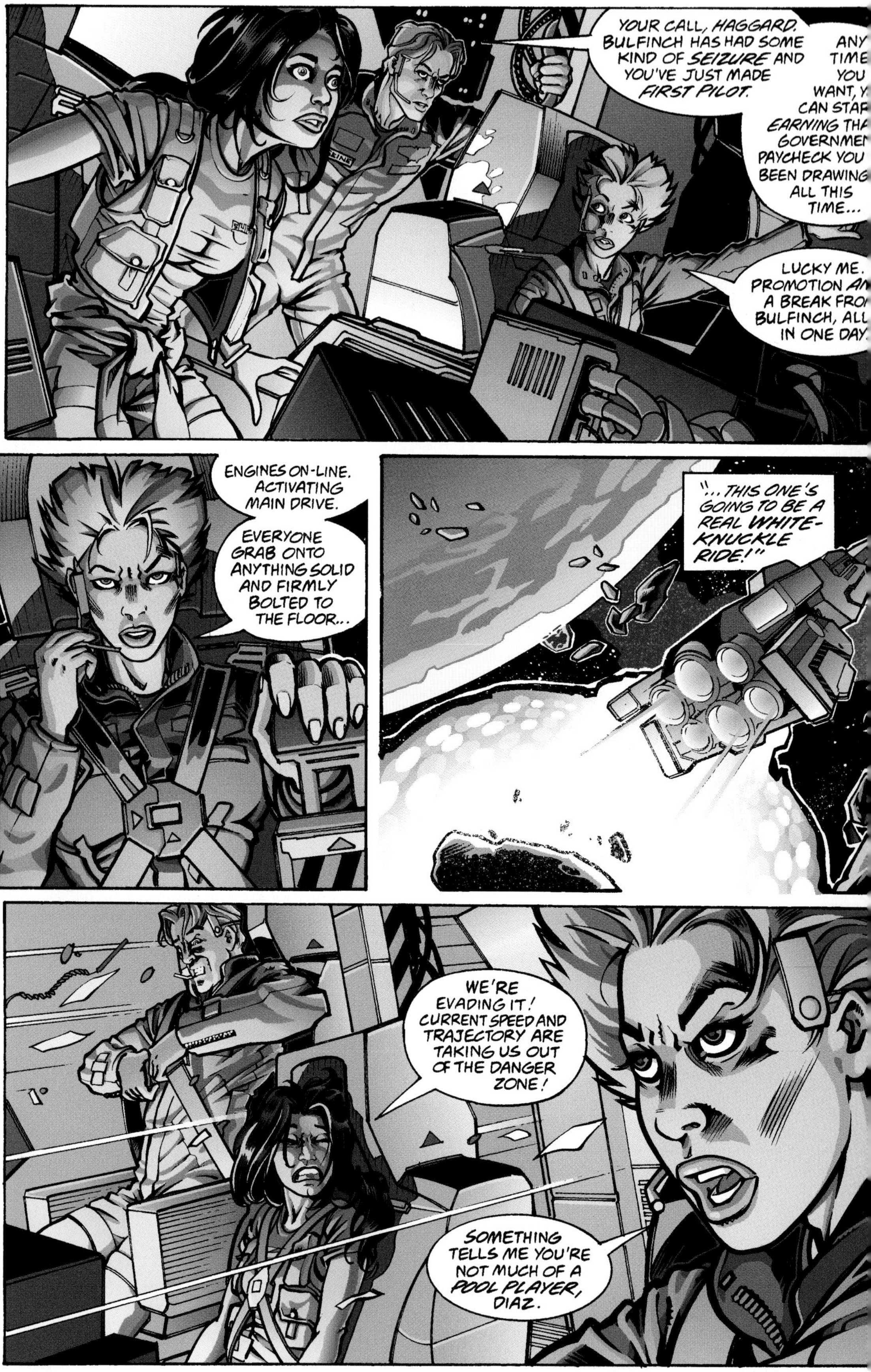
YOUR CALL, HAGGARD. BULFINCH HAS HAD SOME KIND OF SEIZURE AND YOU'VE JUST MADE FIRST PILOT.
ANY TIME YOU WANT, Y CAN STAR EARNING THA GOVERNMEN PAYCHECK YOU BEEN DRAWING ALL THIS TIME...
LUCKY ME. PROMOTION AN A BREAK FRO BULFINCH, ALL IN ONE DAY.
ENGINES ON-LINE. ACTIVATING MAIN DRIVE.
EVERYONE GRAB ONTO ANYTHING SOLID AND FIRMLY BOLTED TO THE FLOOR...
"...THIS ONE'S GOING TO BE A REAL WHITE-KNUCKLE RIDE!"
WE'RE EVADING IT! CURRENT SPEED AND TRAJECTORY ARE TAKING US OUT OF THE DANGER ZONE!
SOMETHING TELLS ME YOU'RE NOT MUCH OF A POOL PLAYER, DIAZ.

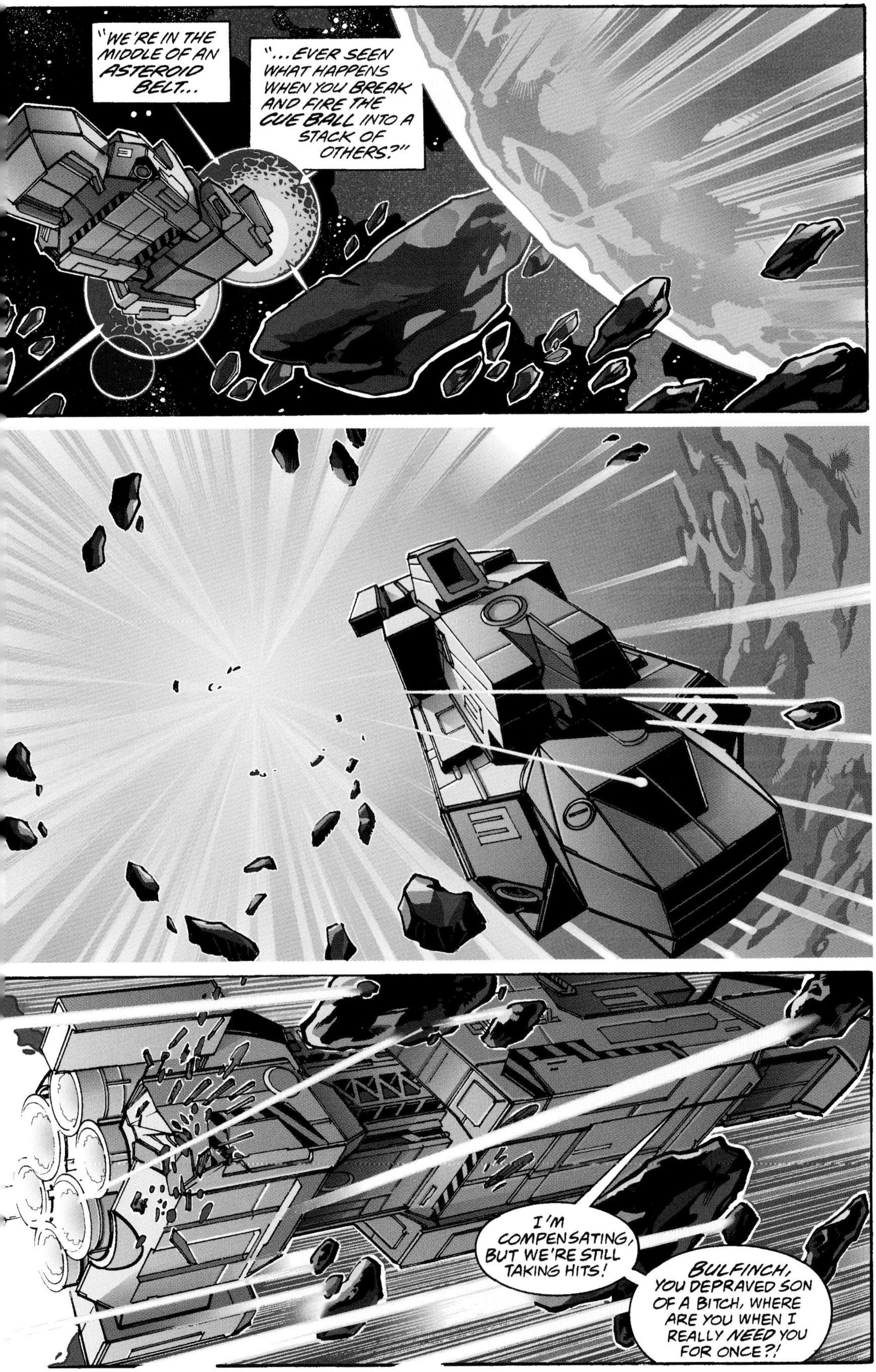

"WE'RE IN THE MIDDLE OF AN ASTEROID BELT...
"...EVER SEEN WHAT HAPPENS WHEN YOU BREAK AND FIRE THE CUE BALL INTO A STACK OF OTHERS?"
I'M COMPENSATING, BUT WE'RE STILL TAKING HITS!
BULFINCH, YOU DEPRAVED SON OF A BITCH, WHERE ARE YOU WHEN I REALLY NEED YOU FOR ONCE?!

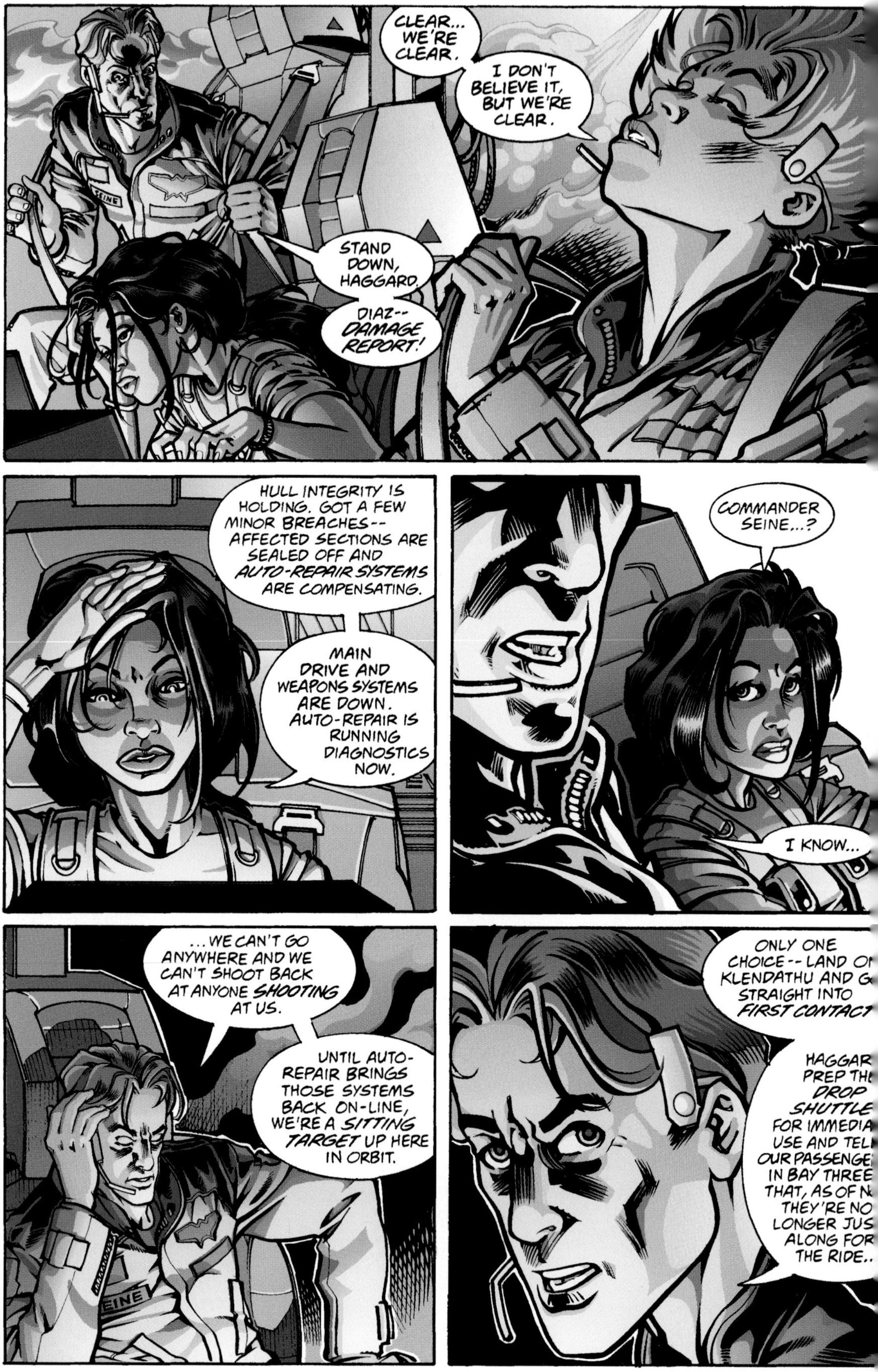
CLEAR... WE'RE CLEAR.
I DON'T BELIEVE IT, BUT WE'RE CLEAR.
STAND DOWN, HAGGARD.
DIAZ-- DAMAGE REPORT!
HULL INTEGRITY IS HOLDING. GOT A FEW MINOR BREACHES-- AFFECTED SECTIONS ARE SEALED OFF AND AUTO-REPAIR SYSTEMS ARE COMPENSATING.
MAIN DRIVE AND WEAPONS SYSTEMS ARE DOWN. AUTO-REPAIR IS RUNNING DIAGNOSTICS NOW.
COMMANDER SEINE...?
I KNOW...
...WE CAN'T GO ANYWHERE AND WE CAN'T SHOOT BACK AT ANYONE SHOOTING AT US.
UNTIL AUTO-REPAIR BRINGS THOSE SYSTEMS BACK ON-LINE, WE'RE A SITTING TARGET UP HERE IN ORBIT.
ONLY ONE CHOICE -- LAND O KLENDATHU AND G STRAIGHT INTO FIRST CONTAC
HAGGAR PREP TH DROP SHUTTLE FOR IMMEDIA USE AND TEL OUR PASSENGE IN BAY THREE THAT, AS OF N THEY'RE NO LONGER JUS ALONG FOR THE RIDE..

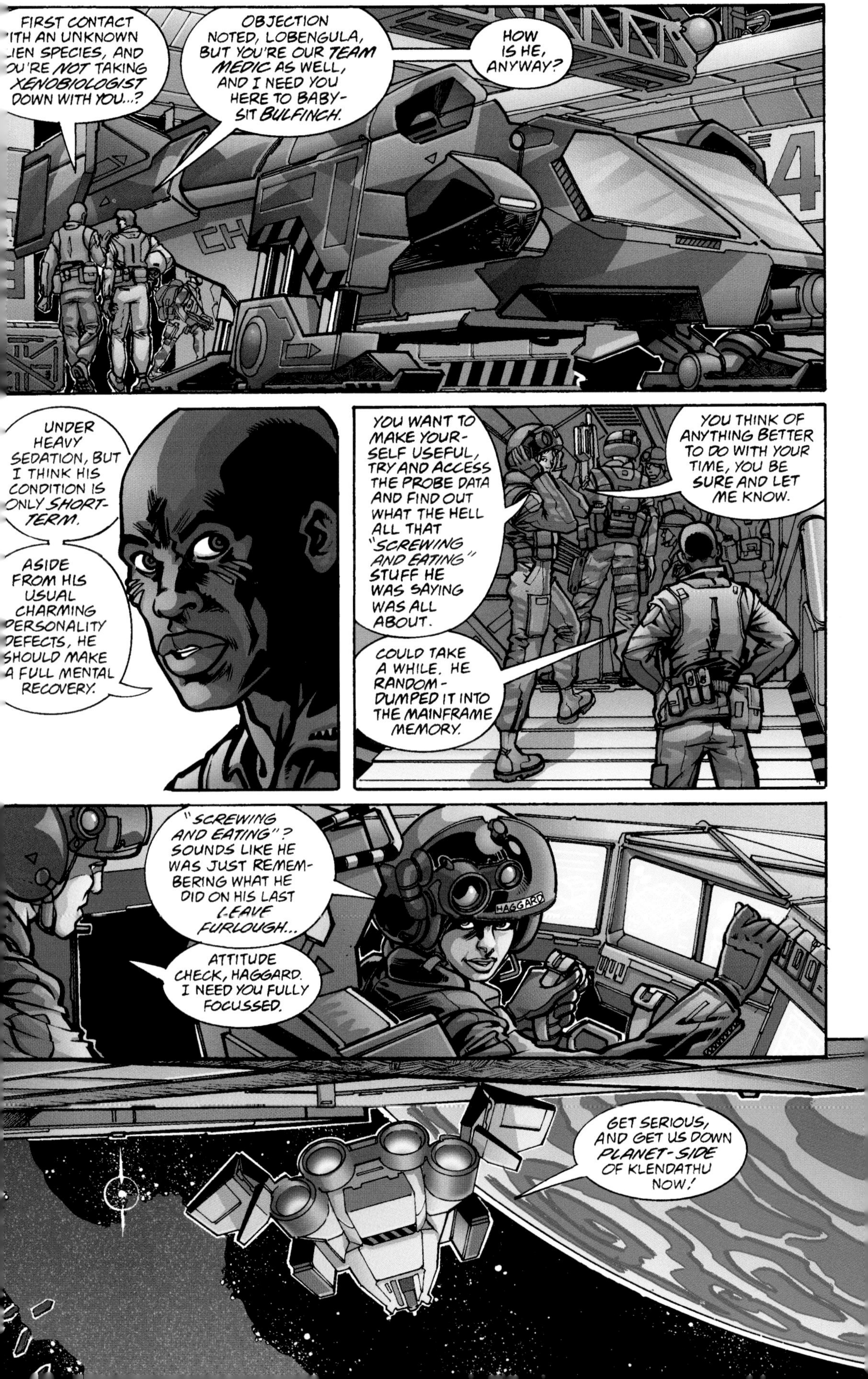

FIRST CONTACT ITH AN UNKNOWN LIEN SPECIES, AND OU'RE NOT TAKING XENOBIOLOGIST DOWN WITH YOU...?
OBJECTION NOTED, LOBENGULA, BUT YOU'RE OUR TEAM MEDIC AS WELL, AND I NEED YOU HERE TO BABY-SIT BULFINCH.
HOW IS HE, ANYWAY?
UNDER HEAVY SEDATION, BUT I THINK HIS CONDITION IS ONLY SHORT-TERM.
ASIDE FROM HIS USUAL CHARMING PERSONALITY DEFECTS, HE SHOULD MAKE A FULL MENTAL RECOVERY.
YOU WANT TO MAKE YOURSELF USEFUL, TRY AND ACCESS THE PROBE DATA AND FIND OUT WHAT THE HELL ALL THAT "SCREWING AND EATING" STUFF HE WAS SAYING WAS ALL ABOUT.
YOU THINK OF ANYTHING BETTER TO DO WITH YOUR TIME, YOU BE SURE AND LET ME KNOW.
COULD TAKE A WHILE. HE RANDOM-DUMPED IT INTO THE MAINFRAME MEMORY.
"SCREWING AND EATING"? SOUNDS LIKE HE WAS JUST REMEMBERING WHAT HE DID ON HIS LAST LEAVE FURLOUGH...
HAGGARD
ATTITUDE CHECK, HAGGARD. I NEED YOU FULLY FOCUSSED.
GET SERIOUS, AND GET US DOWN PLANET-SIDE OF KLENDATHU NOW!

DROP PROBE DATA SAYS KLENDATHU HAS A G-3 TYPE ATMOSPHERE. *EARTH STANDARD.*
ANY CHANCE IT ALSO GAVE US A SUITABLE PLACE TO *LAND?*
SEIN
GOT A LOCK-ON ON ONE OF THE PROBES' POSITIONS BEFORE IT WENT DEAD ON US.
I'M SENDING THE COORDINATES THROUGH TO *YOUR* CONSOLE NOW...
GOT IT. ZEROING IN FOR LANDING NOW.
WHOA... SOME *PRIME REAL ESTATE POSSIBILITIES* HERE!
WHERE DO I SIGN UP FOR MY REGULATION FORTY-ACRES-AND-A-MULE?

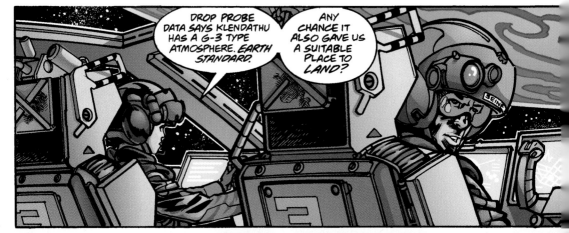

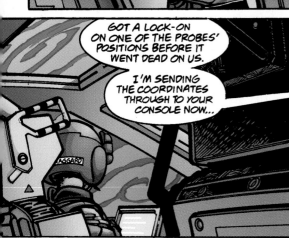

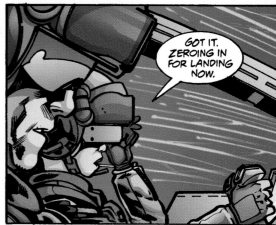

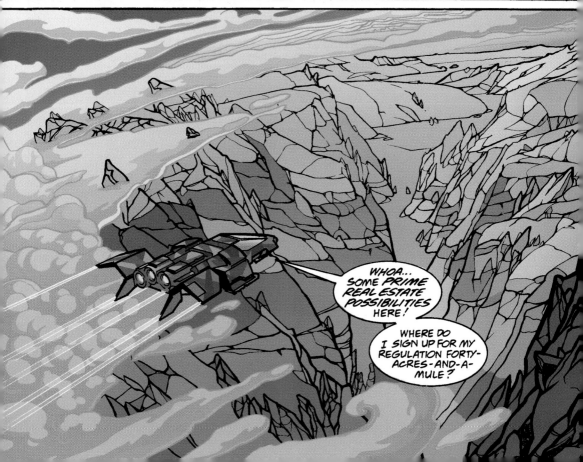

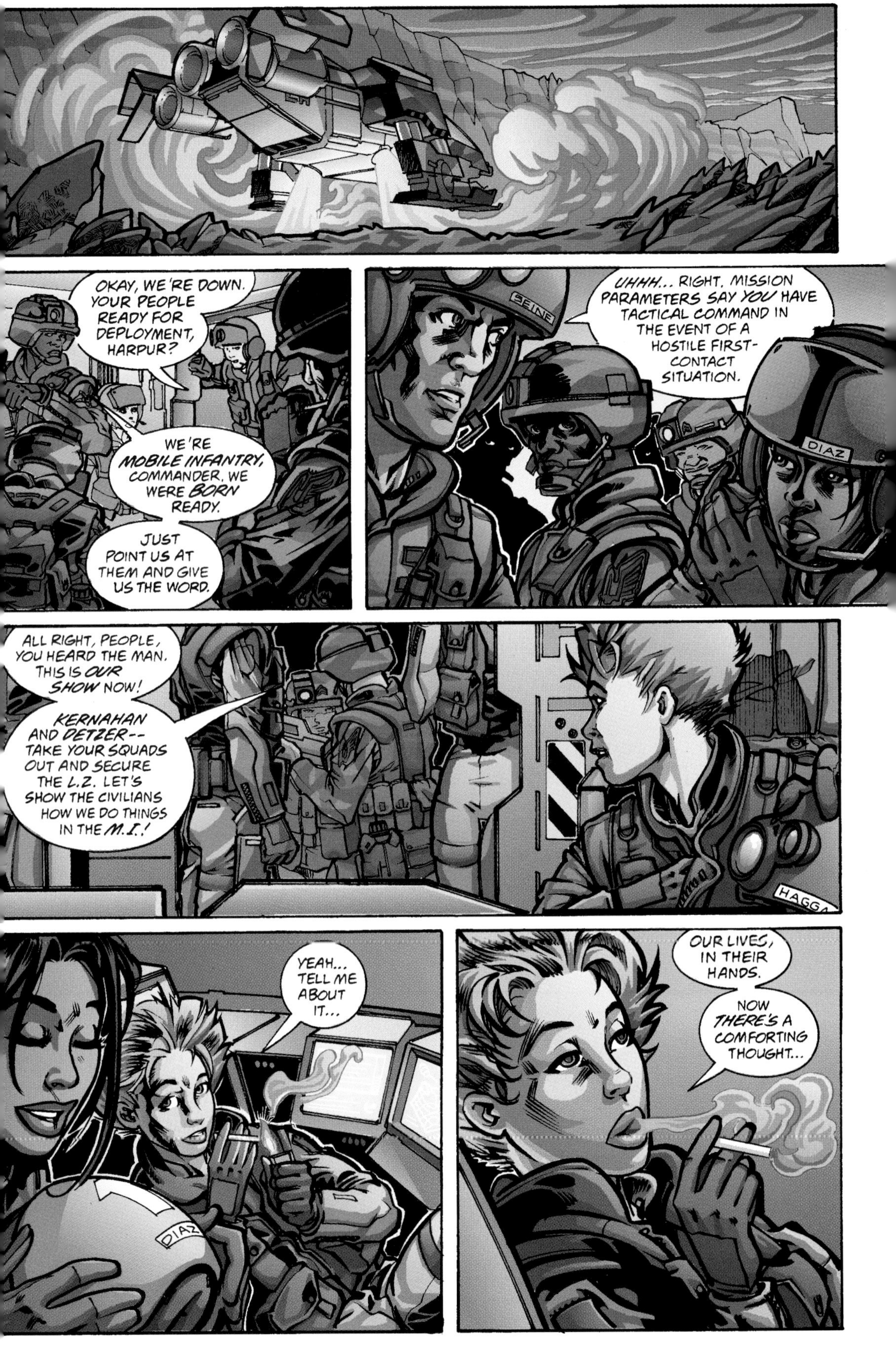
OKAY, WE'RE DOWN. YOUR PEOPLE READY FOR DEPLOYMENT, HARPUR?
WE'RE MOBILE INFANTRY, COMMANDER. WE WERE BORN READY.
JUST POINT US AT THEM AND GIVE US THE WORD.
SEINE
UHHH... RIGHT. MISSION PARAMETERS SAY YOU HAVE TACTICAL COMMAND IN THE EVENT OF A HOSTILE FIRST-CONTACT SITUATION.
DIAZ
ALL RIGHT, PEOPLE, YOU HEARD THE MAN. THIS IS OUR SHOW NOW!
KERNAHAN AND DETZER-- TAKE YOUR SQUADS OUT AND SECURE THE L.Z. LET'S SHOW THE CIVILIANS HOW WE DO THINGS IN THE M.I.!
YEAH... TELL ME ABOUT IT...
DIAZ
OUR LIVES, IN THEIR HANDS.
NOW THERE'S A COMFORTING THOUGHT...

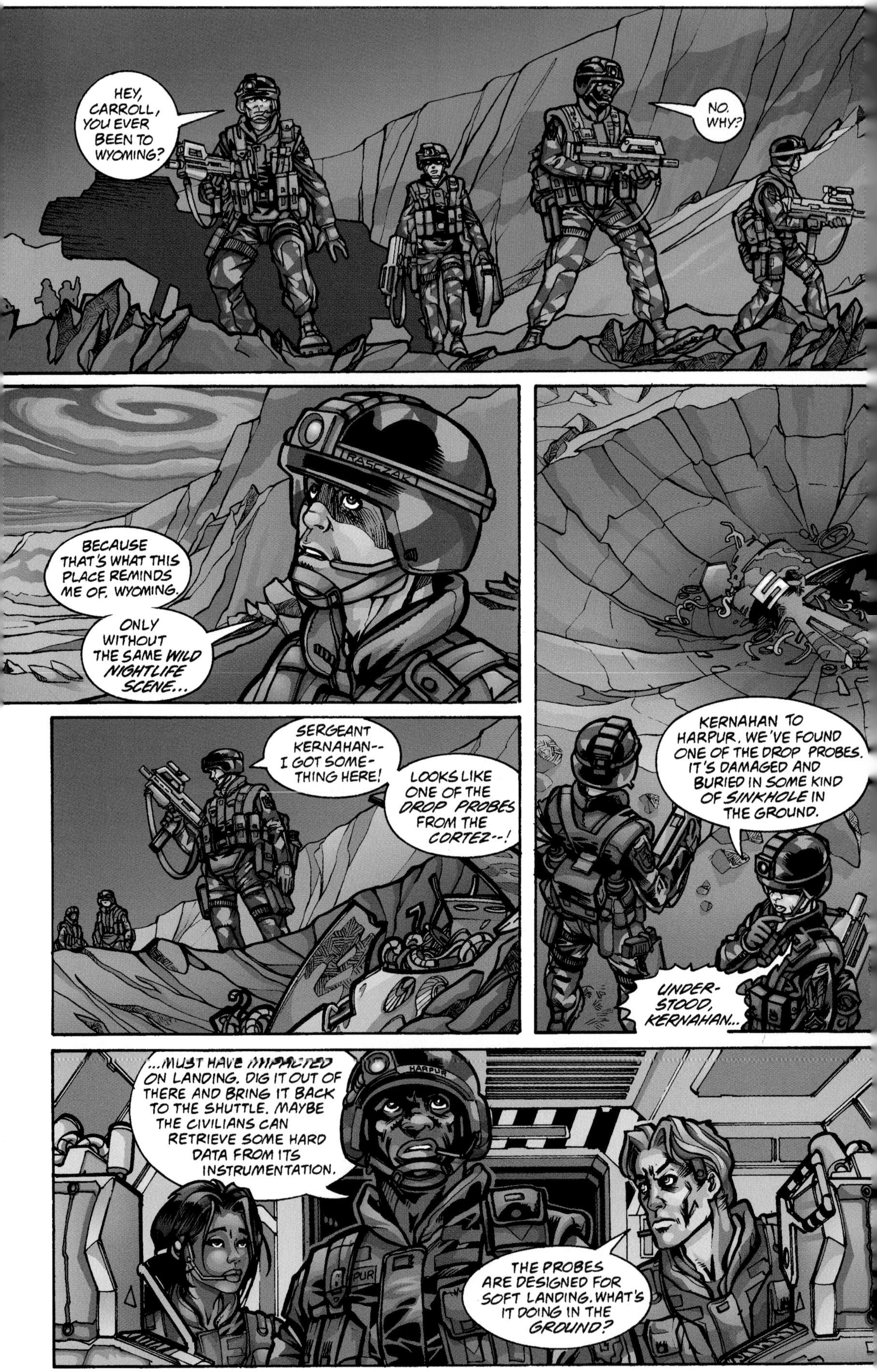
HEY, CARROLL, YOU EVER BEEN TO WYOMING?
NO. WHY?
BECAUSE THAT'S WHAT THIS PLACE REMINDS ME OF. WYOMING.
ONLY WITHOUT THE SAME *WILD NIGHTLIFE SCENE*...
RASCZAK
SERGEANT KERNAHAN-- I GOT SOME-THING HERE!
LOOKS LIKE ONE OF THE *DROP PROBES* FROM THE *CORTEZ*--!
KERNAHAN TO HARPUR. WE'VE FOUND ONE OF THE DROP PROBES. IT'S DAMAGED AND BURIED IN SOME KIND OF *SINKHOLE* IN THE GROUND.
UNDER-STOOD, KERNAHAN...
...MUST HAVE *IMPACTED* ON LANDING. DIG IT OUT OF THERE AND BRING IT BACK TO THE SHUTTLE. MAYBE THE CIVILIANS CAN RETRIEVE SOME HARD DATA FROM ITS INSTRUMENTATION.
HARPUR
THE PROBES ARE DESIGNED FOR SOFT LANDING. WHAT'S IT DOING IN THE *GROUND?*

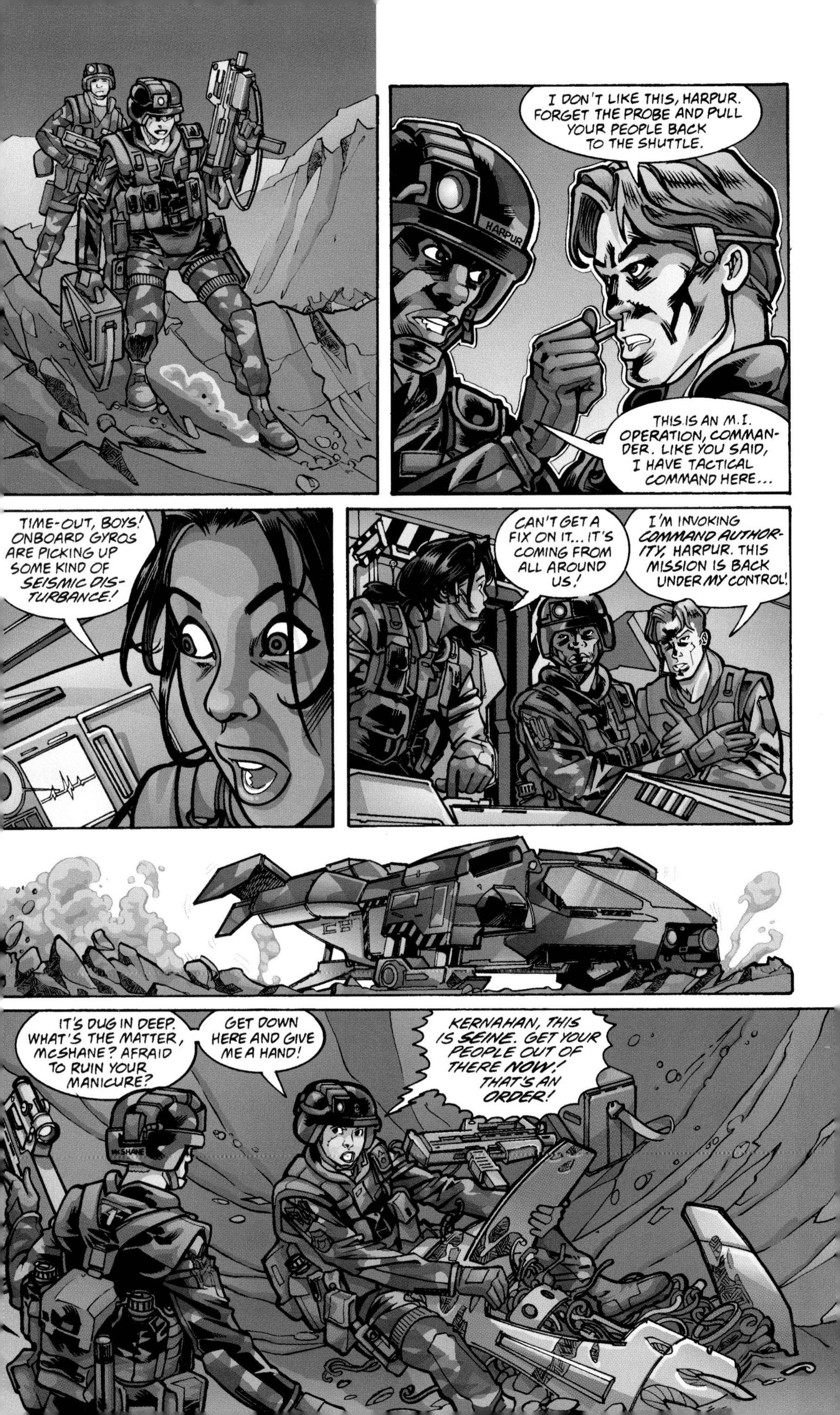

I DON'T LIKE THIS, HARPUR. FORGET THE PROBE AND PULL YOUR PEOPLE BACK TO THE SHUTTLE.
HARPUR
THIS IS AN M.I. OPERATION, COMMANDER. LIKE YOU SAID, I HAVE TACTICAL COMMAND HERE...
TIME-OUT, BOYS! ONBOARD GYROS ARE PICKING UP SOME KIND OF SEISMIC DISTURBANCE!
CAN'T GET A FIX ON IT... IT'S COMING FROM ALL AROUND US!
I'M INVOKING COMMAND AUTHORITY, HARPUR. THIS MISSION IS BACK UNDER MY CONTROL!
IT'S DUG IN DEEP. WHAT'S THE MATTER, McSHANE? AFRAID TO RUIN YOUR MANICURE?
GET DOWN HERE AND GIVE ME A HAND!
KERNAHAN, THIS IS SEINE. GET YOUR PEOPLE OUT OF THERE NOW! THAT'S AN ORDER!
McSHANE

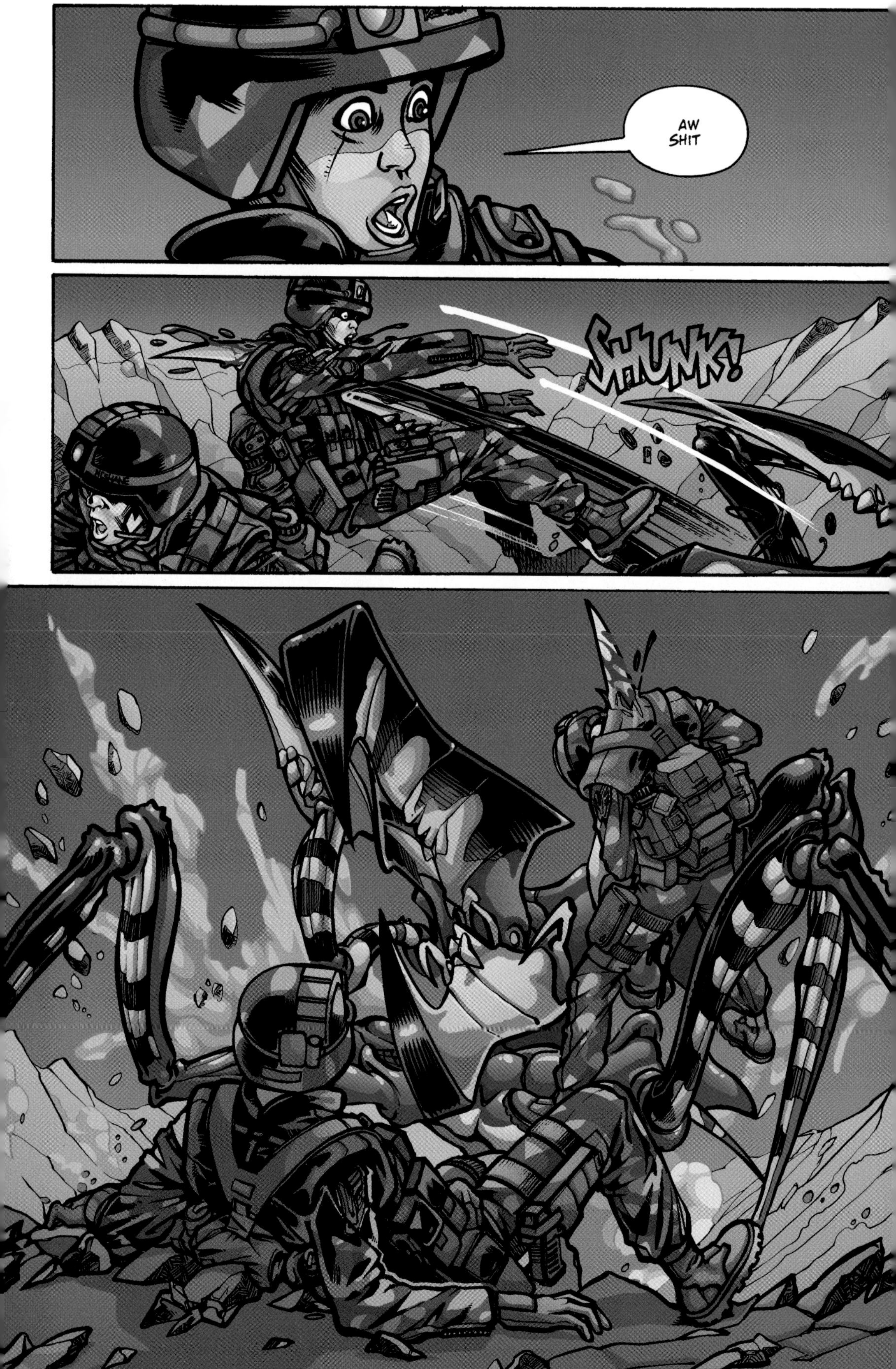
AW SHIT
SHUNK!

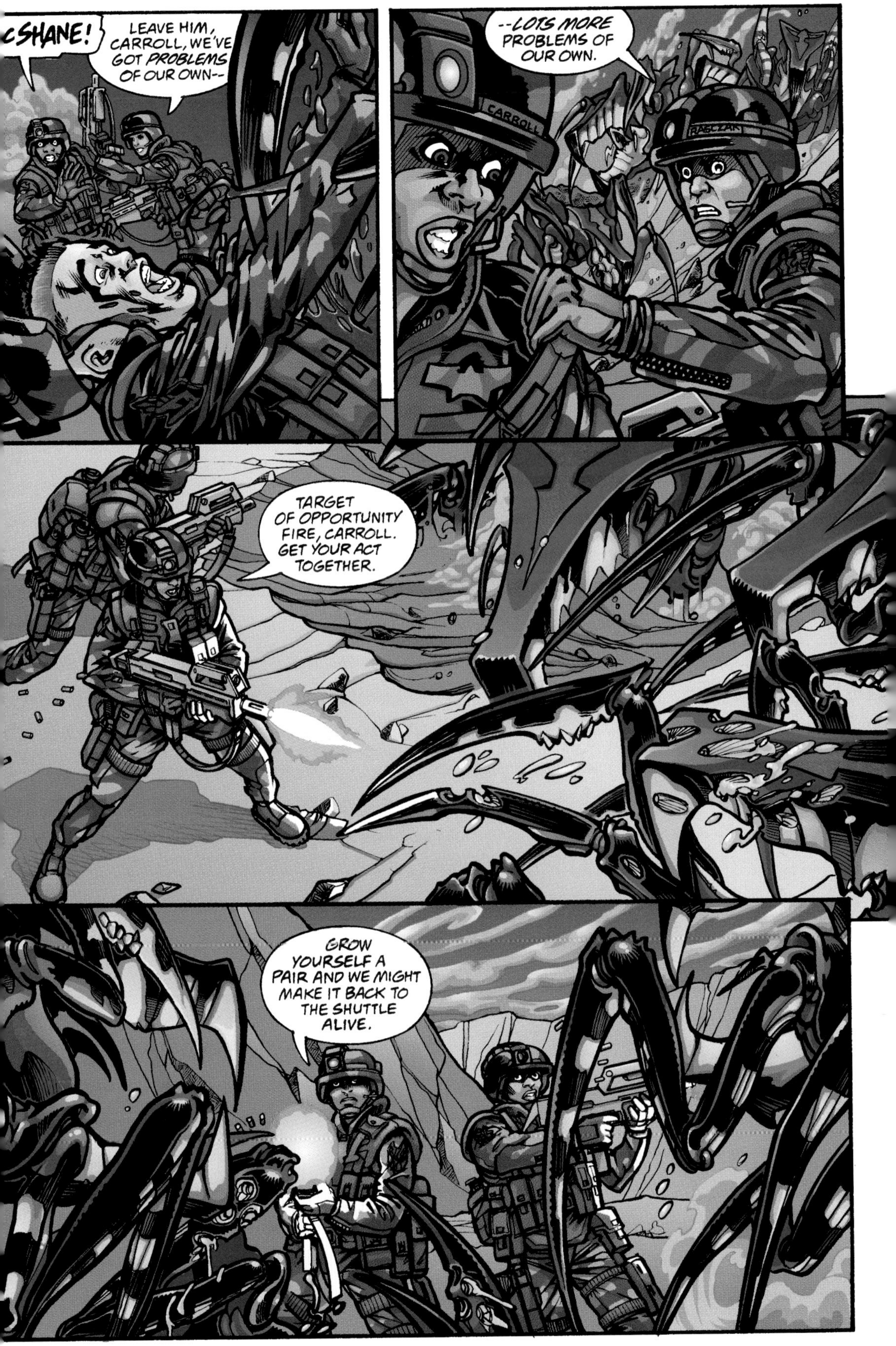
cSHANE!
LEAVE HIM, CARROLL, WE'VE GOT PROBLEMS OF OUR OWN--
--LOTS MORE PROBLEMS OF OUR OWN.
CARROLL
TARGET OF OPPORTUNITY FIRE, CARROLL. GET YOUR ACT TOGETHER.
GROW YOURSELF A PAIR AND WE MIGHT MAKE IT BACK TO THE SHUTTLE ALIVE.

DETZER, THIS IS SEINE. FALL BACK TO THE SHUTTLE. FALL BACK, NOW!

SHEPPER... GONE... CH... THEY JUS... RIPPED H... IN TWO...

THOSE ARE MY PEOPLE OUT THERE ...THOSE ARE MY PEOPLE...

THOSE ARE M... PEOPLE. ... SENT THEM ... THERE. I'LL ... BRING THE... BACK IN...

HARPUR! NO!

MORE SEISMIC MOVEMENT. IT'S CENTERED DIRECTLY ON THE SHUTTLE!

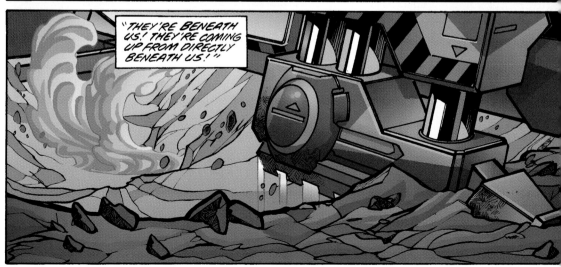

"THEY'RE BENEATH US! THEY'RE COMING UP FROM DIRECTLY BENEATH US!"

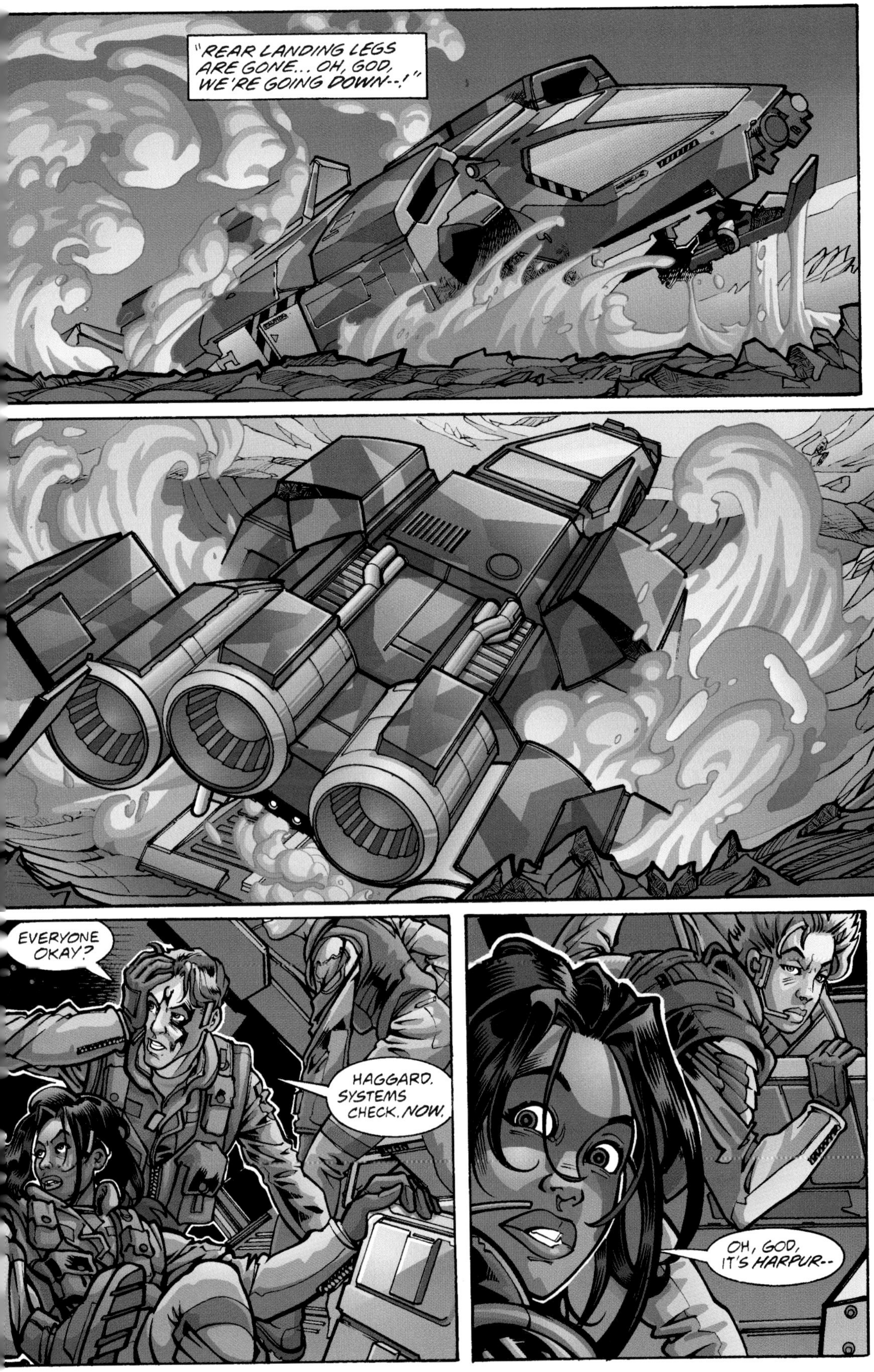
"REAR LANDING LEGS ARE GONE... OH, GOD, WE'RE GOING DOWN--!"
EVERYONE OKAY?
HAGGARD. SYSTEMS CHECK. NOW.
OH, GOD, IT'S HARPUR--

"--IT'S HARPUR. HE'S OUT THERE, AND HE'S STILL ALIVE!"

GG~GGG--GHHK

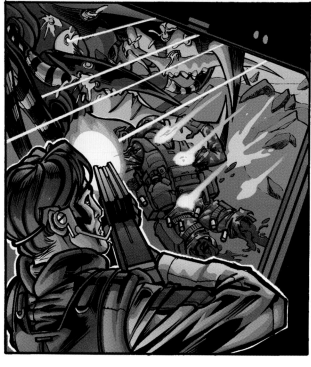

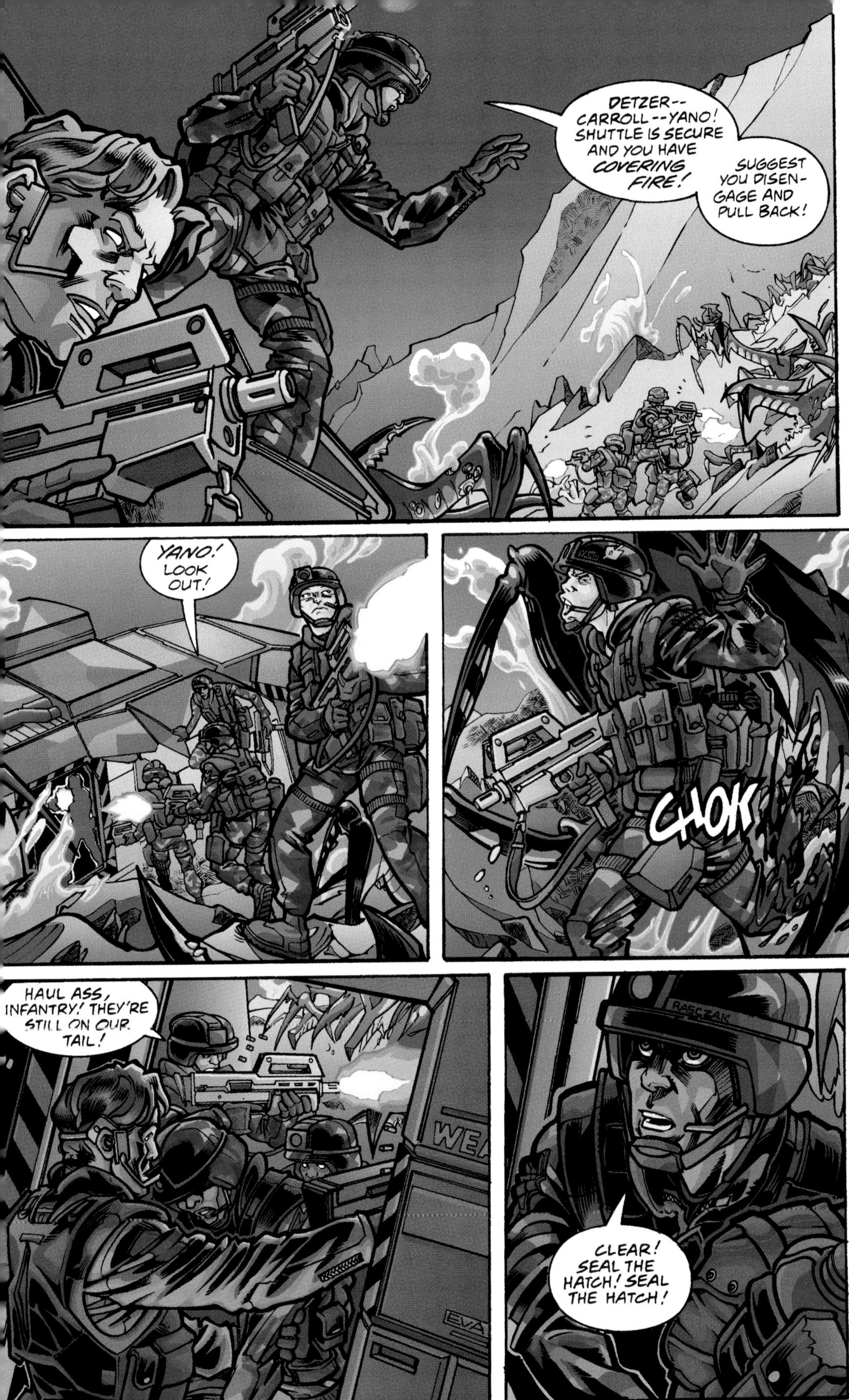
DETZER--
CARROLL--YANO! SHUTTLE IS SECURE AND YOU HAVE COVERING FIRE!
SUGGEST YOU DISENGAGE AND PULL BACK!
YANO! LOOK OUT!
CHOK
HAUL ASS, INFANTRY! THEY'RE STILL ON OUR TAIL!
CLEAR! SEAL THE HATCH! SEAL THE HATCH!

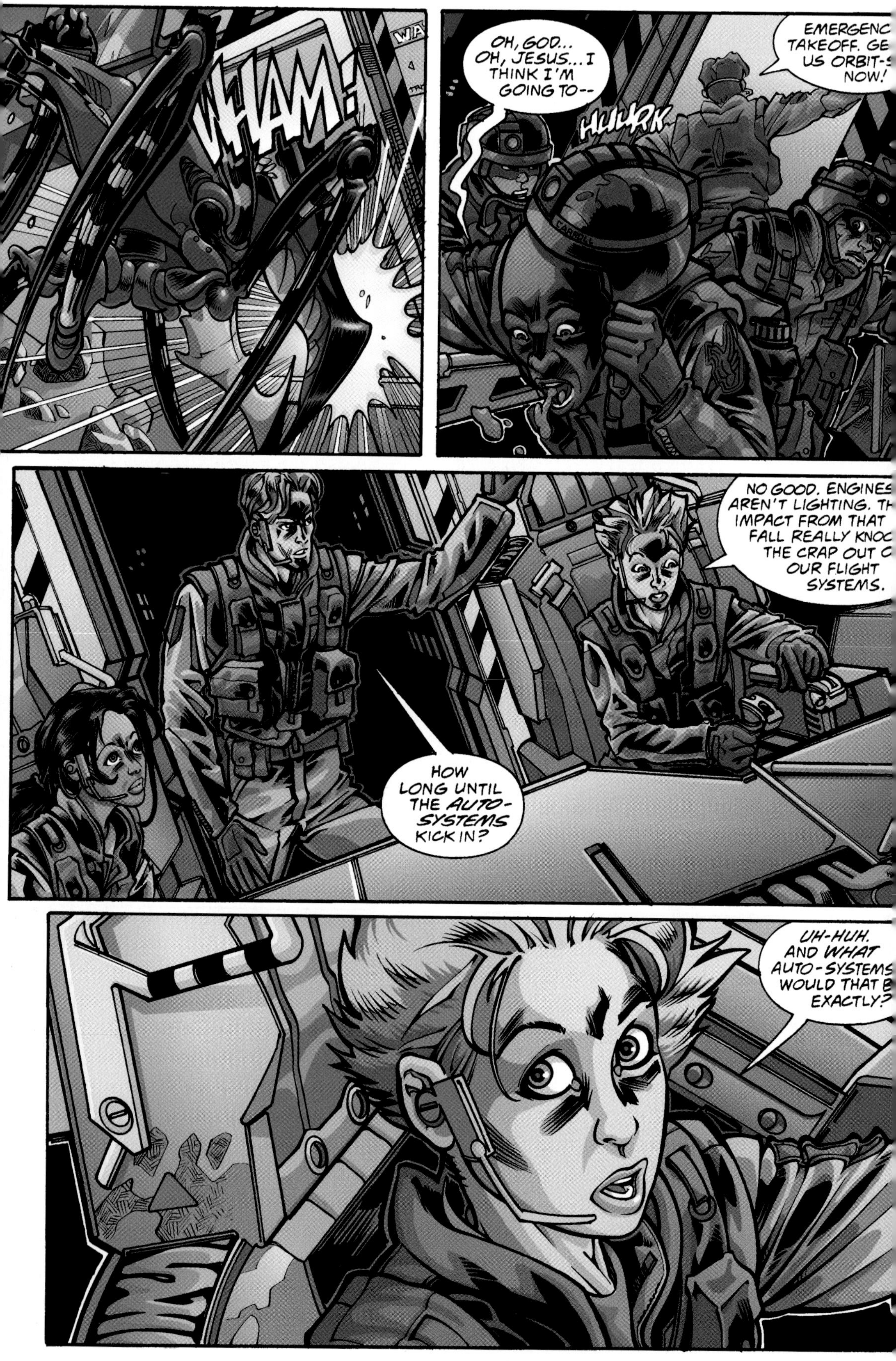
WHAM!
OH, GOD... OH, JESUS... I THINK I'M GOING TO--
HUURK
EMERGENC TAKEOFF. GE US ORBIT-S NOW!
NO GOOD. ENGINES AREN'T LIGHTING. TH IMPACT FROM THAT FALL REALLY KNOC THE CRAP OUT O OUR FLIGHT SYSTEMS.
HOW LONG UNTIL THE *AUTO-SYSTEMS* KICK IN?
UH-HUH. AND *WHAT* AUTO-SYSTEMS WOULD THAT B EXACTLY?

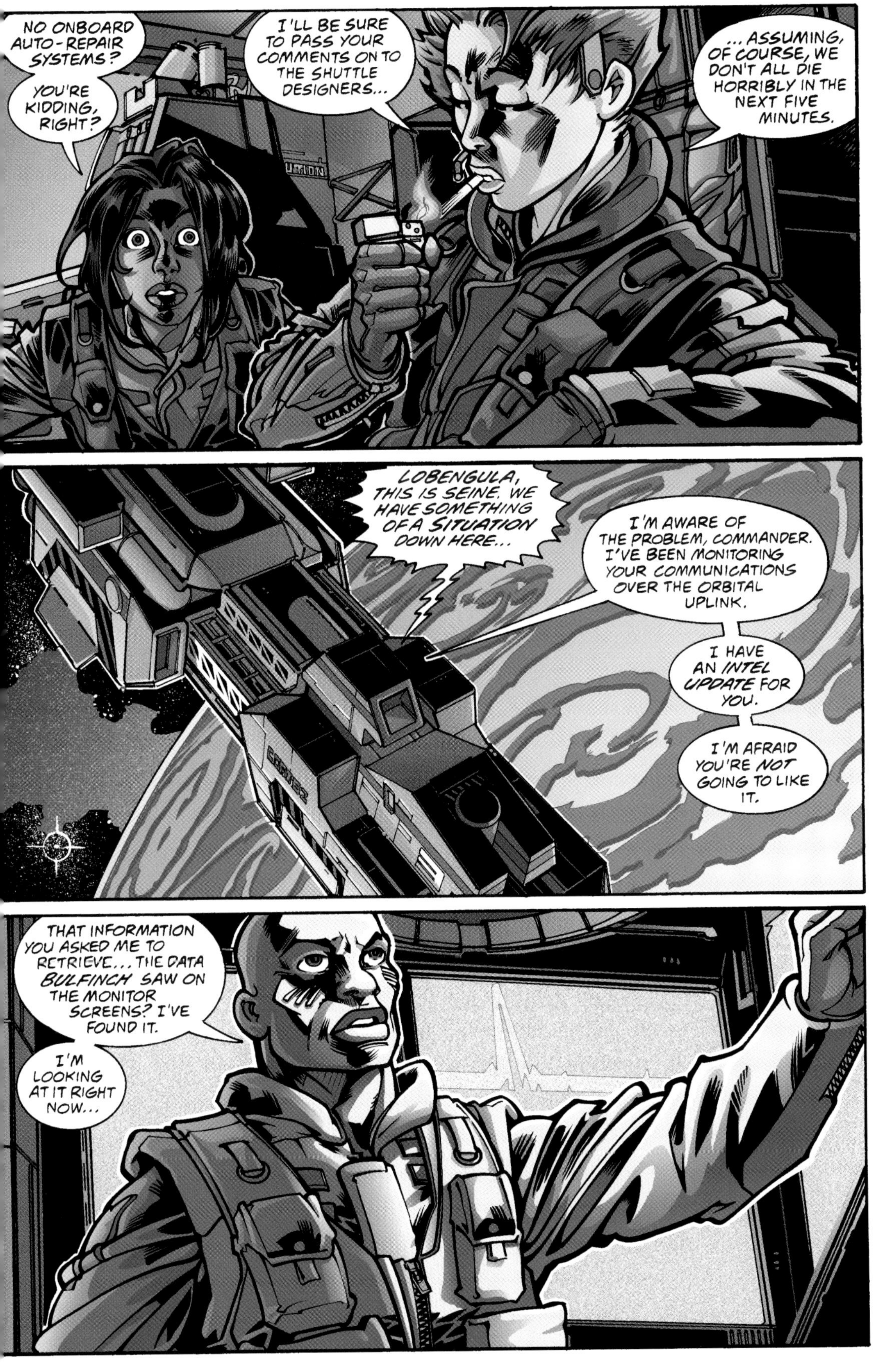
NO ONBOARD AUTO-REPAIR SYSTEMS?
YOU'RE KIDDING, RIGHT?
I'LL BE SURE TO PASS YOUR COMMENTS ON TO THE SHUTTLE DESIGNERS...
...ASSUMING, OF COURSE, WE DON'T ALL DIE HORRIBLY IN THE NEXT FIVE MINUTES.
LOBENGULA, THIS IS SEINE. WE HAVE SOMETHING OF A SITUATION DOWN HERE...
I'M AWARE OF THE PROBLEM, COMMANDER. I'VE BEEN MONITORING YOUR COMMUNICATIONS OVER THE ORBITAL UPLINK.
I HAVE AN INTEL UPDATE FOR YOU.
I'M AFRAID YOU'RE NOT GOING TO LIKE IT.
THAT INFORMATION YOU ASKED ME TO RETRIEVE... THE DATA BULFINCH SAW ON THE MONITOR SCREENS? I'VE FOUND IT.
I'M LOOKING AT IT RIGHT NOW...

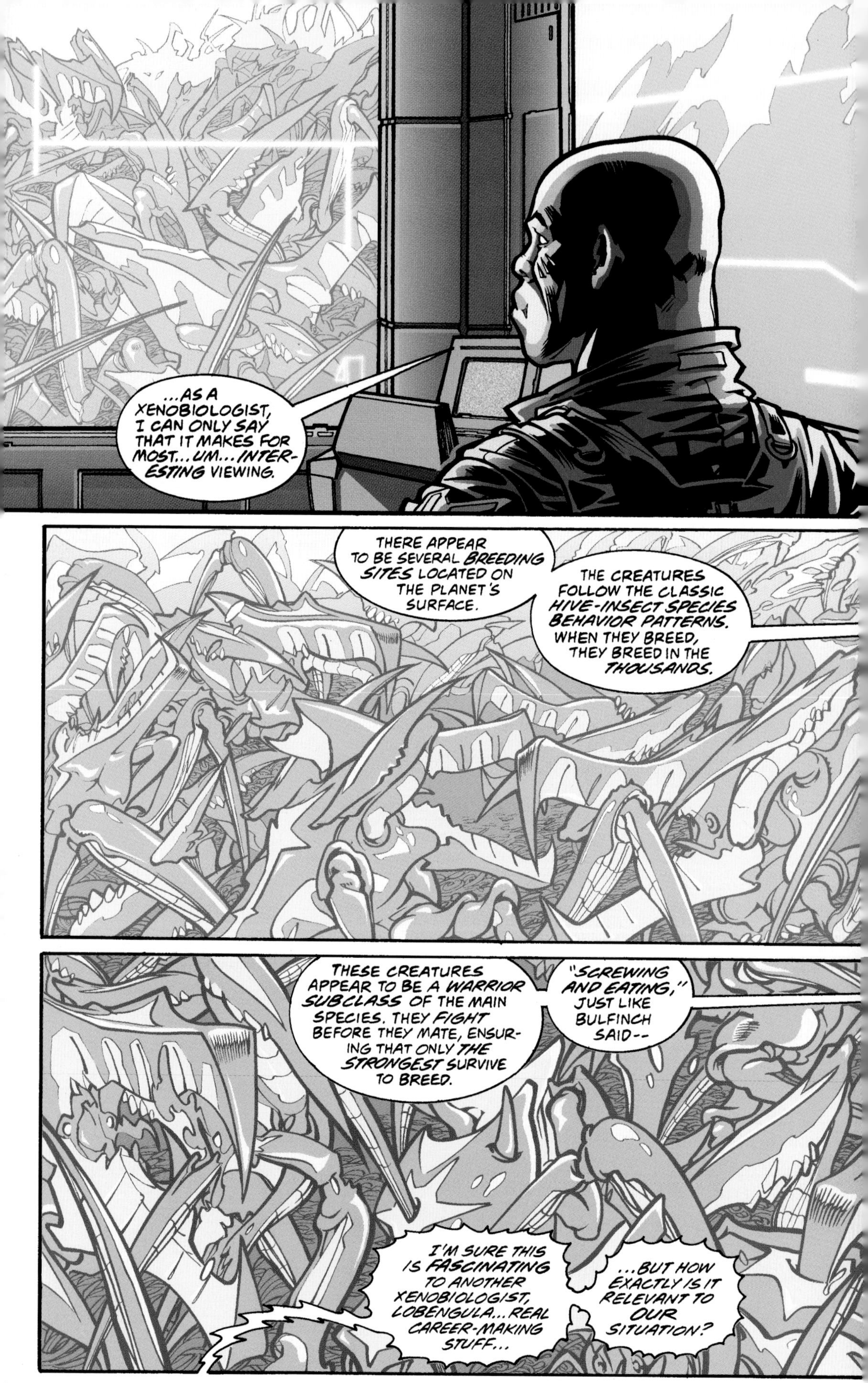
...AS A XENOBIOLOGIST, I CAN ONLY SAY THAT IT MAKES FOR MOST... UM... INTERESTING VIEWING.
THERE APPEAR TO BE SEVERAL BREEDING SITES LOCATED ON THE PLANET'S SURFACE.
THE CREATURES FOLLOW THE CLASSIC HIVE-INSECT SPECIES BEHAVIOR PATTERNS. WHEN THEY BREED, THEY BREED IN THE THOUSANDS.
THESE CREATURES APPEAR TO BE A WARRIOR SUBCLASS OF THE MAIN SPECIES. THEY FIGHT BEFORE THEY MATE, ENSURING THAT ONLY THE STRONGEST SURVIVE TO BREED.
"SCREWING AND EATING," JUST LIKE BULFINCH SAID--
I'M SURE THIS IS FASCINATING TO ANOTHER XENOBIOLOGIST, LOBENGULA... REAL CAREER-MAKING STUFF...
...BUT HOW EXACTLY IS IT RELEVANT TO OUR SITUATION?

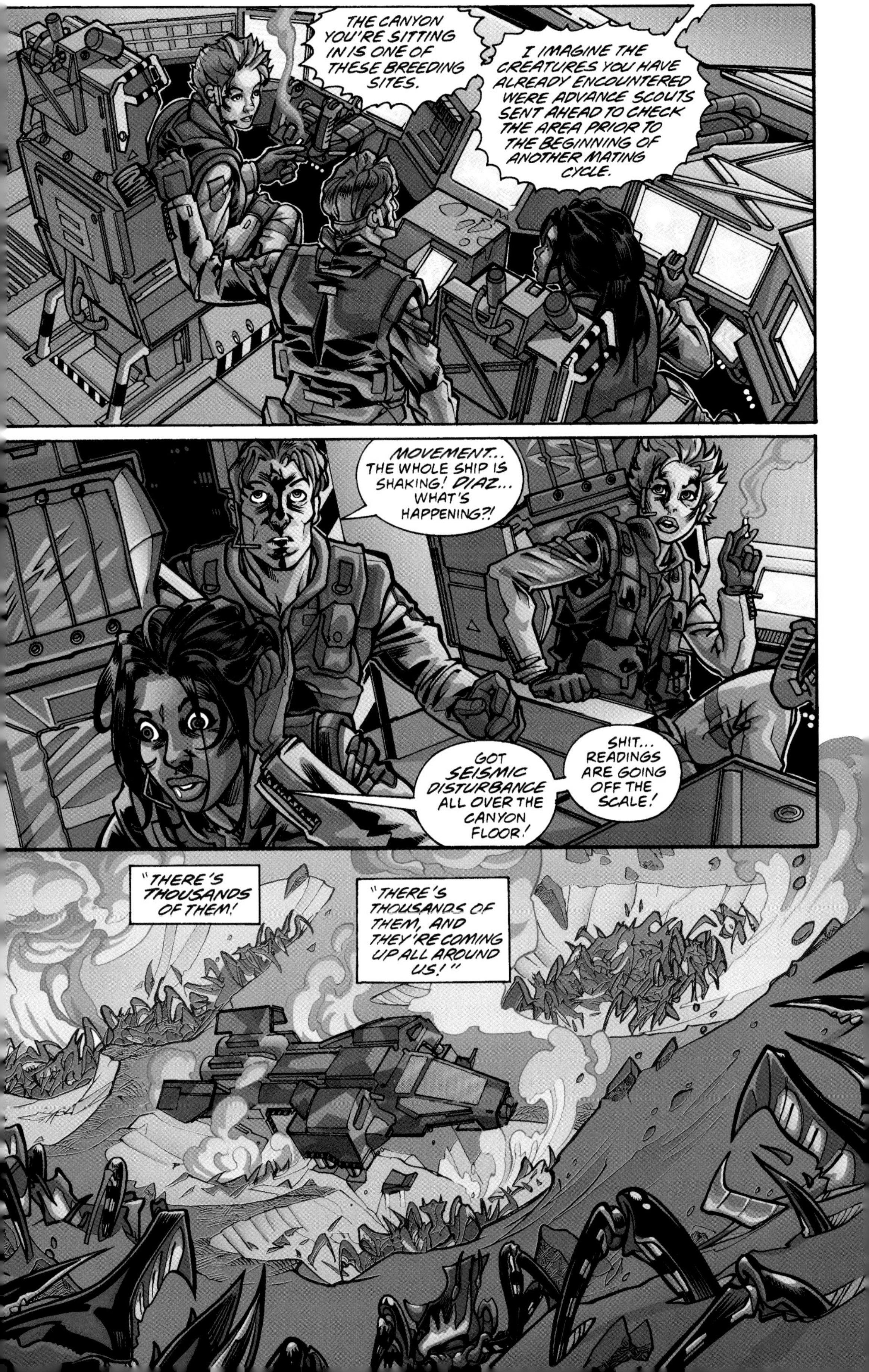
THE CANYON YOU'RE SITTING IN IS ONE OF THESE BREEDING SITES.
I IMAGINE THE CREATURES YOU HAVE ALREADY ENCOUNTERED WERE ADVANCE SCOUTS SENT AHEAD TO CHECK THE AREA PRIOR TO THE BEGINNING OF ANOTHER MATING CYCLE.
MOVEMENT... THE WHOLE SHIP IS SHAKING! DIAZ... WHAT'S HAPPENING?!
GOT SEISMIC DISTURBANCE ALL OVER THE CANYON FLOOR!
SHIT... READINGS ARE GOING OFF THE SCALE!
"THERE'S THOUSANDS OF THEM!
"THERE'S THOUSANDS OF THEM, AND THEY'RE COMING UP ALL AROUND US!"

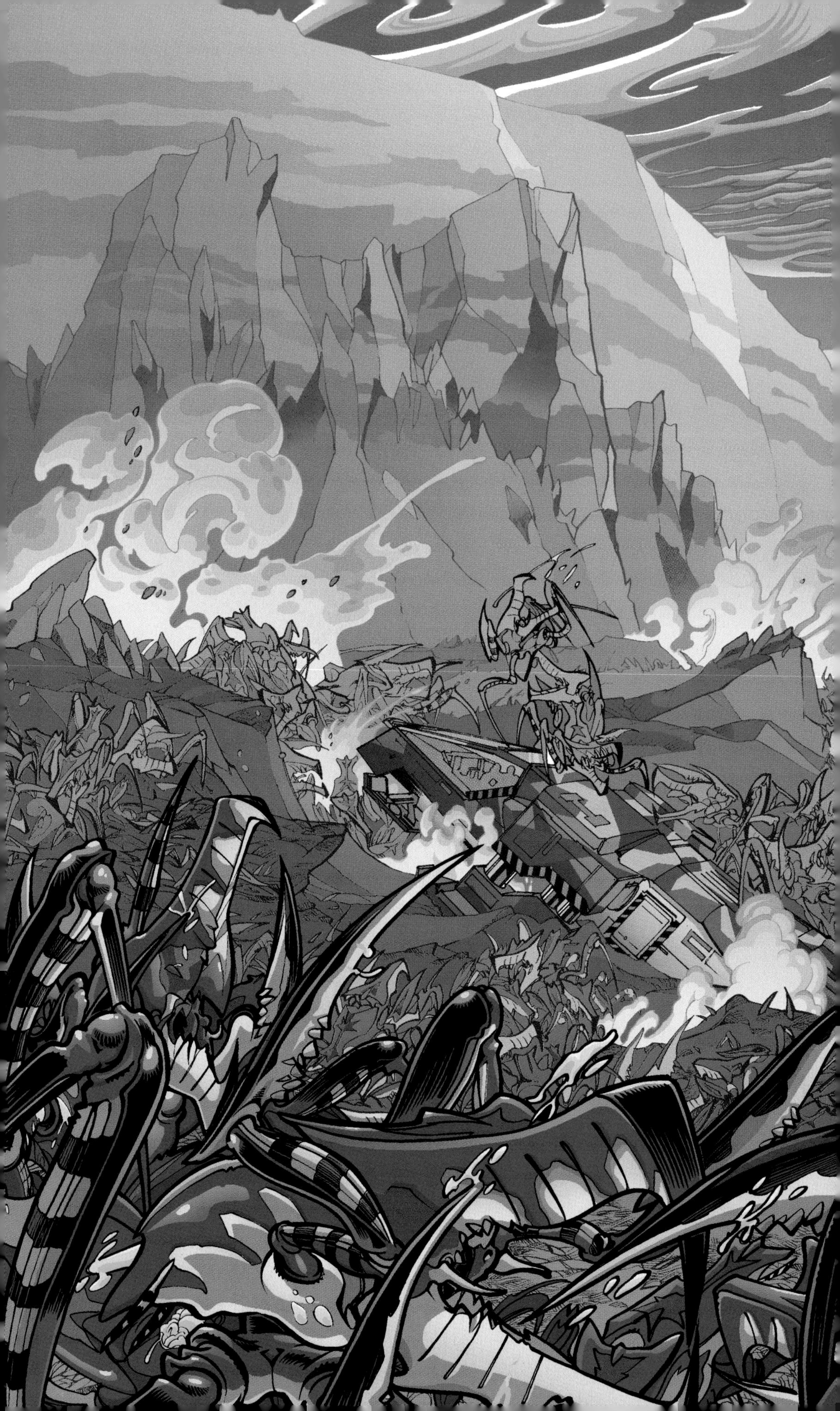

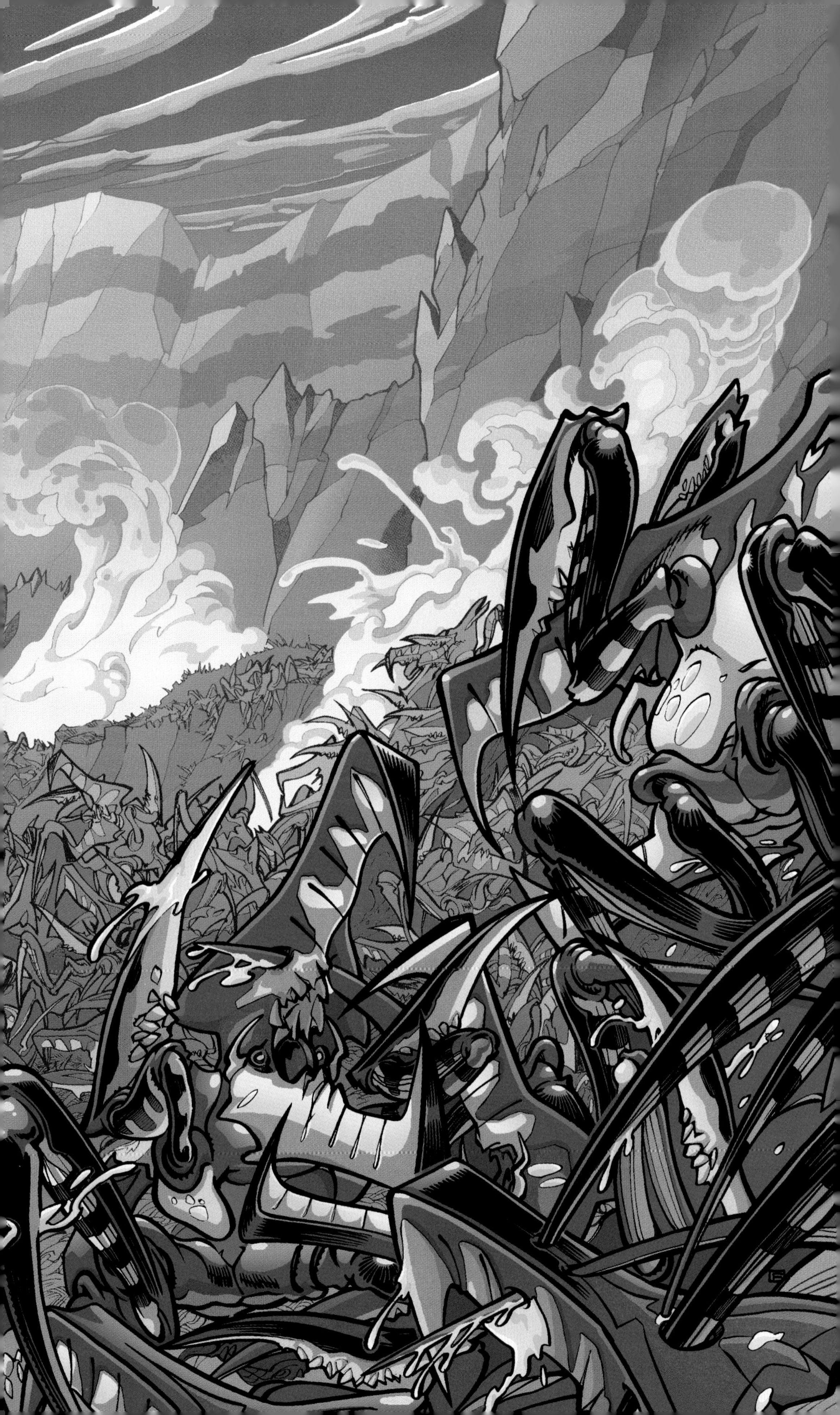

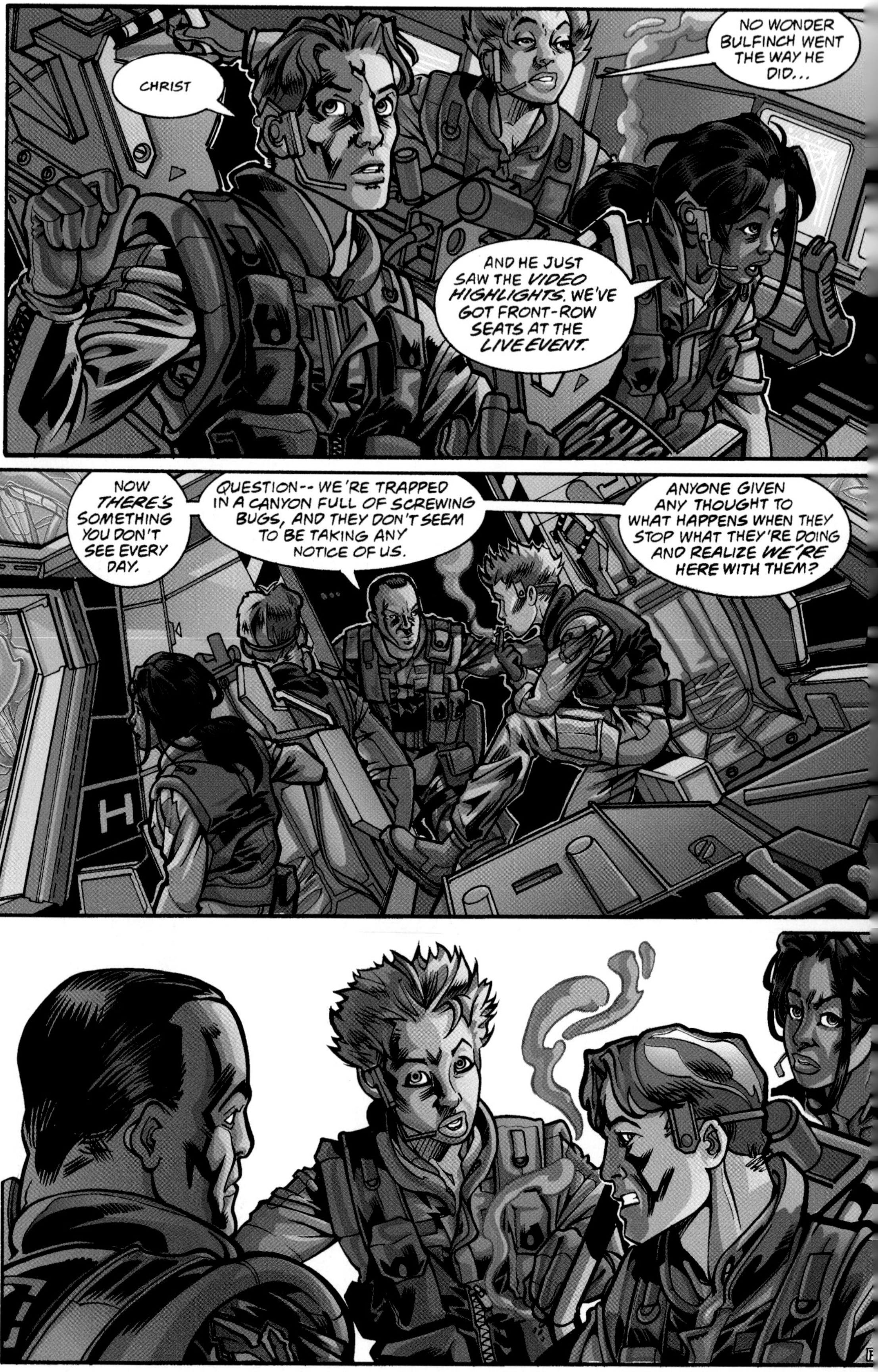
CHRIST
NO WONDER BULFINCH WENT THE WAY HE DID...
AND HE JUST SAW THE VIDEO HIGHLIGHTS. WE'VE GOT FRONT-ROW SEATS AT THE LIVE EVENT.
NOW THERE'S SOMETHING YOU DON'T SEE EVERY DAY.
QUESTION-- WE'RE TRAPPED IN A CANYON FULL OF SCREWING BUGS, AND THEY DON'T SEEM TO BE TAKING ANY NOTICE OF US.
ANYONE GIVEN ANY THOUGHT TO WHAT HAPPENS WHEN THEY STOP WHAT THEY'RE DOING AND REALIZE WE'RE HERE WITH THEM?

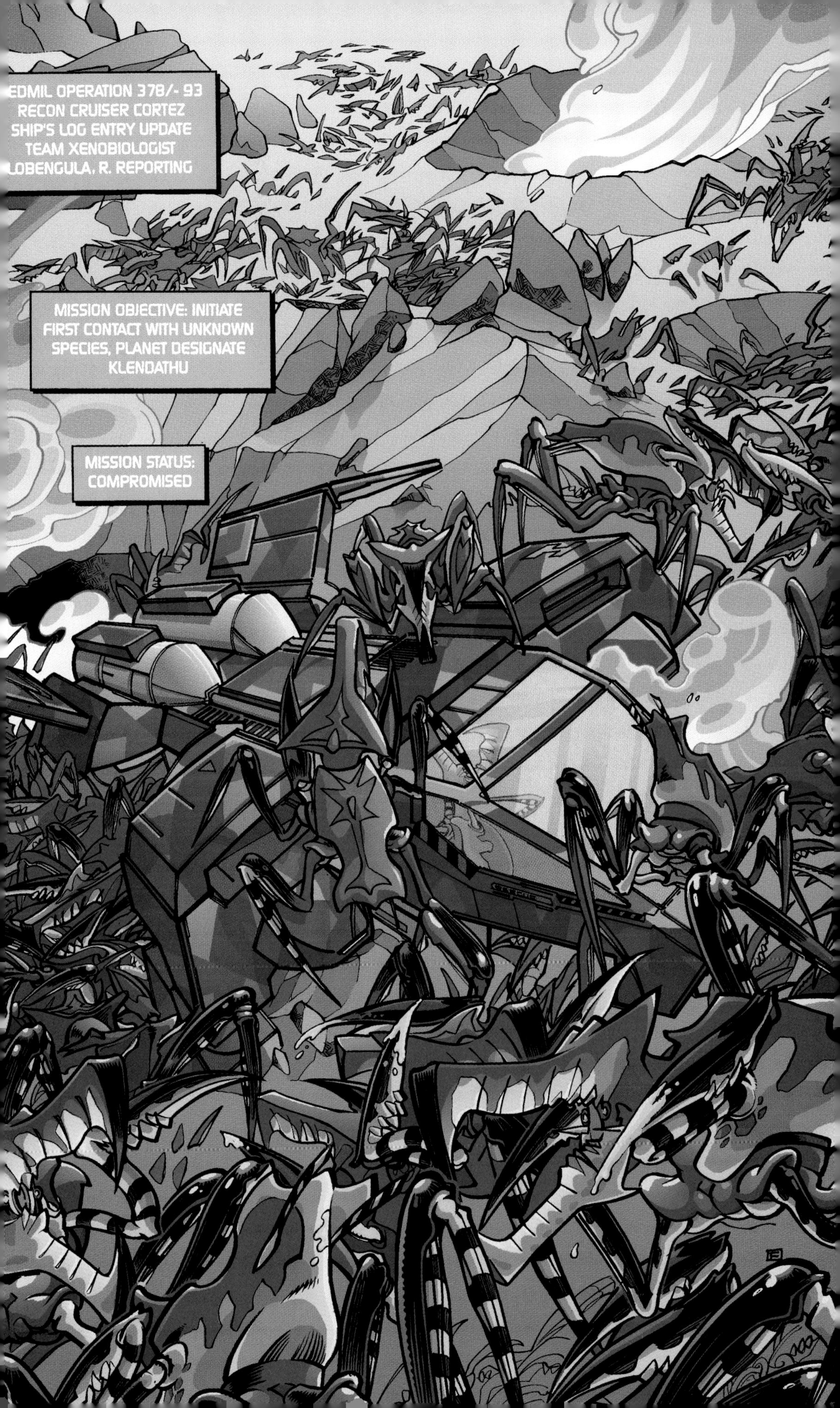
EDMIL OPERATION 378/- 93
RECON CRUISER CORTEZ
SHIP'S LOG ENTRY UPDATE
TEAM XENOBIOLOGIST
LOBENGULA, R. REPORTING
MISSION OBJECTIVE: INITIATE FIRST CONTACT WITH UNKNOWN SPECIES, PLANET DESIGNATE KLENDATHU
MISSION STATUS: COMPROMISED

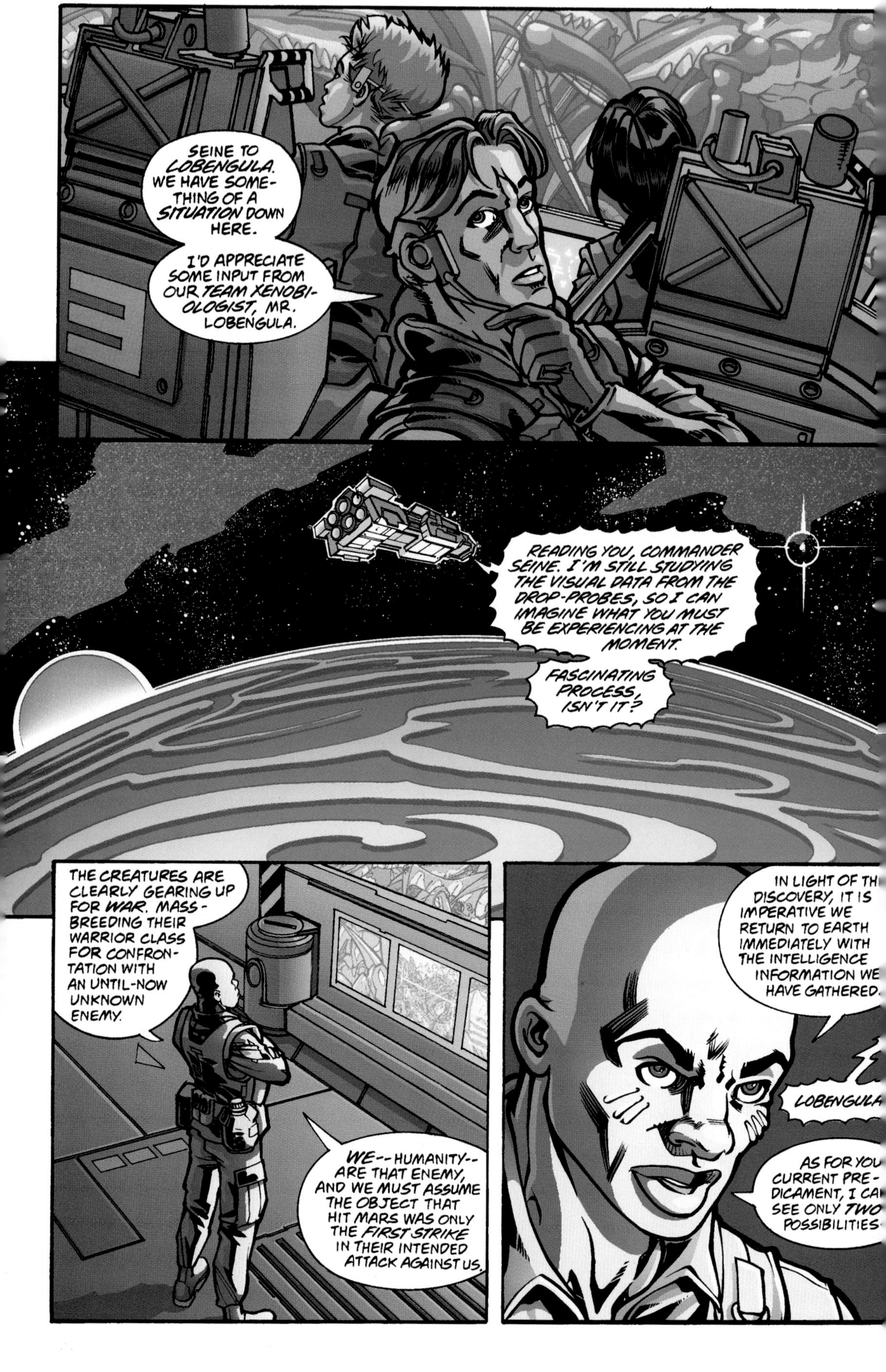
SEINE TO LOBENGULA. WE HAVE SOMETHING OF A SITUATION DOWN HERE.
I'D APPRECIATE SOME INPUT FROM OUR TEAM XENOBIOLOGIST, MR. LOBENGULA.
READING YOU, COMMANDER SEINE. I'M STILL STUDYING THE VISUAL DATA FROM THE DROP-PROBES, SO I CAN IMAGINE WHAT YOU MUST BE EXPERIENCING AT THE MOMENT.
FASCINATING PROCESS, ISN'T IT?
THE CREATURES ARE CLEARLY GEARING UP FOR WAR. MASS-BREEDING THEIR WARRIOR CLASS FOR CONFRONTATION WITH AN UNTIL-NOW UNKNOWN ENEMY.
WE--HUMANITY--ARE THAT ENEMY, AND WE MUST ASSUME THE OBJECT THAT HIT MARS WAS ONLY THE FIRST STRIKE IN THEIR INTENDED ATTACK AGAINST US.
IN LIGHT OF TH DISCOVERY, IT IS IMPERATIVE WE RETURN TO EARTH IMMEDIATELY WITH THE INTELLIGENCE INFORMATION WE HAVE GATHERED.
LOBENGULA
AS FOR YOU CURRENT PREDICAMENT, I CA SEE ONLY TWO POSSIBILITIES

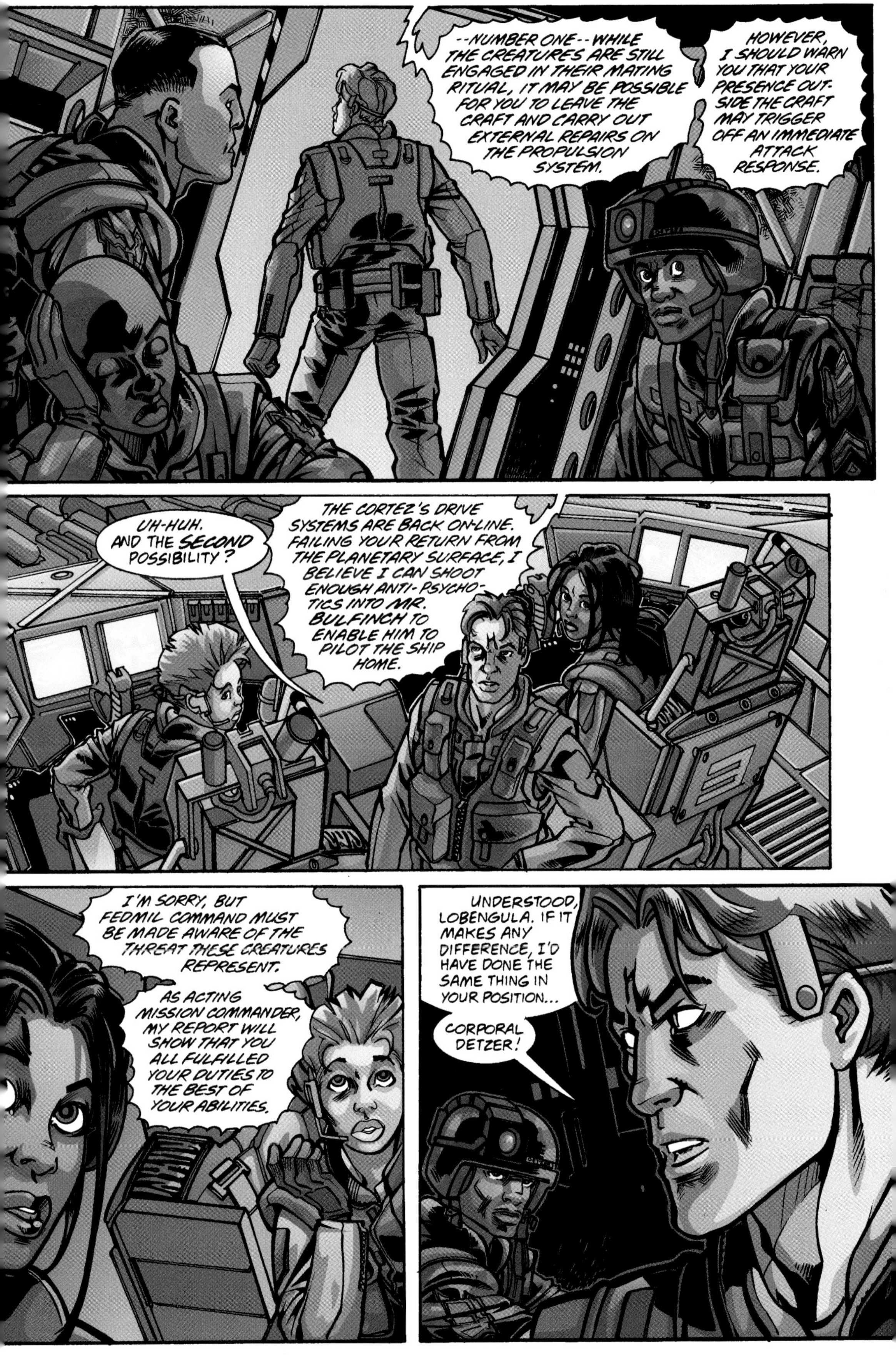
--NUMBER ONE--WHILE THE CREATURES ARE STILL ENGAGED IN THEIR MATING RITUAL, IT MAY BE POSSIBLE FOR YOU TO LEAVE THE CRAFT AND CARRY OUT EXTERNAL REPAIRS ON THE PROPULSION SYSTEM.
HOWEVER, I SHOULD WARN YOU THAT YOUR PRESENCE OUTSIDE THE CRAFT MAY TRIGGER OFF AN IMMEDIATE ATTACK RESPONSE.
UH-HUH. AND THE SECOND POSSIBILITY?
THE CORTEZ'S DRIVE SYSTEMS ARE BACK ON-LINE. FAILING YOUR RETURN FROM THE PLANETARY SURFACE, I BELIEVE I CAN SHOOT ENOUGH ANTI-PSYCHOTICS INTO MR. BULFINCH TO ENABLE HIM TO PILOT THE SHIP HOME.
I'M SORRY, BUT FEDMIL COMMAND MUST BE MADE AWARE OF THE THREAT THESE CREATURES REPRESENT.
AS ACTING MISSION COMMANDER, MY REPORT WILL SHOW THAT YOU ALL FULFILLED YOUR DUTIES TO THE BEST OF YOUR ABILITIES.
UNDERSTOOD, LOBENGULA. IF IT MAKES ANY DIFFERENCE, I'D HAVE DONE THE SAME THING IN YOUR POSITION...
CORPORAL DETZER!

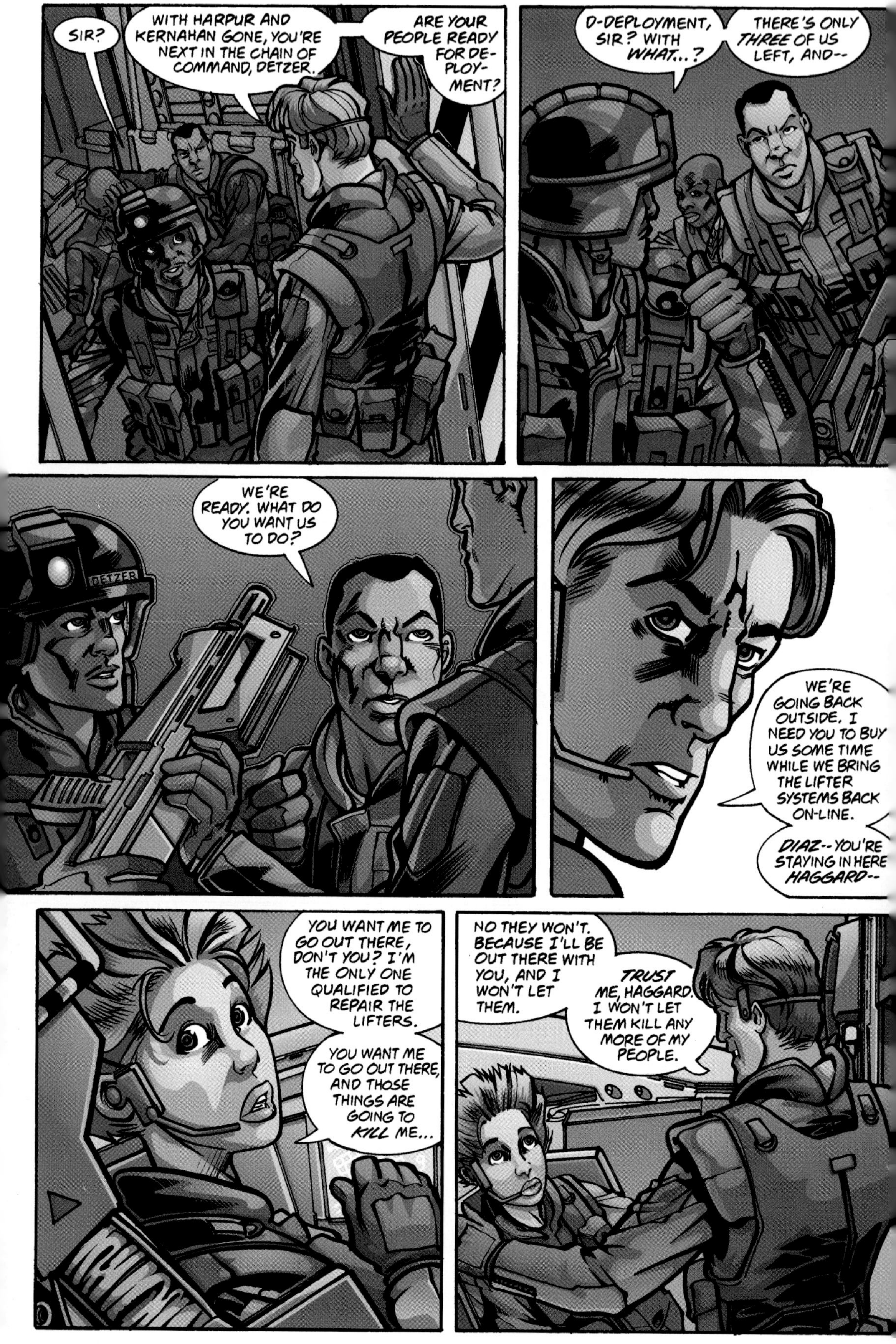
SIR?
WITH HARPUR AND KERNAHAN GONE, YOU'RE NEXT IN THE CHAIN OF COMMAND, DETZER.
ARE YOUR PEOPLE READY FOR DE-PLOY-MENT?
D-DEPLOYMENT, SIR? WITH WHAT...?
THERE'S ONLY THREE OF US LEFT, AND--
WE'RE READY. WHAT DO YOU WANT US TO DO?
DETZER
WE'RE GOING BACK OUTSIDE. I NEED YOU TO BUY US SOME TIME WHILE WE BRING THE LIFTER SYSTEMS BACK ON-LINE.
DIAZ--YOU'RE STAYING IN HERE HAGGARD--
YOU WANT ME TO GO OUT THERE, DON'T YOU? I'M THE ONLY ONE QUALIFIED TO REPAIR THE LIFTERS.
YOU WANT ME TO GO OUT THERE, AND THOSE THINGS ARE GOING TO KILL ME...
NO THEY WON'T. BECAUSE I'LL BE OUT THERE WITH YOU, AND I WON'T LET THEM.
TRUST ME, HAGGARD. I WON'T LET THEM KILL ANY MORE OF MY PEOPLE.

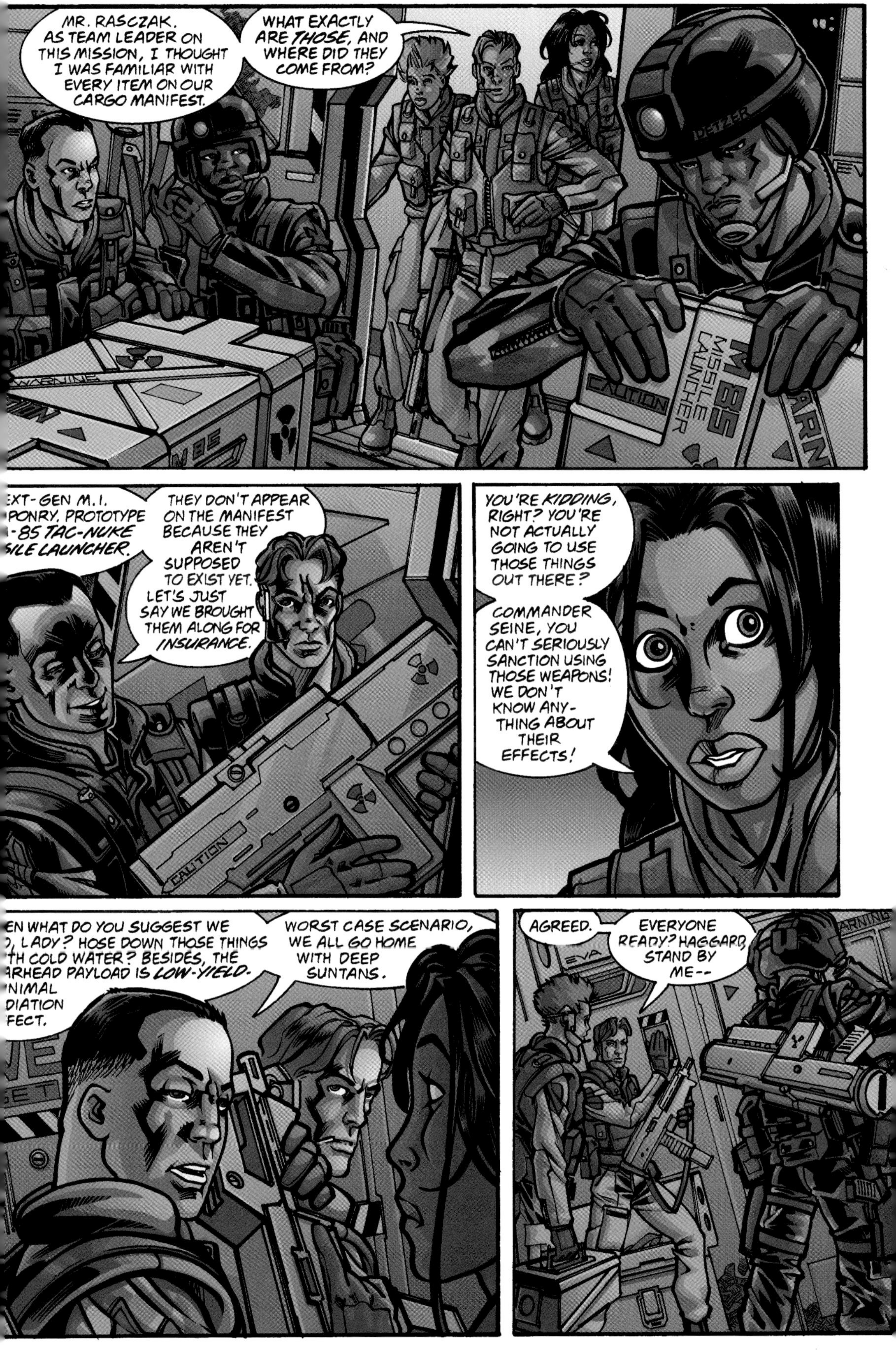
MR. RASCZAK. AS TEAM LEADER ON THIS MISSION, I THOUGHT I WAS FAMILIAR WITH EVERY ITEM ON OUR CARGO MANIFEST.
WHAT EXACTLY ARE THOSE, AND WHERE DID THEY COME FROM?
DETZER
M 85 MISSILE LAUNCHER
CAUTION
WARNING
EXT-GEN M.I. PONRY. PROTOTYPE -85 TAC-NUKE SILE LAUNCHER.
THEY DON'T APPEAR ON THE MANIFEST BECAUSE THEY AREN'T SUPPOSED TO EXIST YET. LET'S JUST SAY WE BROUGHT THEM ALONG FOR INSURANCE.
CAUTION
YOU'RE KIDDING, RIGHT? YOU'RE NOT ACTUALLY GOING TO USE THOSE THINGS OUT THERE?
COMMANDER SEINE, YOU CAN'T SERIOUSLY SANCTION USING THOSE WEAPONS! WE DON'T KNOW ANY-THING ABOUT THEIR EFFECTS!
EN WHAT DO YOU SUGGEST WE , LADY? HOSE DOWN THOSE THINGS TH COLD WATER? BESIDES, THE ARHEAD PAYLOAD IS LOW-YIELD. NIMAL DIATION FECT.
WORST CASE SCENARIO, WE ALL GO HOME WITH DEEP SUNTANS.
AGREED.
EVERYONE READY? HAGGARD, STAND BY ME--
EVA

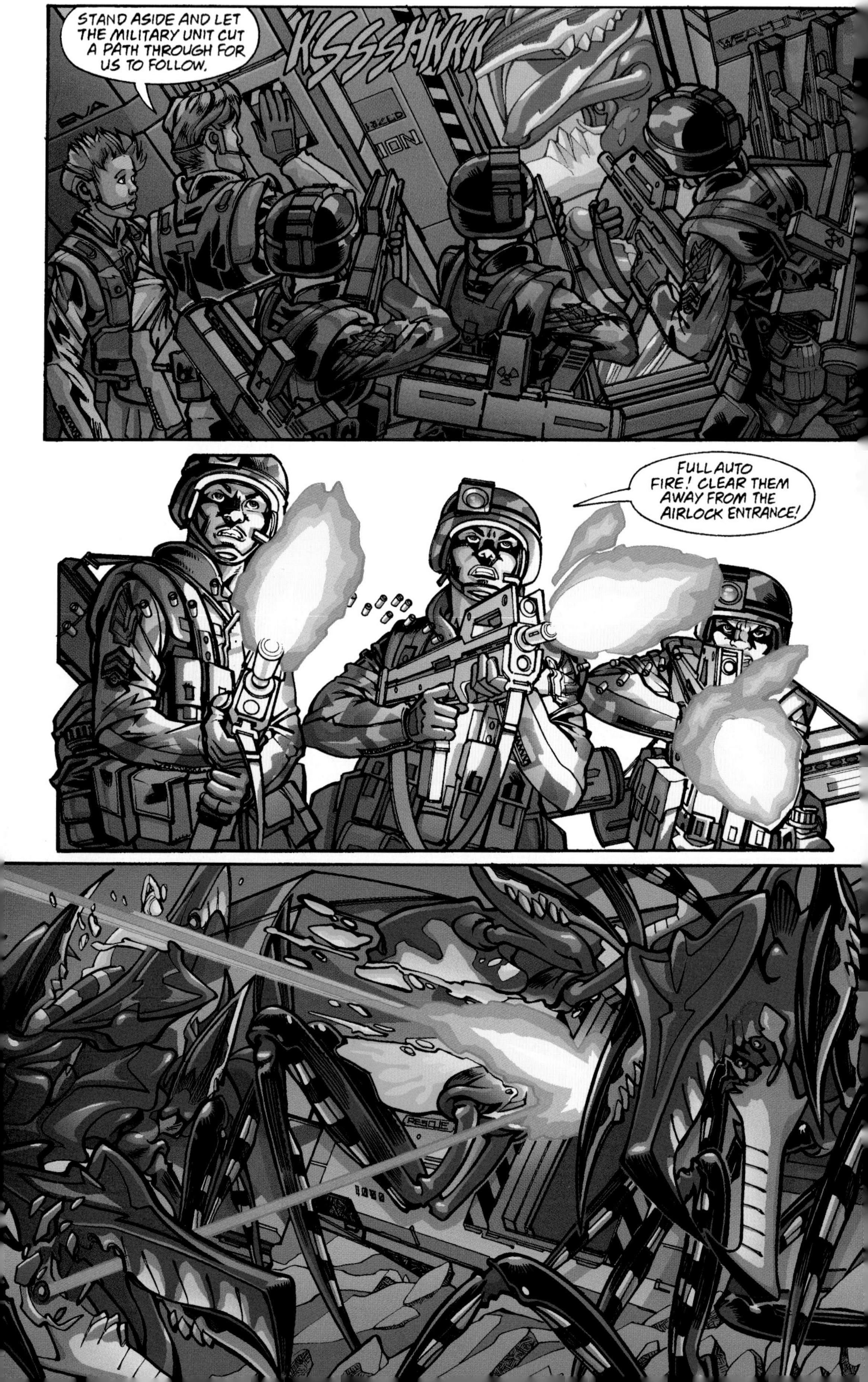
STAND ASIDE AND LET THE MILITARY UNIT CUT A PATH THROUGH FOR US TO FOLLOW.
KSSSSHKKK
FULL AUTO FIRE! CLEAR THEM AWAY FROM THE AIRLOCK ENTRANCE!

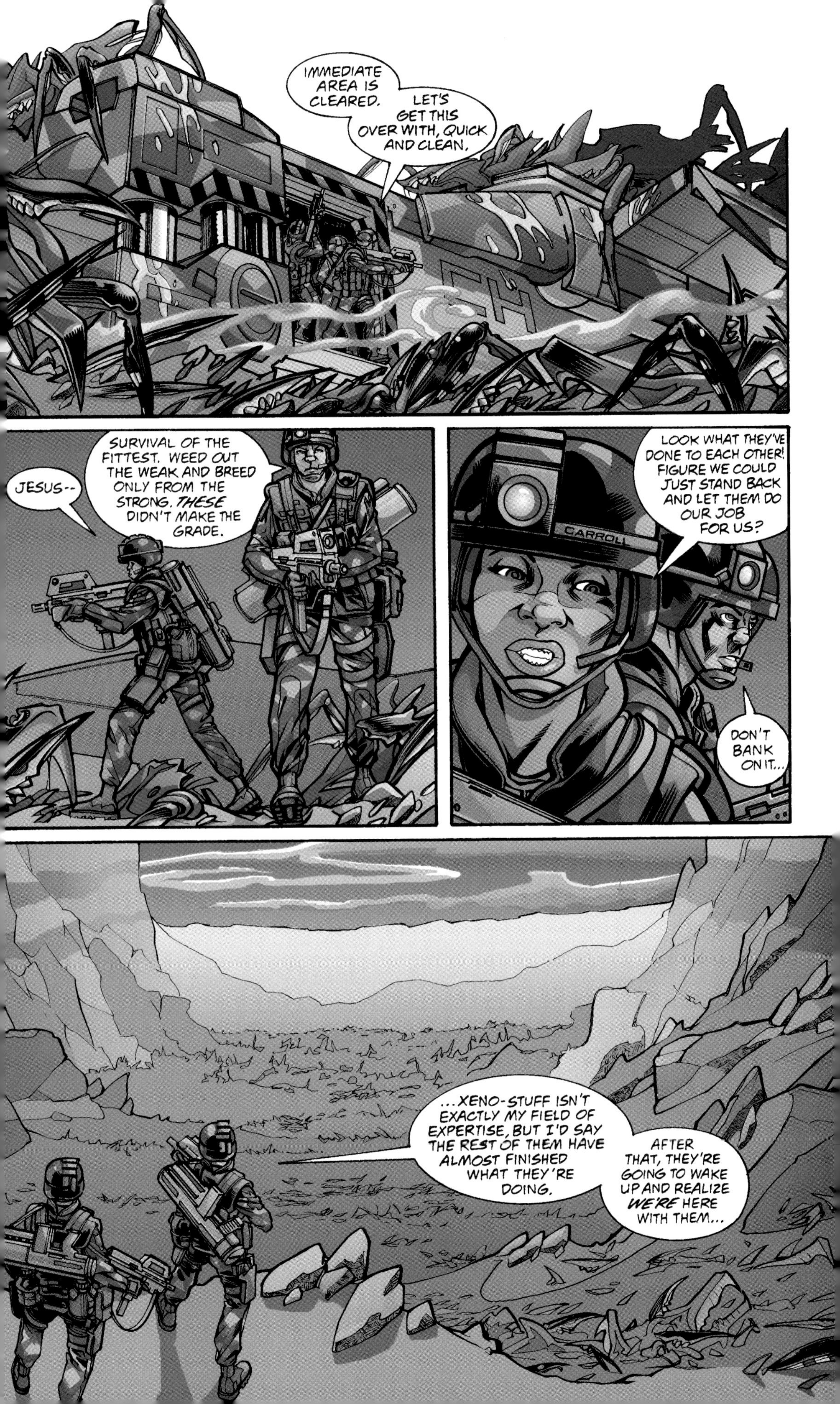
IMMEDIATE AREA IS CLEARED.
LET'S GET THIS OVER WITH, QUICK AND CLEAN.
JESUS--
SURVIVAL OF THE FITTEST. WEED OUT THE WEAK AND BREED ONLY FROM THE STRONG. THESE DIDN'T MAKE THE GRADE.
CARROLL
LOOK WHAT THEY'VE DONE TO EACH OTHER! FIGURE WE COULD JUST STAND BACK AND LET THEM DO OUR JOB FOR US?
DON'T BANK ON IT...
...XENO-STUFF ISN'T EXACTLY MY FIELD OF EXPERTISE, BUT I'D SAY THE REST OF THEM HAVE ALMOST FINISHED WHAT THEY'RE DOING.
AFTER THAT, THEY'RE GOING TO WAKE UP AND REALIZE WE'RE HERE WITH THEM...

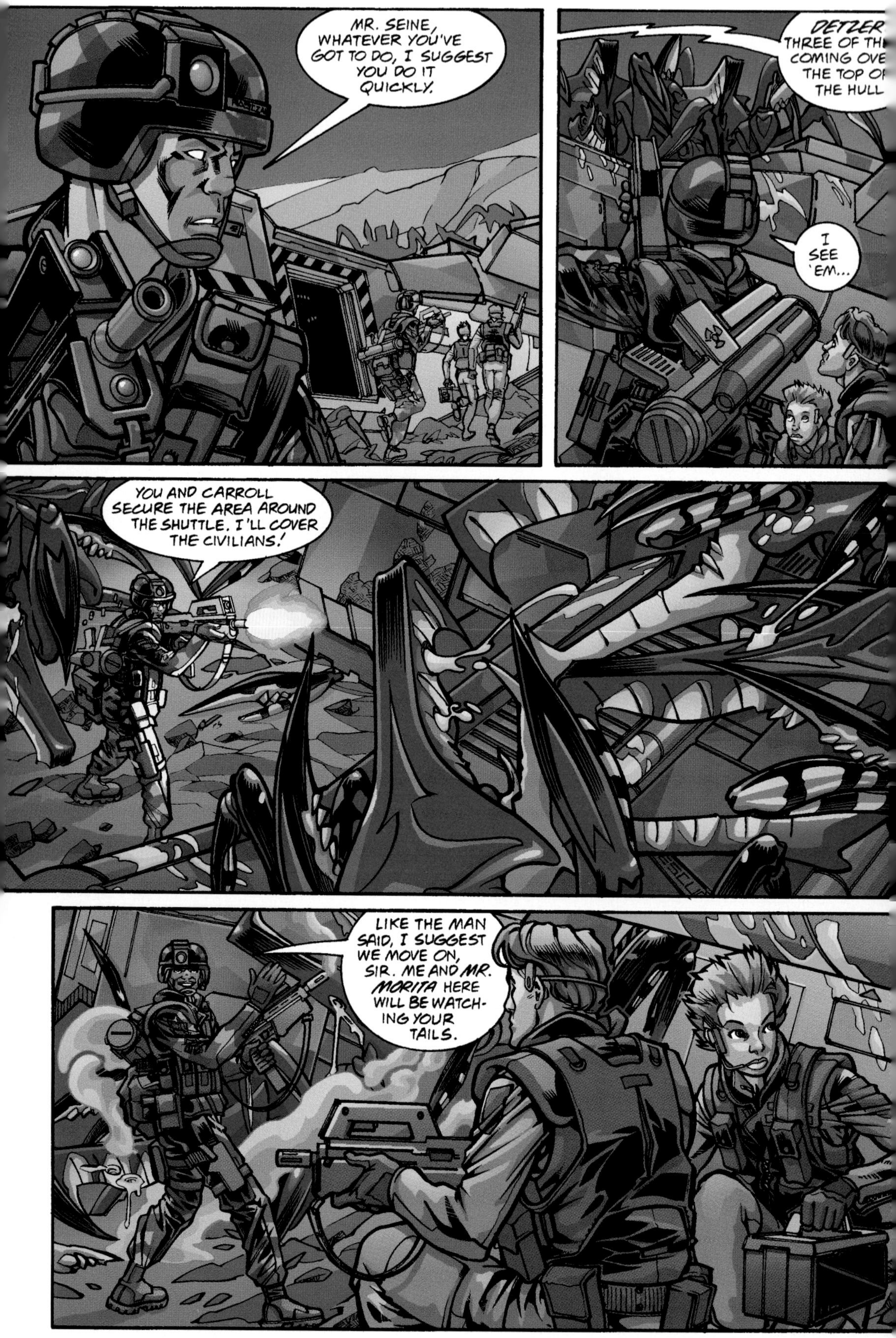

MR. SEINE, WHATEVER YOU'VE GOT TO DO, I SUGGEST YOU DO IT QUICKLY.
DETZER THREE OF TH COMING OVE THE TOP OF THE HULL
I SEE 'EM...
YOU AND CARROLL SECURE THE AREA AROUND THE SHUTTLE. I'LL COVER THE CIVILIANS!
LIKE THE MAN SAID, I SUGGEST WE MOVE ON, SIR. ME AND MR. MORITA HERE WILL BE WATCHING YOUR TAILS.

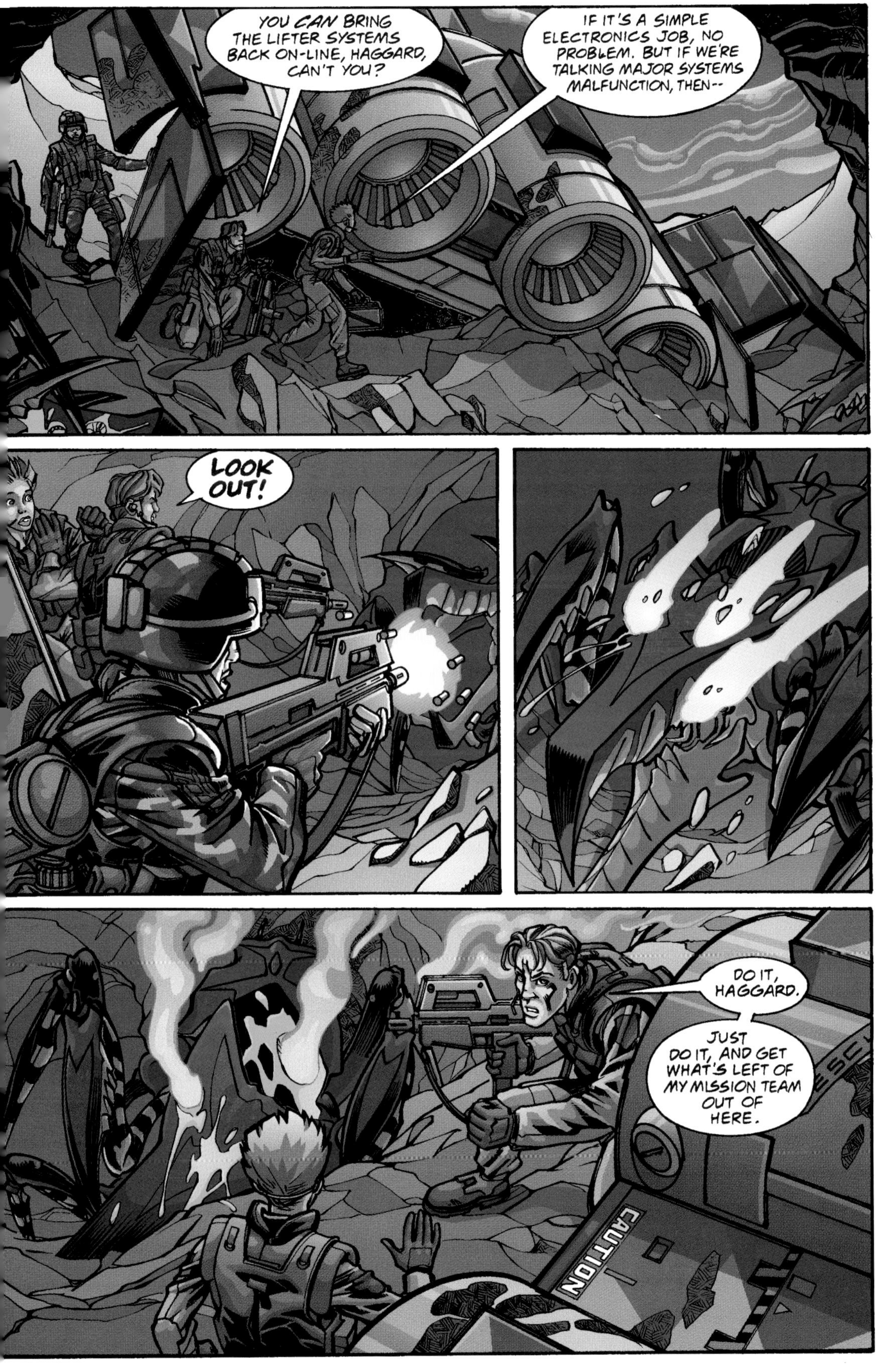
YOU CAN BRING THE LIFTER SYSTEMS BACK ON-LINE, HAGGARD, CAN'T YOU?
IF IT'S A SIMPLE ELECTRONICS JOB, NO PROBLEM. BUT IF WE'RE TALKING MAJOR SYSTEMS MALFUNCTION, THEN--
LOOK OUT!
DO IT, HAGGARD.
JUST DO IT, AND GET WHAT'S LEFT OF MY MISSION TEAM OUT OF HERE.
CAUTION

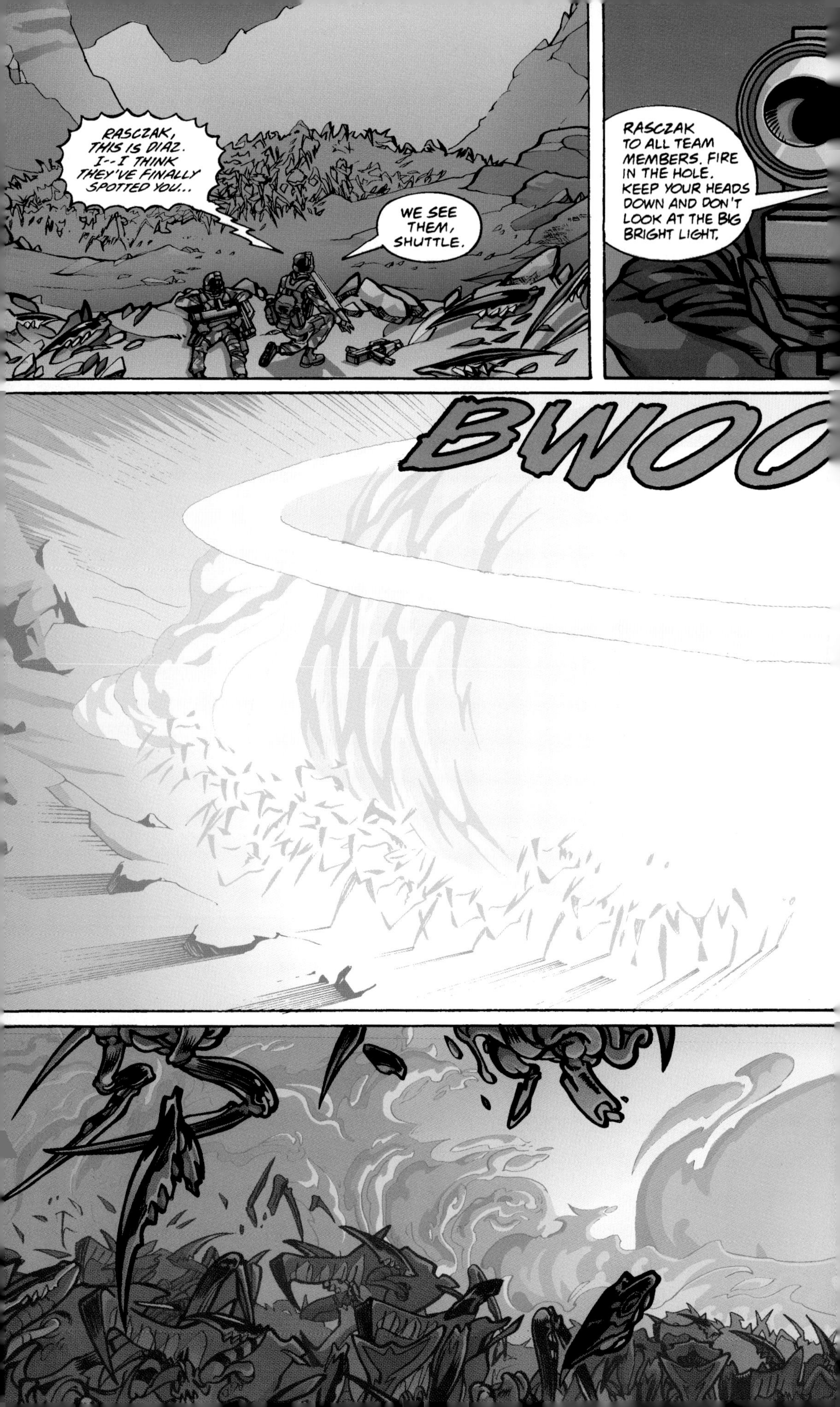
RASCZAK, THIS IS DIAZ. I--I THINK THEY'VE FINALLY SPOTTED YOU...
WE SEE THEM, SHUTTLE.
RASCZAK TO ALL TEAM MEMBERS. FIRE IN THE HOLE. KEEP YOUR HEADS DOWN AND DON'T LOOK AT THE BIG BRIGHT LIGHT.
BWOO

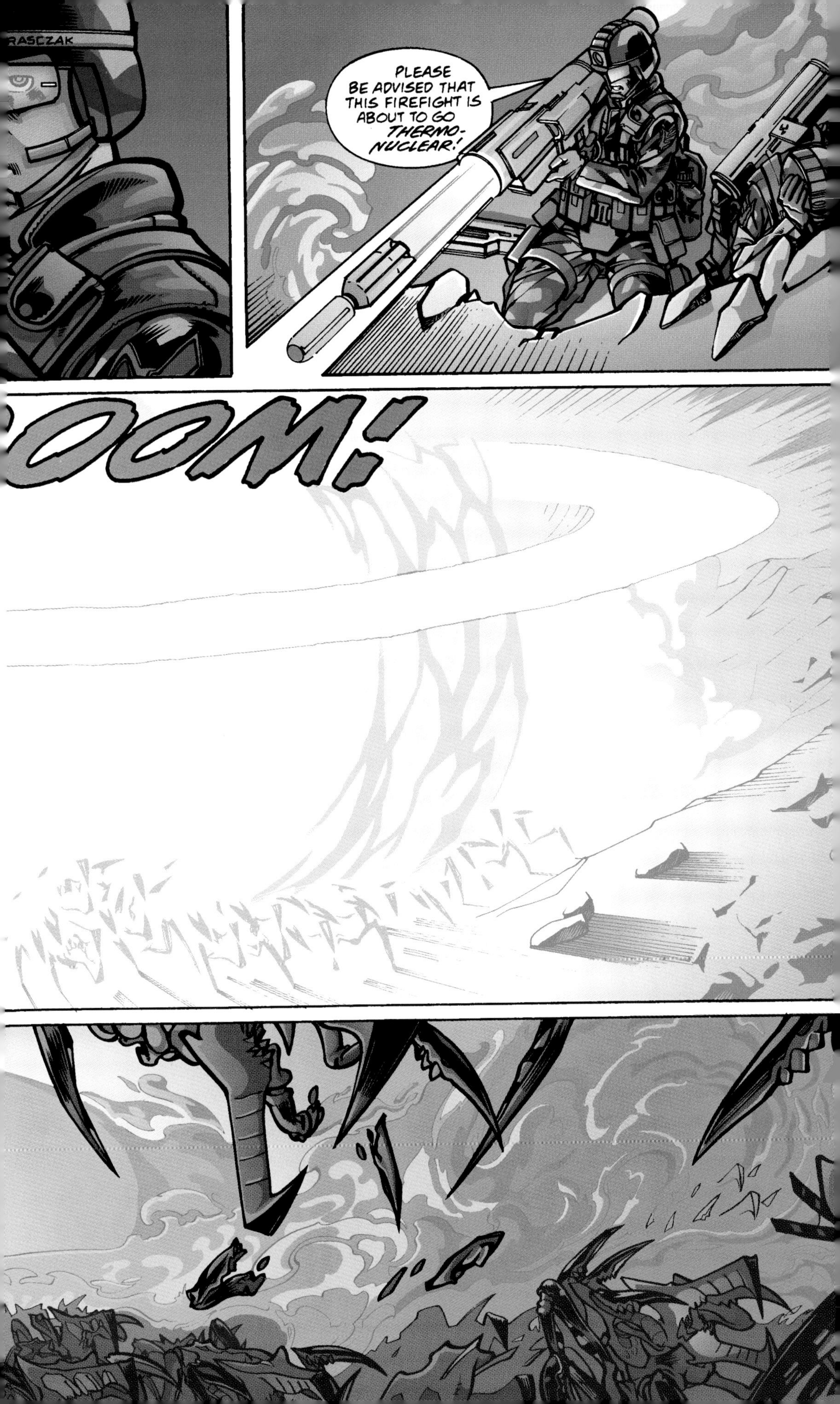
RASCZAK
PLEASE BE ADVISED THAT THIS FIREFIGHT IS ABOUT TO GO THERMO-NUCLEAR!
OOM!

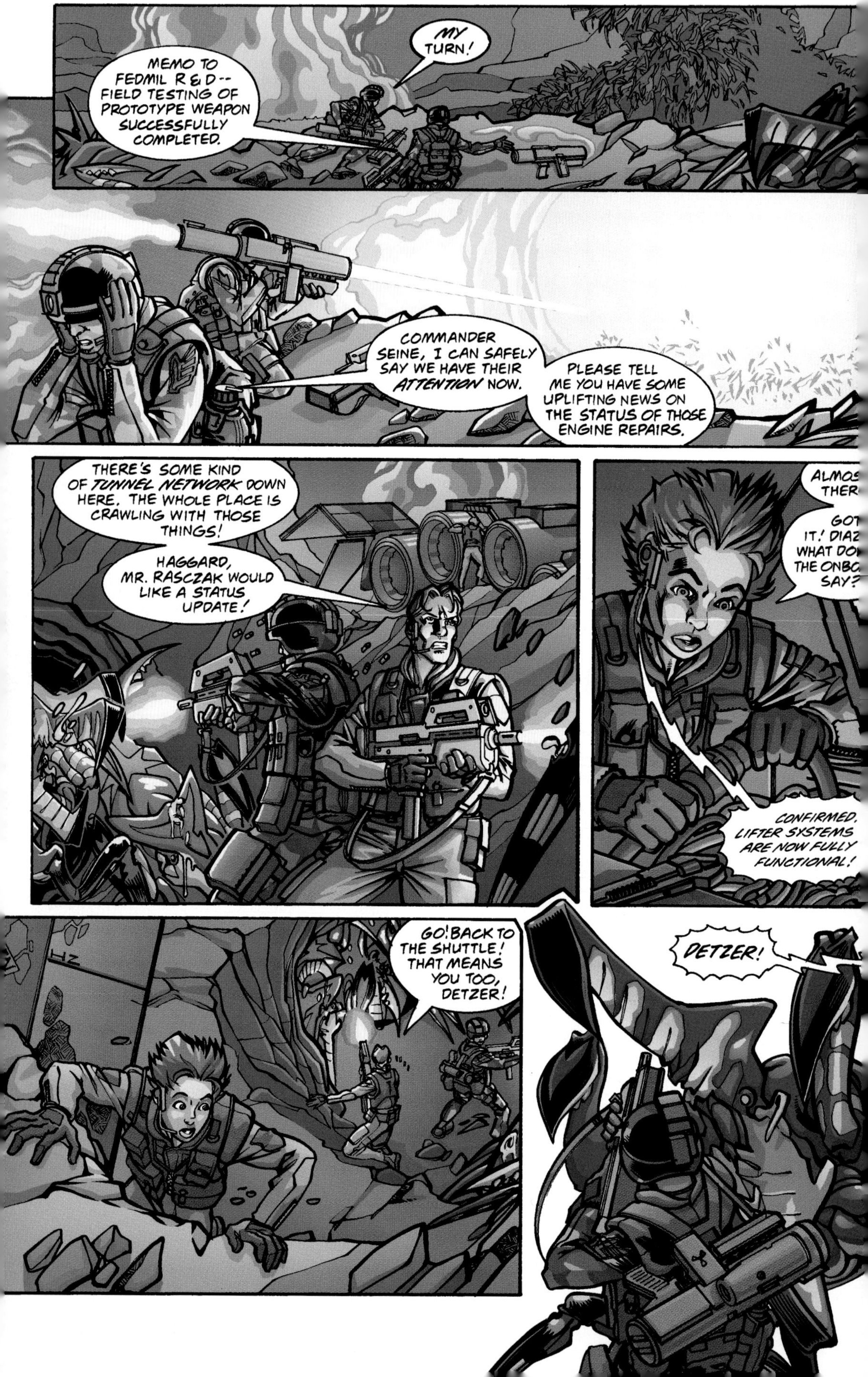
MEMO TO FEDMIL R&D-- FIELD TESTING OF PROTOTYPE WEAPON SUCCESSFULLY COMPLETED.
MY TURN!
COMMANDER SEINE, I CAN SAFELY SAY WE HAVE THEIR ATTENTION NOW.
PLEASE TELL ME YOU HAVE SOME UPLIFTING NEWS ON THE STATUS OF THOSE ENGINE REPAIRS.
THERE'S SOME KIND OF TUNNEL NETWORK DOWN HERE. THE WHOLE PLACE IS CRAWLING WITH THOSE THINGS!
HAGGARD, MR. RASCZAK WOULD LIKE A STATUS UPDATE!
ALMOS THER
GOT IT! DIAZ WHAT DO THE ONBO SAY?
CONFIRMED. LIFTER SYSTEMS ARE NOW FULLY FUNCTIONAL!
GO! BACK TO THE SHUTTLE! THAT MEANS YOU TOO, DETZER!
DETZER!

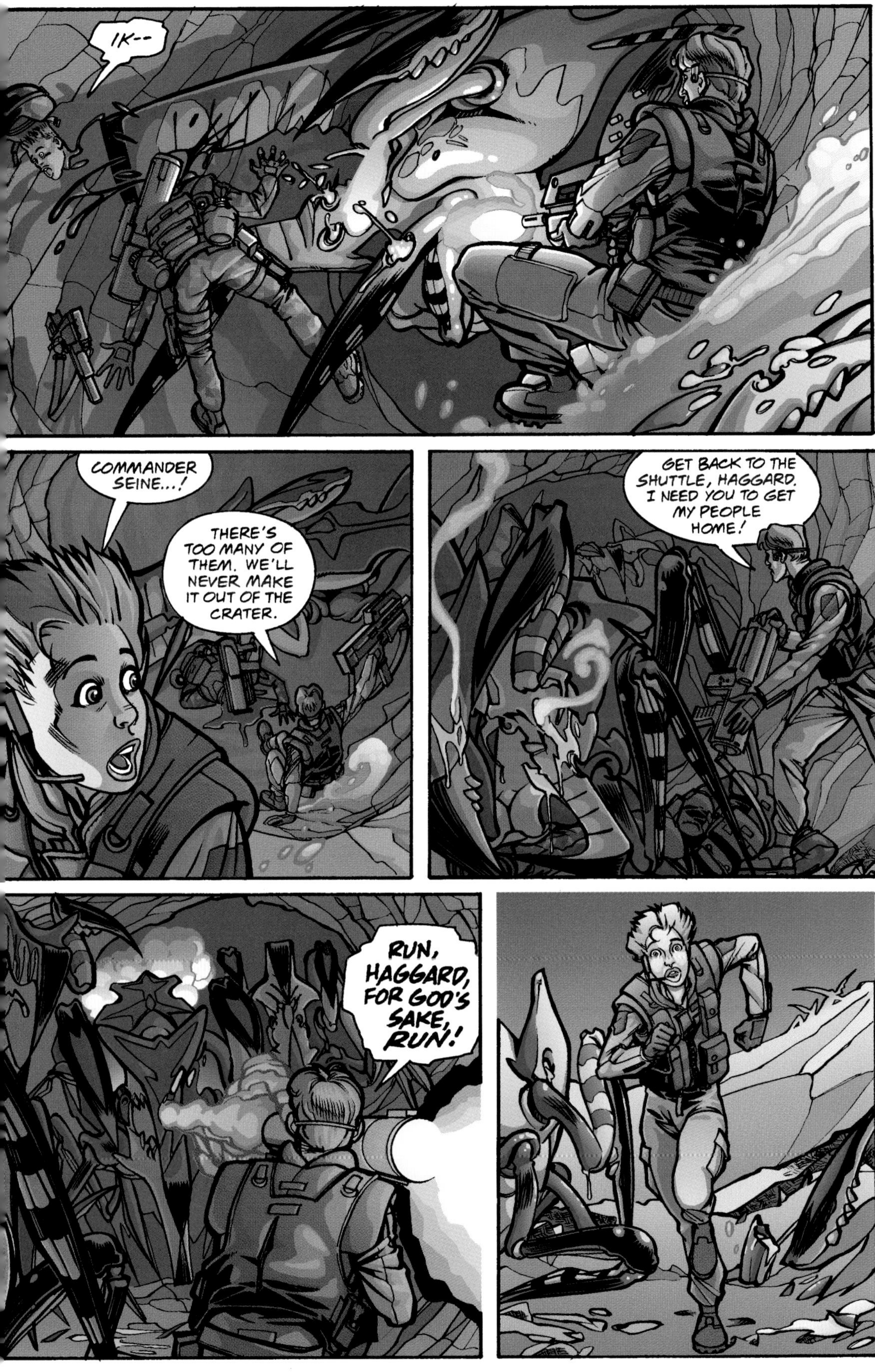
IK--
COMMANDER SEINE...!
THERE'S TOO MANY OF THEM. WE'LL NEVER MAKE IT OUT OF THE CRATER.
GET BACK TO THE SHUTTLE, HAGGARD. I NEED YOU TO GET MY PEOPLE HOME!
RUN, HAGGARD, FOR GOD'S SAKE, RUN!

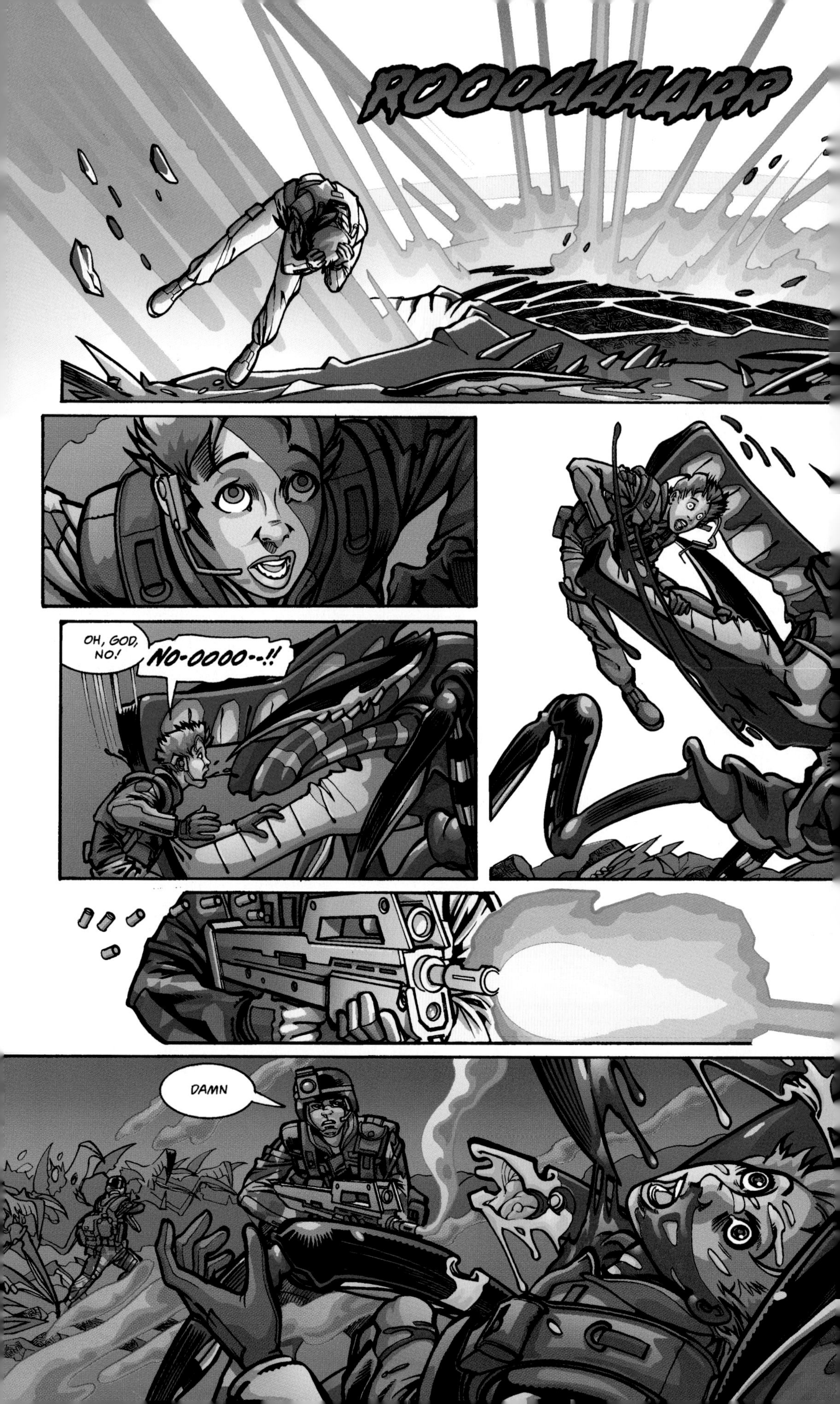
ROOOAAAAARR
OH, GOD, NO!
NO-OOOO--!!
DAMN

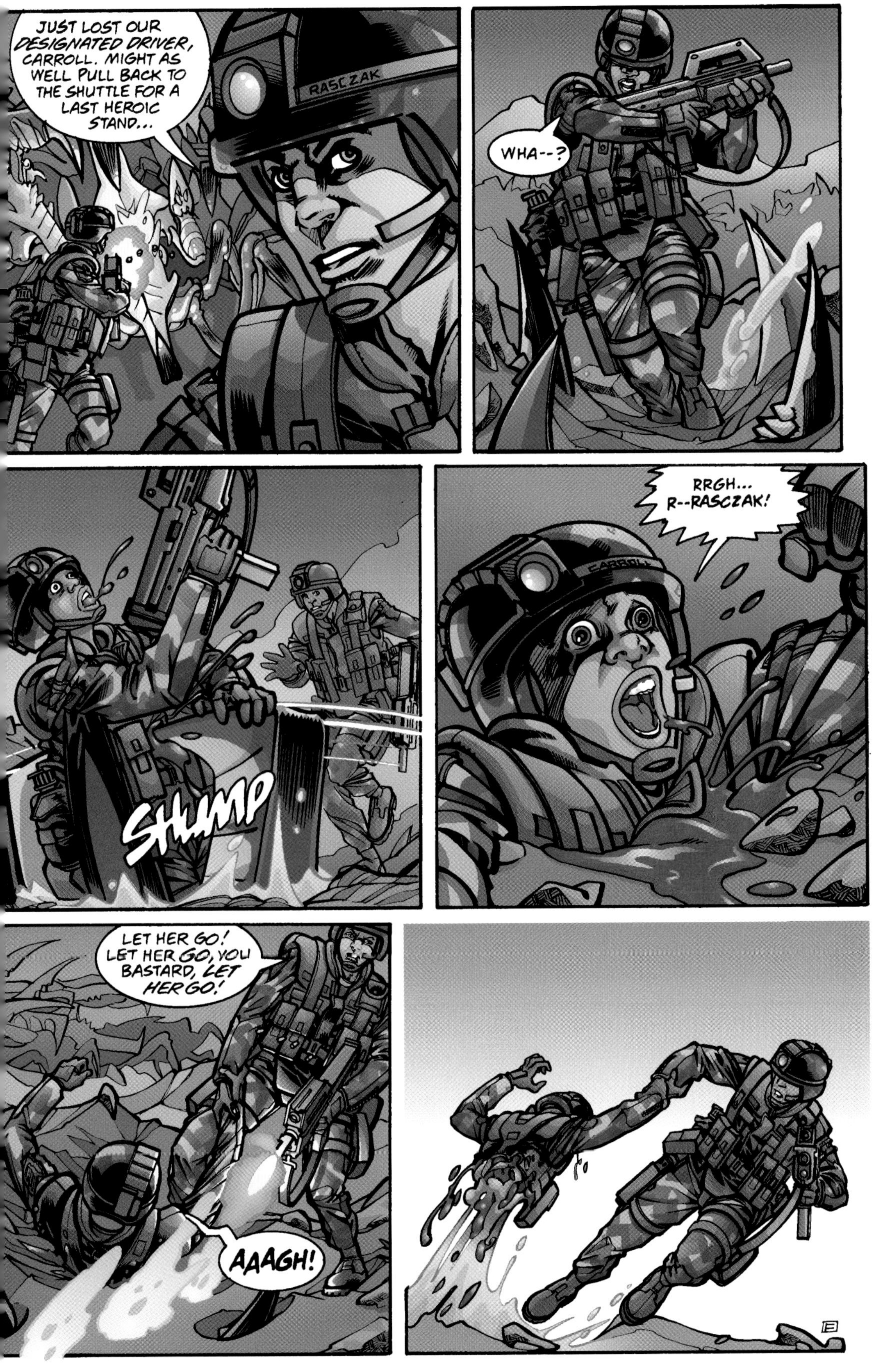

JUST LOST OUR DESIGNATED DRIVER, CARROLL. MIGHT AS WELL PULL BACK TO THE SHUTTLE FOR A LAST HEROIC STAND...
RASCZAK
WHA--?
SHUMP
RRGH... R--RASCZAK!
LET HER GO! LET HER GO, YOU BASTARD, LET HER GO!
AAAGH!

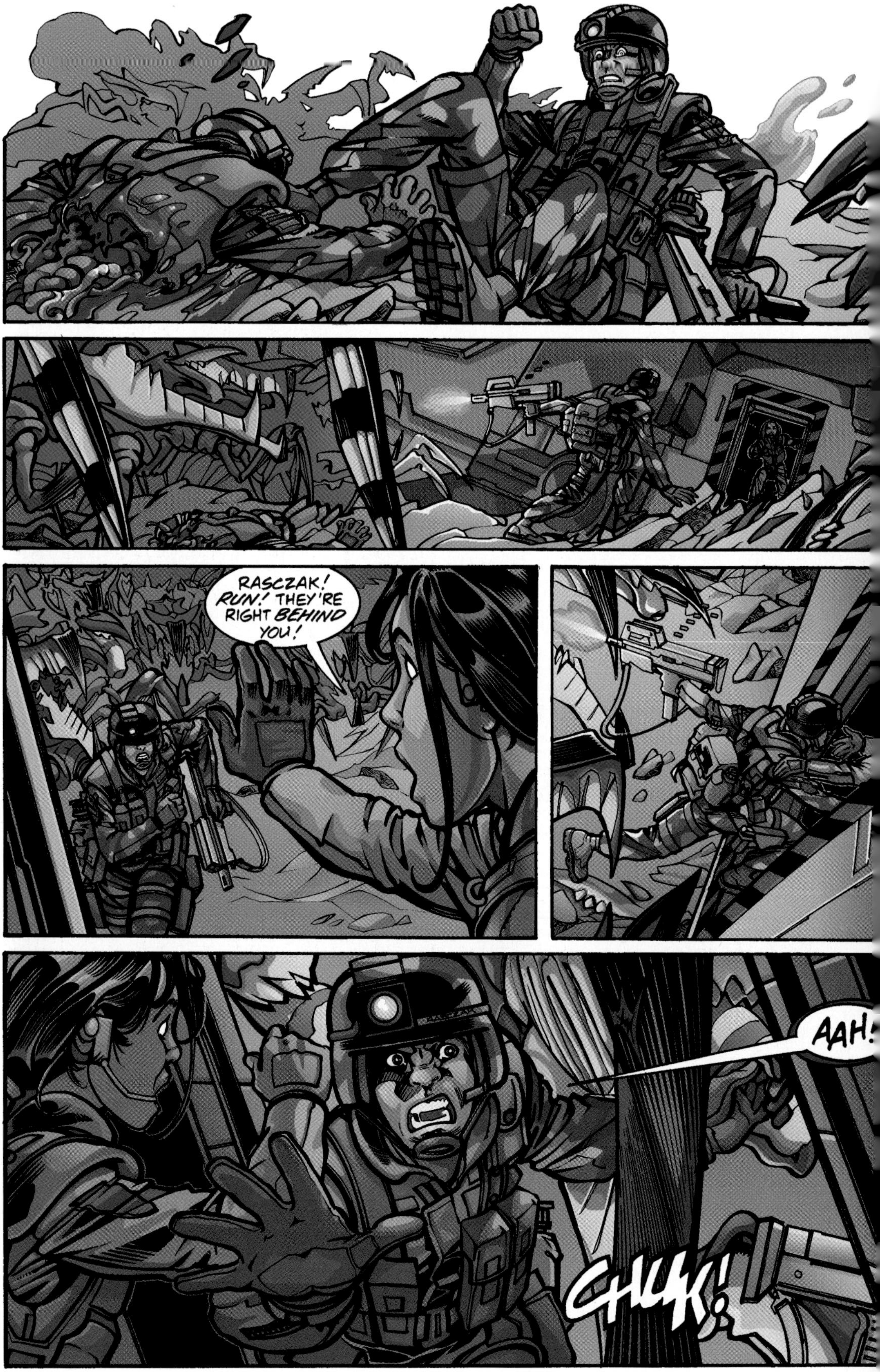
RASCZAK! RUN! THEY'RE RIGHT BEHIND YOU!
AAH!
CHUK!

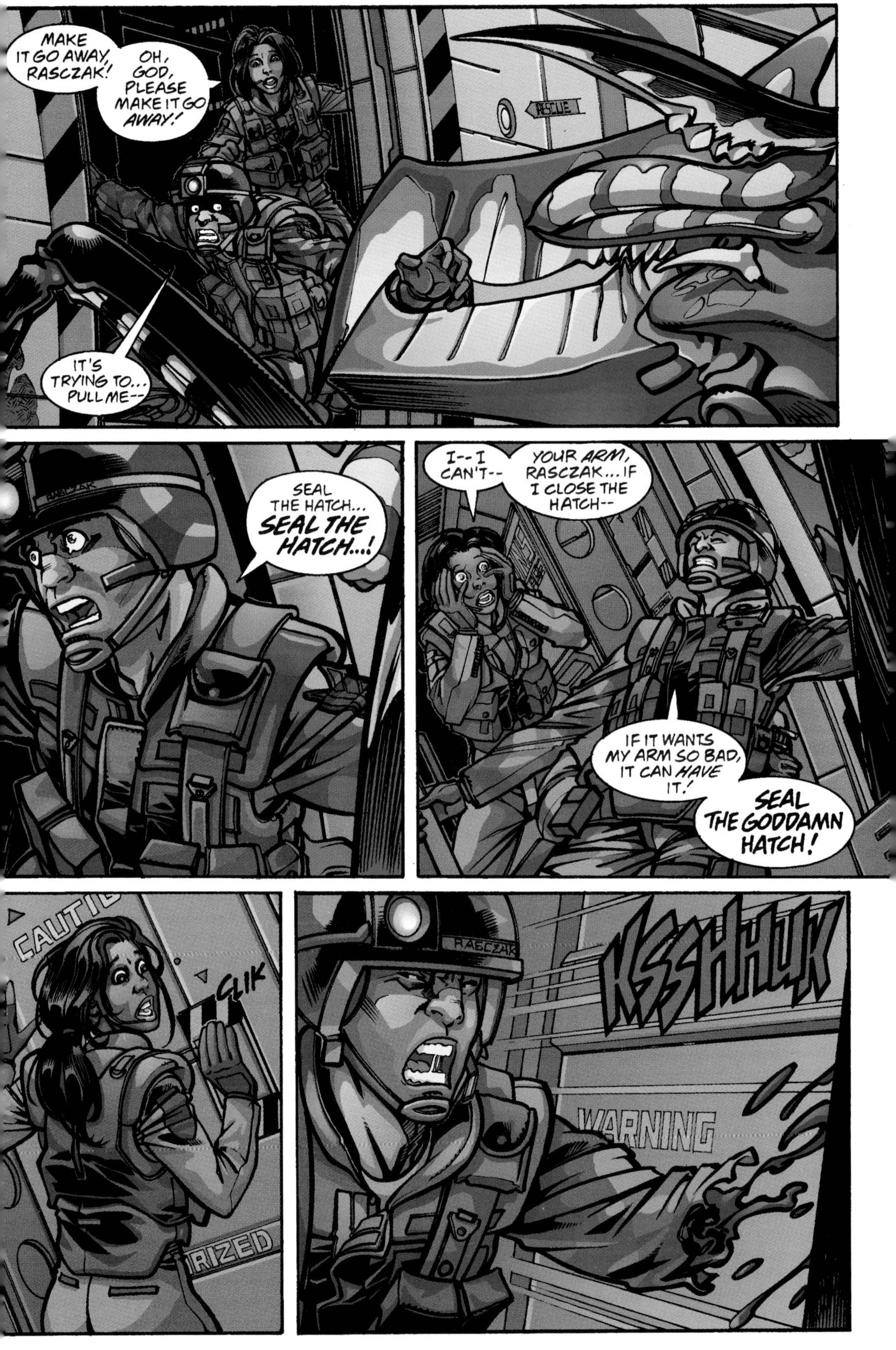

MAKE IT GO AWAY, RASCZAK!
OH, GOD, PLEASE MAKE IT GO AWAY!
RESCUE
IT'S TRYING TO... PULL ME--
RASCZAK
SEAL THE HATCH... SEAL THE HATCH...!
I-- I CAN'T--
YOUR ARM, RASCZAK... IF I CLOSE THE HATCH--
IF IT WANTS MY ARM SO BAD, IT CAN HAVE IT!
SEAL THE GODDAMN HATCH!
CAUTI
CLIK
RIZED
RASCZAK
KSSHHUK
WARNING

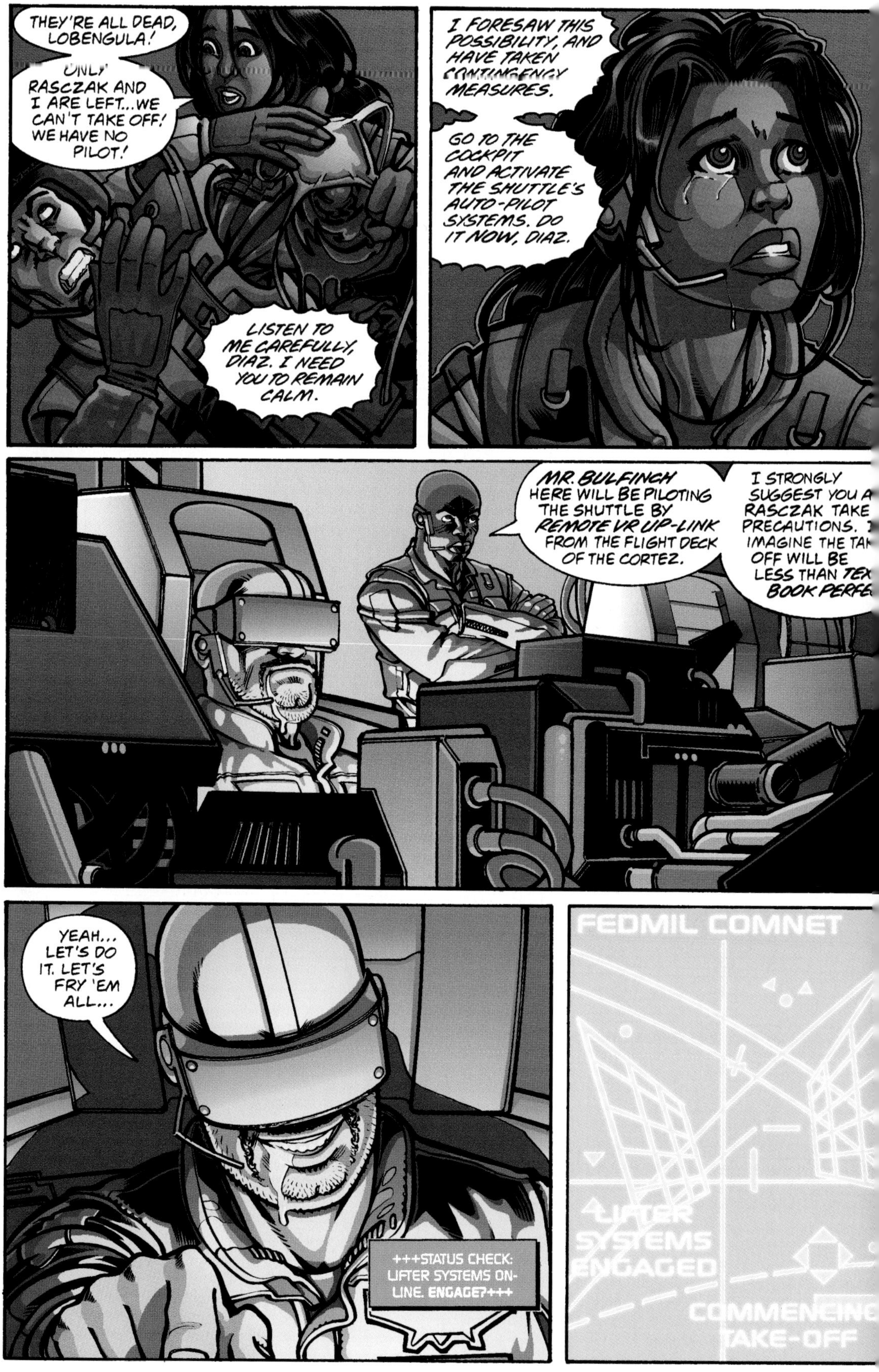
THEY'RE ALL DEAD, LOBENGULA!
ONLY RASCZAK AND I ARE LEFT... WE CAN'T TAKE OFF! WE HAVE NO PILOT!
LISTEN TO ME CAREFULLY, DIAZ. I NEED YOU TO REMAIN CALM.
I FORESAW THIS POSSIBILITY, AND HAVE TAKEN CONTINGENCY MEASURES.
GO TO THE COCKPIT AND ACTIVATE THE SHUTTLE'S AUTO-PILOT SYSTEMS. DO IT NOW, DIAZ.
MR. BULFINCH HERE WILL BE PILOTING THE SHUTTLE BY REMOTE VR UP-LINK FROM THE FLIGHT DECK OF THE CORTEZ.
I STRONGLY SUGGEST YOU A RASCZAK TAKE PRECAUTIONS. I IMAGINE THE TAK OFF WILL BE LESS THAN TEX BOOK PERFE
YEAH... LET'S DO IT. LET'S FRY 'EM ALL...
+++STATUS CHECK: LIFTER SYSTEMS ON-LINE. ENGAGE?+++
FEDMIL COMNET
LIFTER SYSTEMS ENGAGED
COMMENCING TAKE-OFF

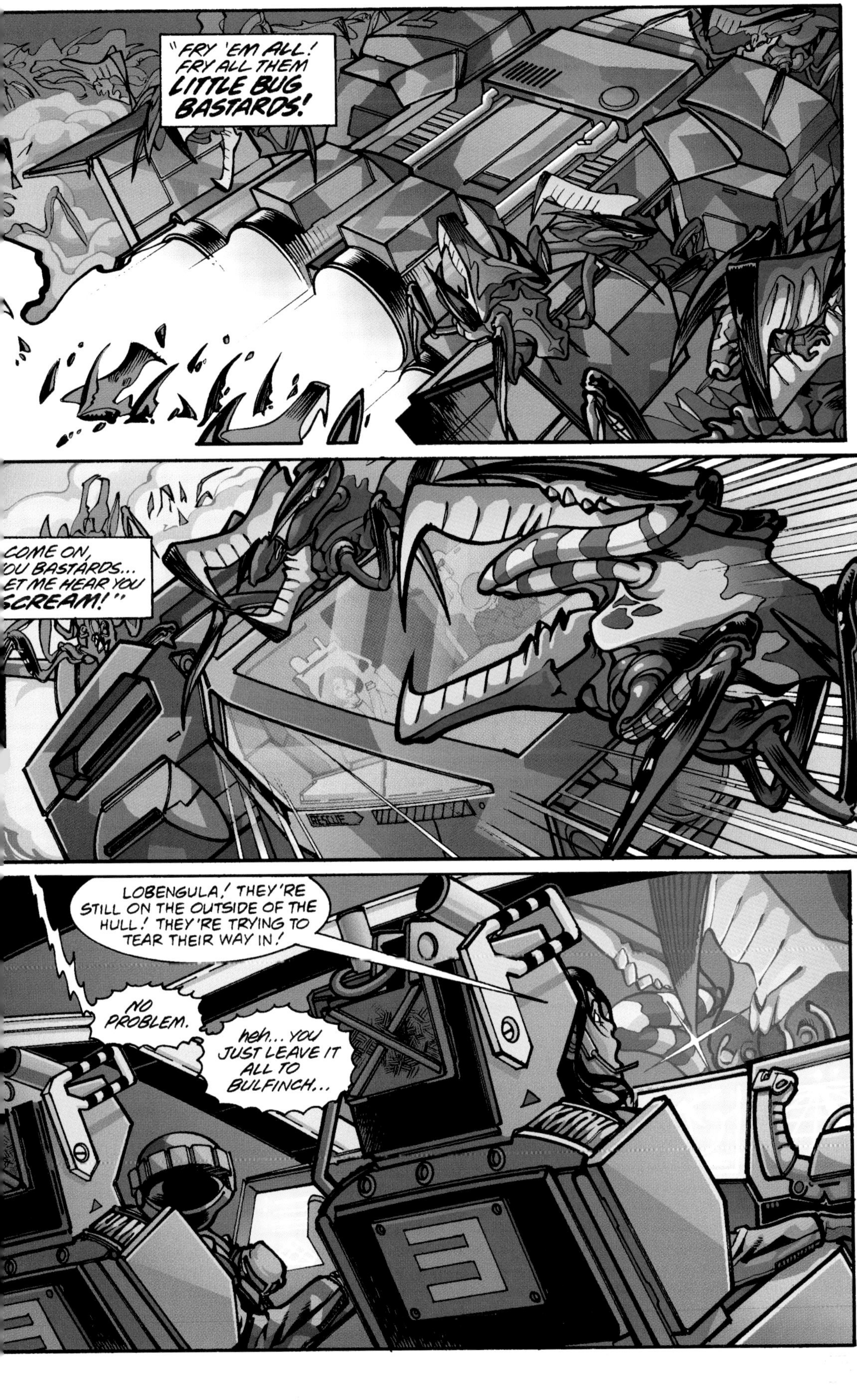
"FRY 'EM ALL! FRY ALL THEM LITTLE BUG BASTARDS!
COME ON, YOU BASTARDS... LET ME HEAR YOU SCREAM!"
RESCUE
LOBENGULA! THEY'RE STILL ON THE OUTSIDE OF THE HULL! THEY'RE TRYING TO TEAR THEIR WAY IN!
NO PROBLEM.
heh... YOU JUST LEAVE IT ALL TO BULFINCH...

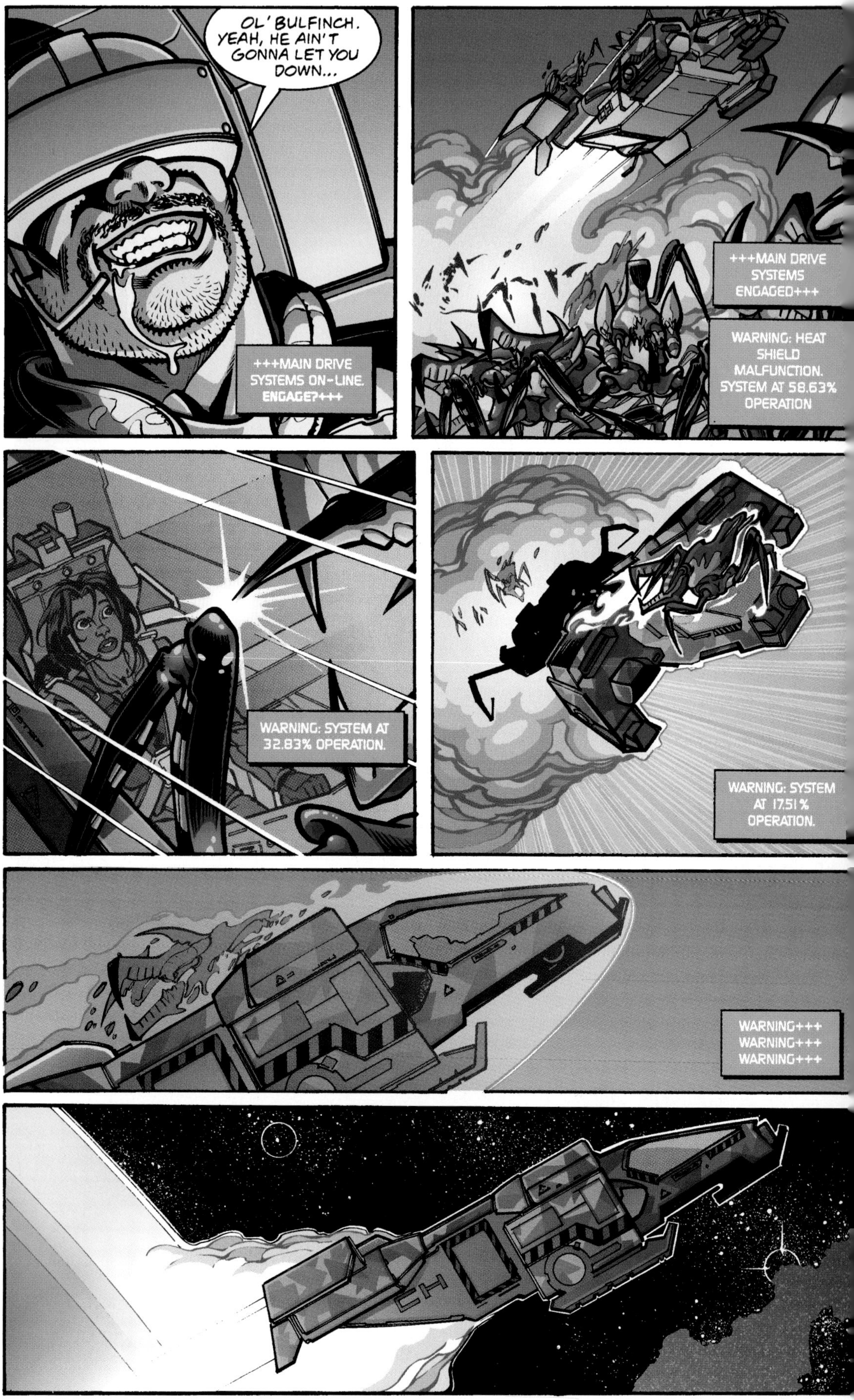
OL' BULFINCH. YEAH, HE AIN'T GONNA LET YOU DOWN...
+++MAIN DRIVE SYSTEMS ON-LINE. ENGAGE?+++
+++MAIN DRIVE SYSTEMS ENGAGED+++
WARNING: HEAT SHIELD MALFUNCTION. SYSTEM AT 58.63% OPERATION
WARNING: SYSTEM AT 32.83% OPERATION.
WARNING: SYSTEM AT 17.51% OPERATION.
WARNING+++
WARNING+++
WARNING+++

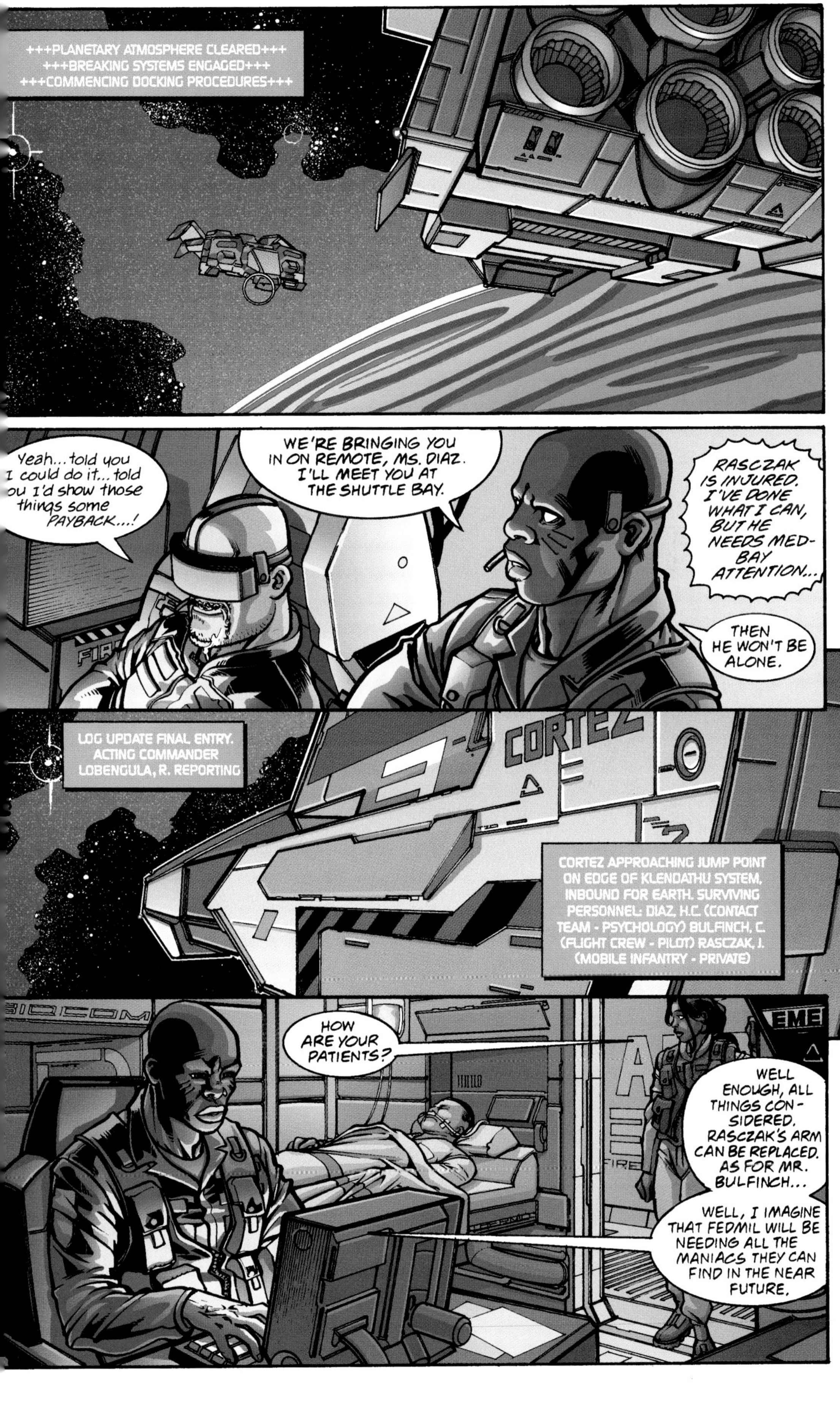
+++PLANETARY ATMOSPHERE CLEARED+++
+++BREAKING SYSTEMS ENGAGED+++
+++COMMENCING DOCKING PROCEDURES+++
Yeah... told you I could do it... told you I'd show those things some PAYBACK...!
WE'RE BRINGING YOU IN ON REMOTE, MS. DIAZ. I'LL MEET YOU AT THE SHUTTLE BAY.
RASCZAK IS INJURED. I'VE DONE WHAT I CAN, BUT HE NEEDS MED-BAY ATTENTION...
THEN HE WON'T BE ALONE.
LOG UPDATE FINAL ENTRY. ACTING COMMANDER LOBENGULA, R. REPORTING
CORTEZ
CORTEZ APPROACHING JUMP POINT ON EDGE OF KLENDATHU SYSTEM, INBOUND FOR EARTH. SURVIVING PERSONNEL: DIAZ, H.C. (CONTACT TEAM - PSYCHOLOGY) BULFINCH, C. (FLIGHT CREW - PILOT) RASCZAK, J. (MOBILE INFANTRY - PRIVATE)
HOW ARE YOUR PATIENTS?
WELL ENOUGH, ALL THINGS CON-SIDERED. RASCZAK'S ARM CAN BE REPLACED. AS FOR MR. BULFINCH...
WELL, I IMAGINE THAT FEDMIL WILL BE NEEDING ALL THE MANIACS THEY CAN FIND IN THE NEAR FUTURE.

YOU REALLY THINK IT'S GOING TO BE THAT BAD?

ABSOLUTELY.

WE'VE JUST EXPERIENCED THE FIRST SKIRMISH BETWEEN TWO AMBITIOUS AND MUTUALLY ANTAGONISTIC IMPERIAL SPECIES. MANKIND AND THE ARACHNIDS.

THIS TIME, WE WERE LUCKY. THEY HAD NEVER EXPERIE[N]... TECHNOLOGICAL WEAPO[NS] BEFORE. BUT THEY'RE SMART. THEY'LL ADAPT.

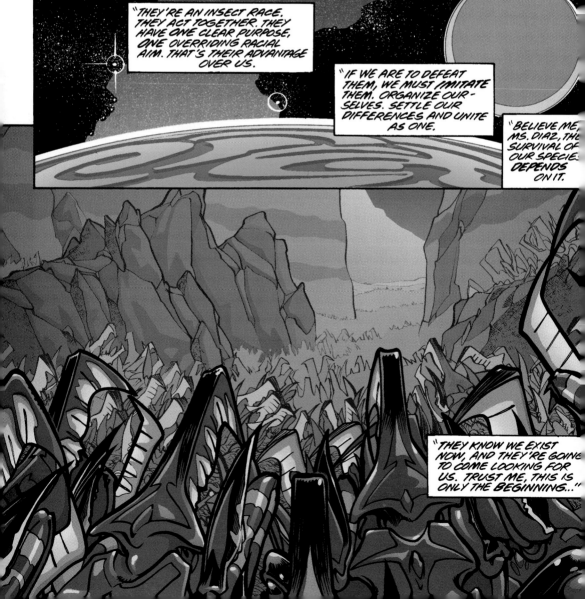

"THEY'RE AN INSECT RACE. THEY ACT TOGETHER. THEY HAVE ONE CLEAR PURPOSE, ONE OVERRIDING RACIAL AIM. THAT'S THEIR ADVANTAGE OVER US.

"IF WE ARE TO DEFEAT THEM, WE MUST IMITATE THEM. ORGANIZE OUR-SELVES. SETTLE OUR DIFFERENCES AND UNITE AS ONE.

"BELIEVE ME, MS. DIAZ, TH[E] SURVIVAL OF OUR SPECIE[S] DEPENDS ON IT.

"THEY KNOW WE EXIST NOW, AND THEY'RE GOING TO COME LOOKING FOR US. TRUST ME, THIS IS ONLY THE BEGINNING..."

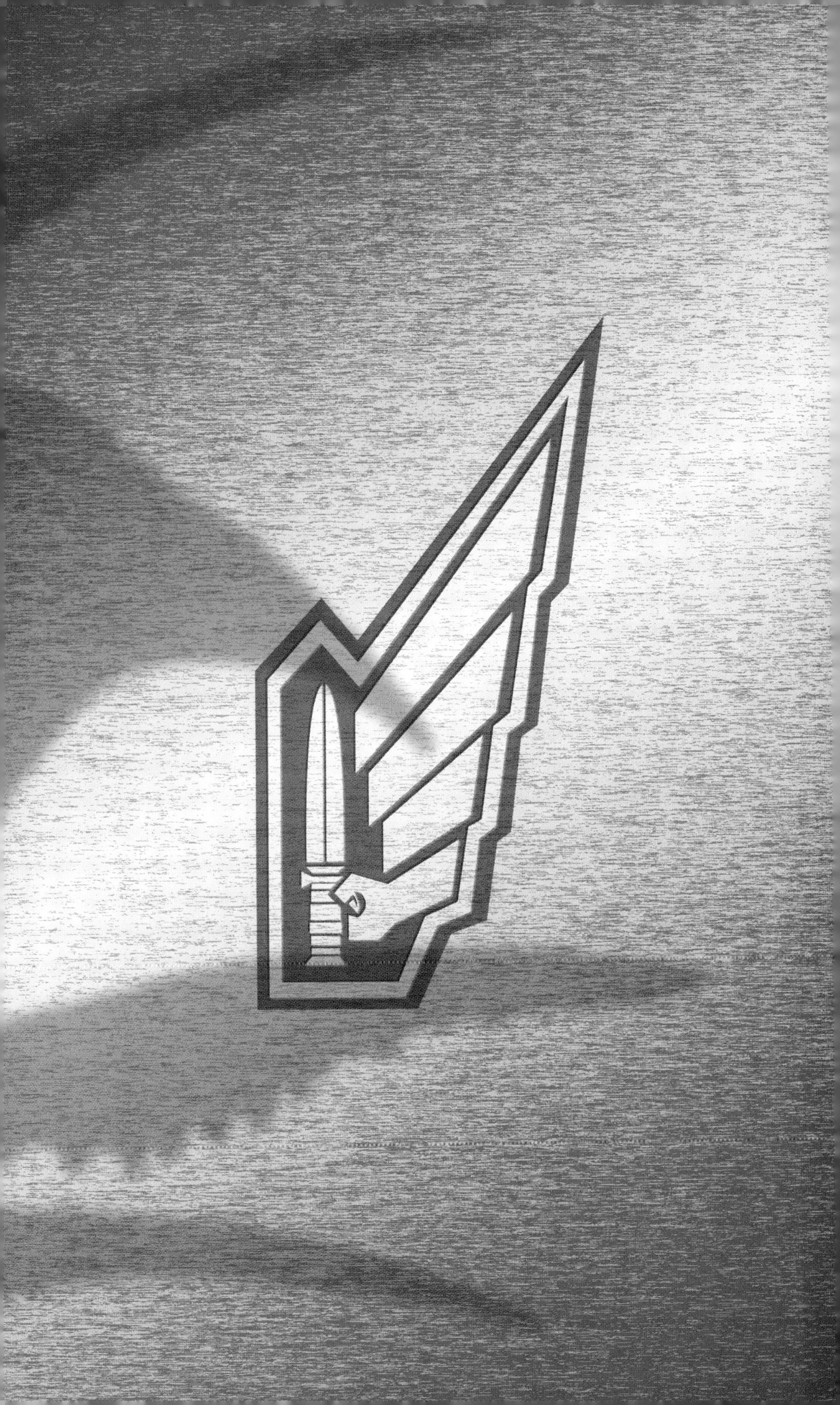

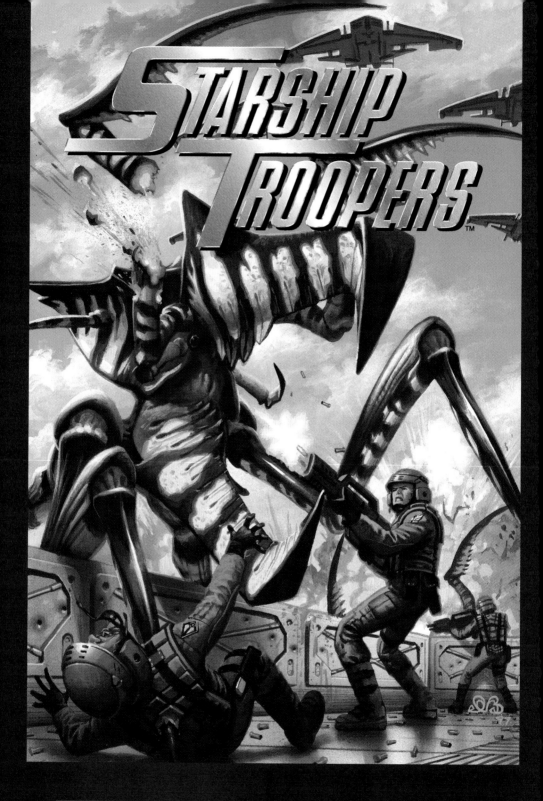

STARSHIP TROOPERS™

BRUTE CREATIONS

DEN BEAUVAIS
COVER ART

"HOW WILL THE SERPENT EVER LOSE ITS VENOM, WHILE THE SERVANTS OF GOD POSSESS THE SAME DISPOSITION, AND CONTINUE TO MAKE WAR UPON IT?

MEN MUST BECOME HARMLESS BEFORE THE BRUTE CREATION, AND WHEN MEN LOSE THEIR VICIOUS DISPOSITIONS AND CEASE TO DESTROY THE ANIMAL RACE...

"...THE LION AND THE LAMB CAN DWELL TOGETHER."

--JOSEPH SMITH, FOUNDER OF THE CHURCH OF JESUS CHRIST OF LATTER-DAY SAINTS

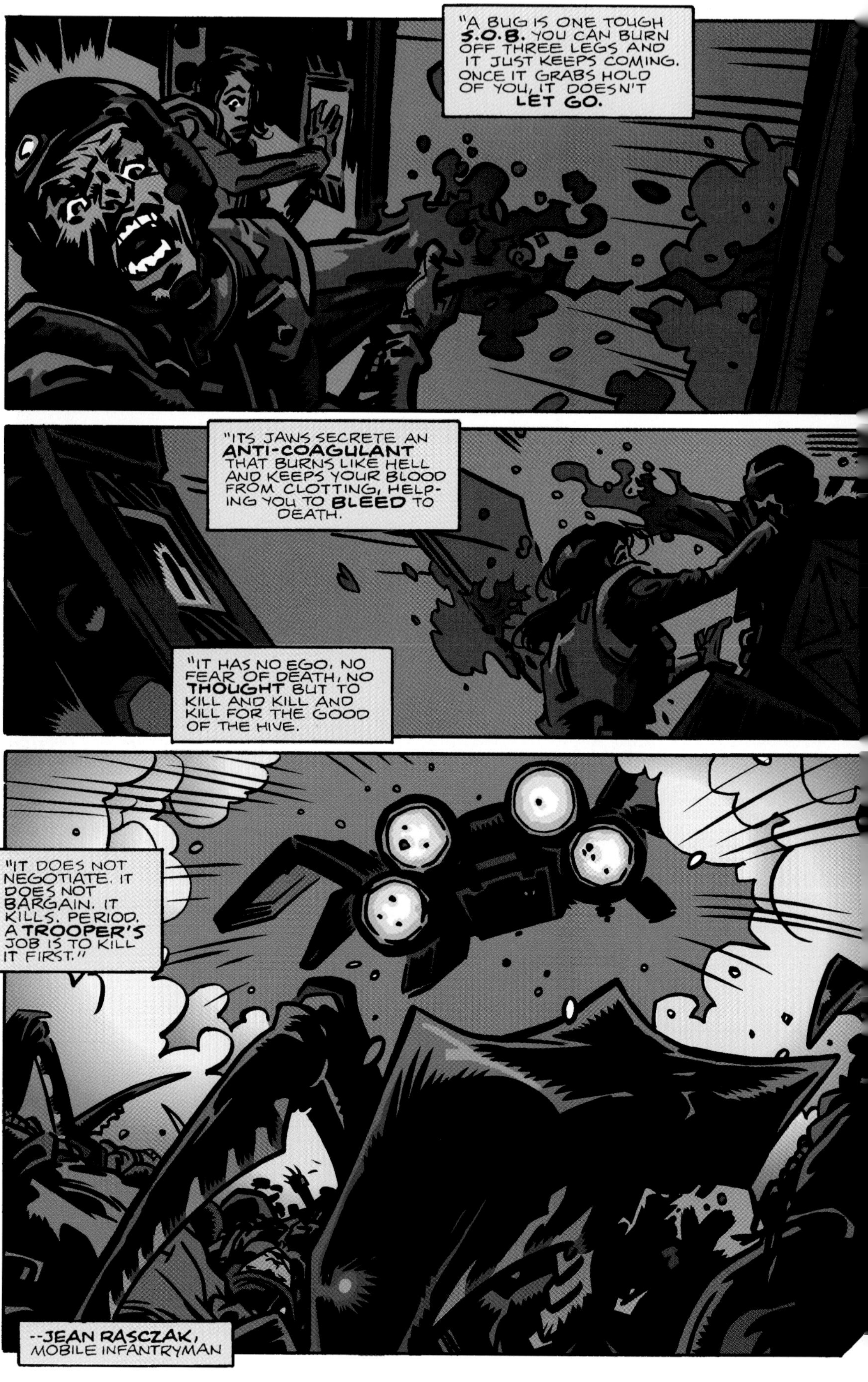
"A BUG IS ONE TOUGH S.O.B. YOU CAN BURN OFF THREE LEGS AND IT JUST KEEPS COMING. ONCE IT GRABS HOLD OF YOU, IT DOESN'T LET GO.
"ITS JAWS SECRETE AN ANTI-COAGULANT THAT BURNS LIKE HELL AND KEEPS YOUR BLOOD FROM CLOTTING, HELPING YOU TO BLEED TO DEATH.
"IT HAS NO EGO, NO FEAR OF DEATH, NO THOUGHT BUT TO KILL AND KILL AND KILL FOR THE GOOD OF THE HIVE.
"IT DOES NOT NEGOTIATE. IT DOES NOT BARGAIN. IT KILLS. PERIOD. A TROOPER'S JOB IS TO KILL IT FIRST."
--JEAN RASCZAK, MOBILE INFANTRYMAN

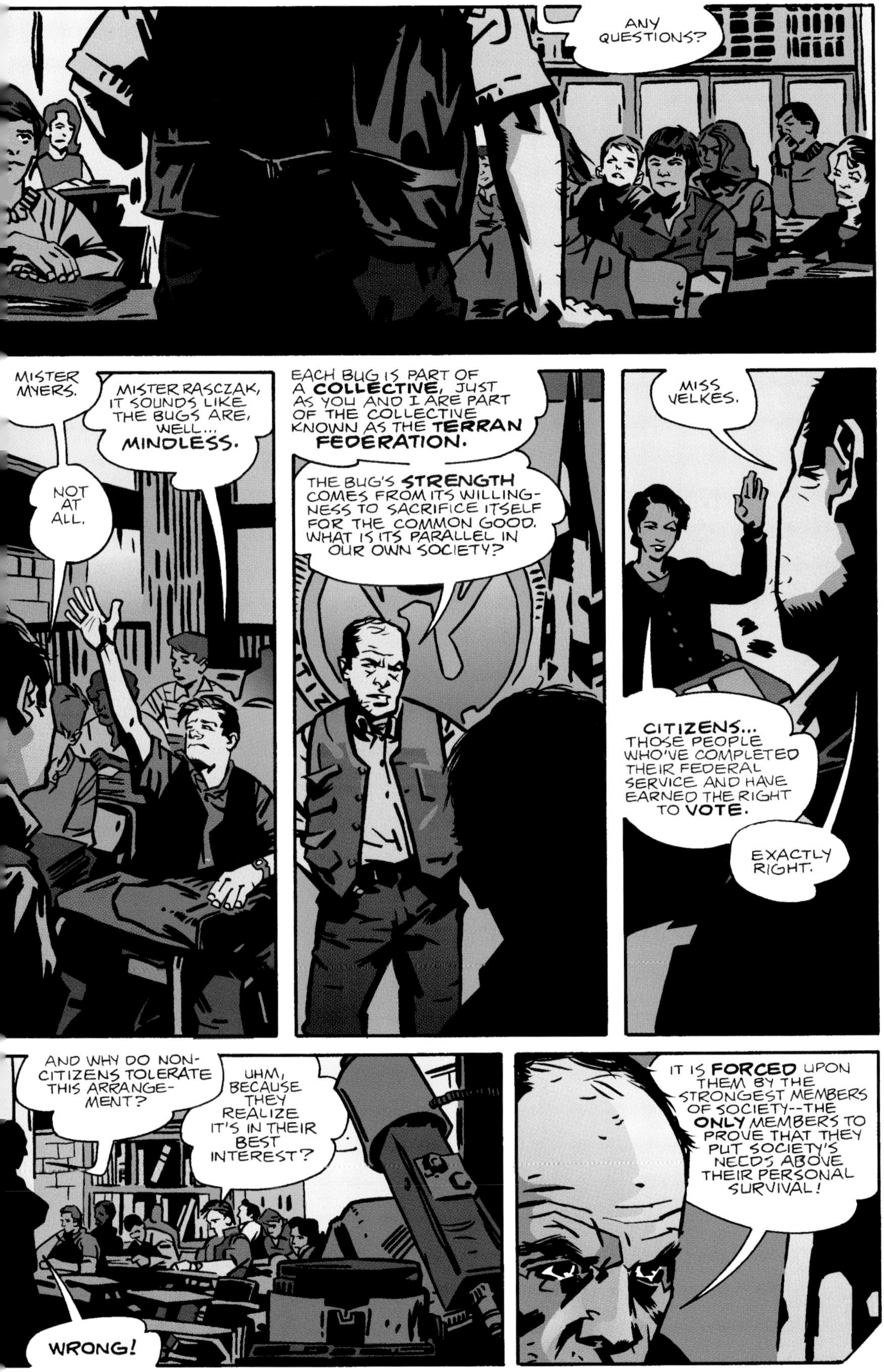

ANY QUESTIONS?
MISTER MYERS.
MISTER RASCZAK, IT SOUNDS LIKE THE BUGS ARE, WELL... MINDLESS.
NOT AT ALL.
EACH BUG IS PART OF A COLLECTIVE, JUST AS YOU AND I ARE PART OF THE COLLECTIVE KNOWN AS THE TERRAN FEDERATION.
THE BUG'S STRENGTH COMES FROM ITS WILLINGNESS TO SACRIFICE ITSELF FOR THE COMMON GOOD. WHAT IS ITS PARALLEL IN OUR OWN SOCIETY?
MISS VELKES.
CITIZENS... THOSE PEOPLE WHO'VE COMPLETED THEIR FEDERAL SERVICE AND HAVE EARNED THE RIGHT TO VOTE.
EXACTLY RIGHT.
AND WHY DO NON-CITIZENS TOLERATE THIS ARRANGEMENT?
UHM, BECAUSE THEY REALIZE IT'S IN THEIR BEST INTEREST?
WRONG!
IT IS FORCED UPON THEM BY THE STRONGEST MEMBERS OF SOCIETY--THE ONLY MEMBERS TO PROVE THAT THEY PUT SOCIETY'S NEEDS ABOVE THEIR PERSONAL SURVIVAL!

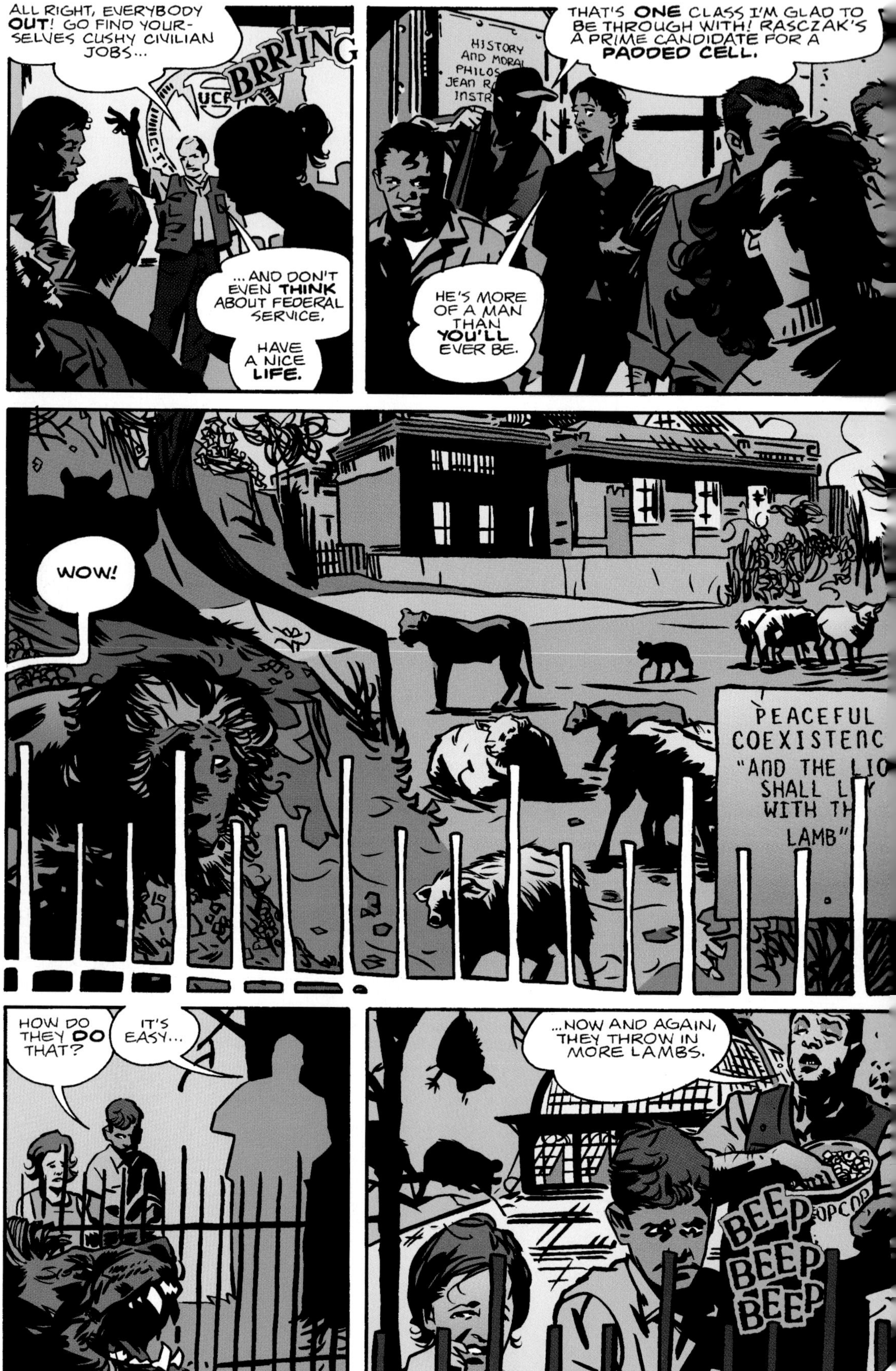
ALL RIGHT, EVERYBODY OUT! GO FIND YOURSELVES CUSHY CIVILIAN JOBS...
BRRING
...AND DON'T EVEN THINK ABOUT FEDERAL SERVICE.
HAVE A NICE LIFE.
HISTORY AND MORAL PHILOS
JEAN R
INSTR
THAT'S ONE CLASS I'M GLAD TO BE THROUGH WITH! RASCZAK'S A PRIME CANDIDATE FOR A PADDED CELL.
HE'S MORE OF A MAN THAN YOU'LL EVER BE.
WOW!
PEACEFUL COEXISTENC
"AND THE LIO
SHALL L
WITH TH
LAMB"
HOW DO THEY DO THAT?
IT'S EASY...
...NOW AND AGAIN, THEY THROW IN MORE LAMBS.
BEEP BEEP BEEP

YEAH.

RASCZAK, I'VE GOT AN ASSIGNMENT FOR YOU.

NOT INTERESTED. I'VE TAUGHT MY LAST CLASS, REMEMBER? NEXT WEEK I'M BACK ON **ACTIVE DUTY.**

CHANGE OF PLANS. YOU LEAVE THIS AFTERNOON FOR **DANTANA.**

DANTANA...THREE HUNDRED MORMON **EXTREMISTS** HAD JUST SETTLED THERE. THE PROBLEM WAS, THE DANTANA SYSTEM WAS INSIDE THE ARACHNID QUARANTINE ZONE...

...BUG TERRITORY.

SINCE THEY LOST **UTAH** IN THE UPRISINGS, THE MORMONS HAD BEEN ON THE RUN, JUST LIKE OLD TIMES.

DESPERATION HAD TAKEN THE MOST RADICAL GROUP TO DANTANA...THAT, AND **STUBBORN-NESS.**

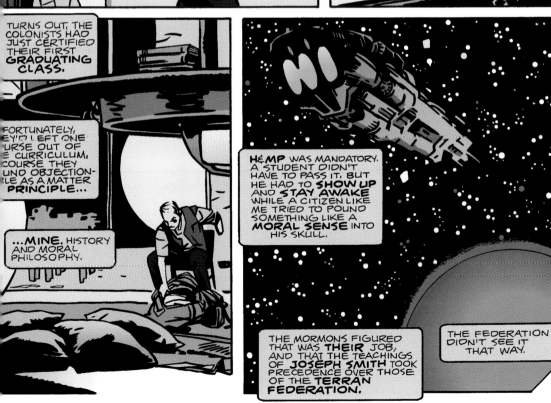

TURNS OUT, THE COLONISTS HAD JUST CERTIFIED THEIR FIRST **GRADUATING CLASS.**

FORTUNATELY, [TH]EY'D LEFT ONE [CO]URSE OUT OF [TH]E CURRICULUM, [A] COURSE THEY [FO]UND OBJECTION[AB]LE AS A MATTER [OF] **PRINCIPLE...**

...**MINE.** HISTORY AND MORAL PHILOSOPHY.

H & MP WAS MANDATORY. A STUDENT DIDN'T HAVE TO PASS IT, BUT HE HAD TO **SHOW UP** AND **STAY AWAKE** WHILE A CITIZEN LIKE ME TRIED TO POUND SOMETHING LIKE A **MORAL SENSE** INTO HIS SKULL.

THE MORMONS FIGURED THAT WAS **THEIR** JOB, AND THAT THE TEACHINGS OF **JOSEPH SMITH** TOOK PRECEDENCE OVER THOSE OF THE **TERRAN FEDERATION.**

THE FEDERATION DIDN'T SEE IT THAT WAY.

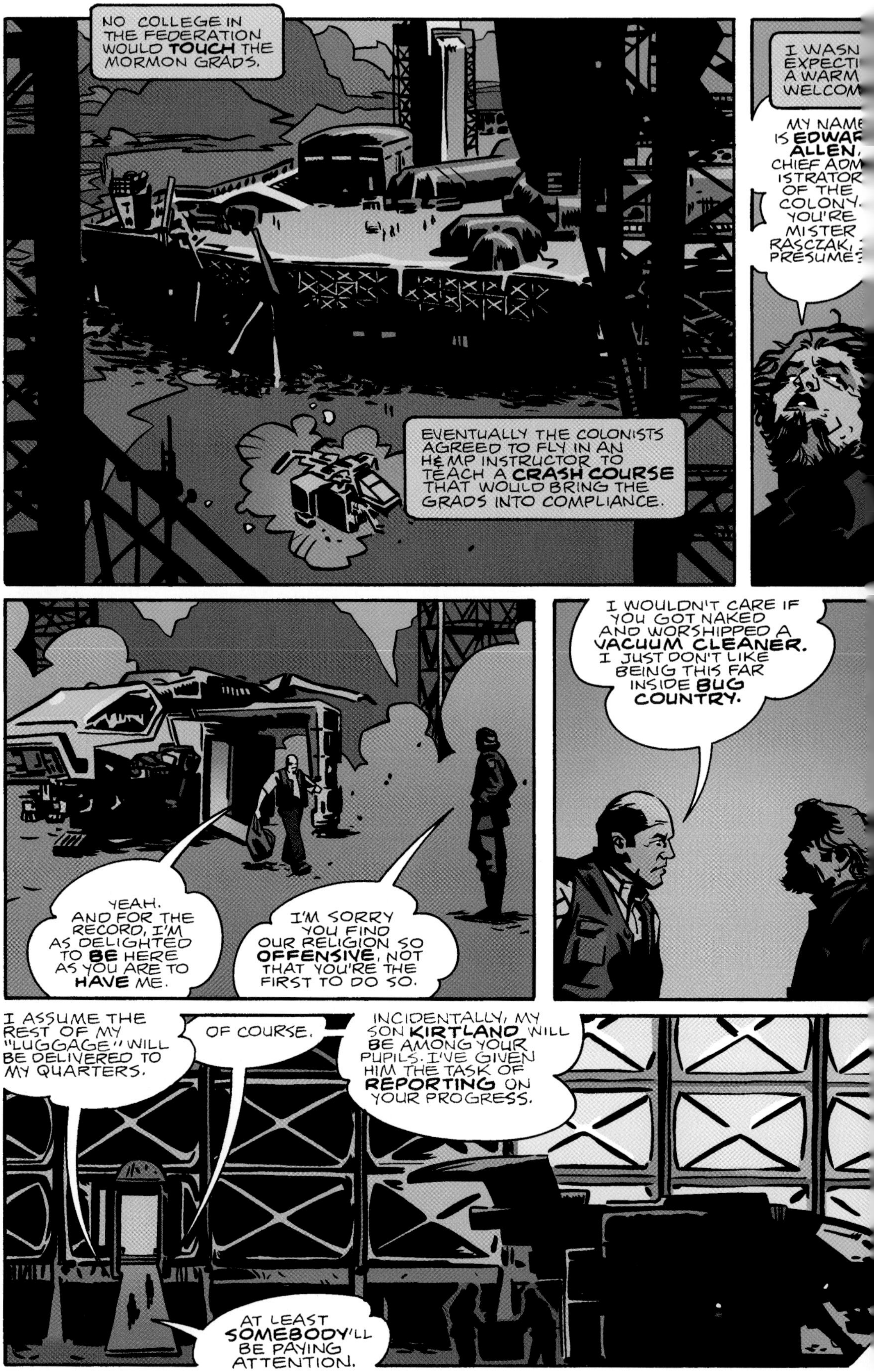
NO COLLEGE IN THE FEDERATION WOULD TOUCH THE MORMON GRADS.
EVENTUALLY THE COLONISTS AGREED TO FLY IN AN H&MP INSTRUCTOR TO TEACH A CRASH COURSE THAT WOULD BRING THE GRADS INTO COMPLIANCE.
I WASN EXPECTI A WARM WELCOM
MY NAME IS EDWAR ALLEN, CHIEF ADM ISTRATOR OF THE COLONY. YOU'RE MISTER RASCZAK, PRESUME?
YEAH. AND FOR THE RECORD, I'M AS DELIGHTED TO BE HERE AS YOU ARE TO HAVE ME.
I'M SORRY YOU FIND OUR RELIGION SO OFFENSIVE, NOT THAT YOU'RE THE FIRST TO DO SO.
I WOULDN'T CARE IF YOU GOT NAKED AND WORSHIPPED A VACUUM CLEANER. I JUST DON'T LIKE BEING THIS FAR INSIDE BUG COUNTRY.
I ASSUME THE REST OF MY "LUGGAGE" WILL BE DELIVERED TO MY QUARTERS.
OF COURSE.
INCIDENTALLY, MY SON KIRTLAND WILL BE AMONG YOUR PUPILS. I'VE GIVEN HIM THE TASK OF REPORTING ON YOUR PROGRESS.
AT LEAST SOMEBODY'LL BE PAYING ATTENTION.

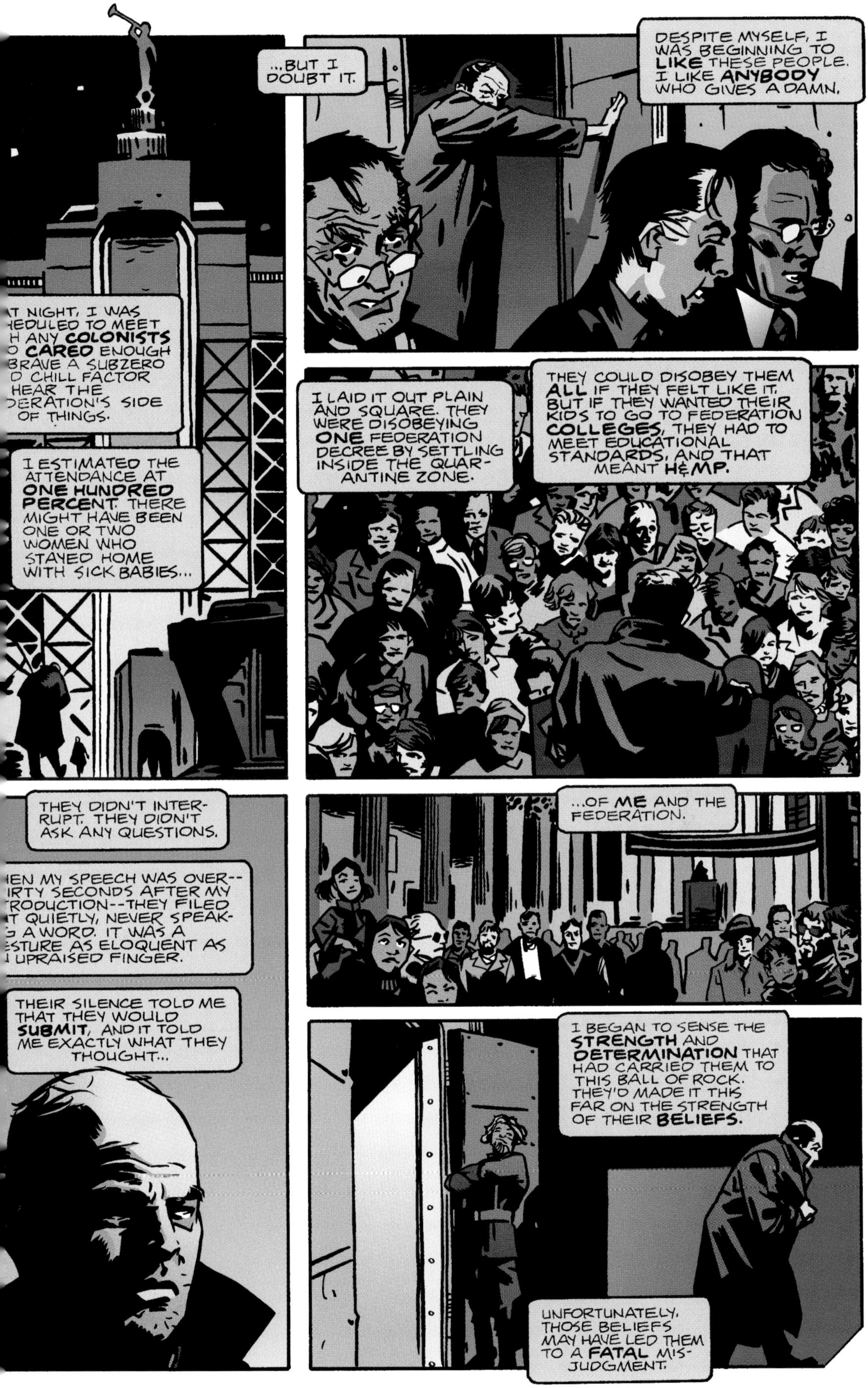

...BUT I DOUBT IT.
DESPITE MYSELF, I WAS BEGINNING TO LIKE THESE PEOPLE. I LIKE ANYBODY WHO GIVES A DAMN.
T NIGHT, I WAS HEDULED TO MEET H ANY COLONISTS O CARED ENOUGH BRAVE A SUBZERO D CHILL FACTOR HEAR THE DERATION'S SIDE OF THINGS.
I ESTIMATED THE ATTENDANCE AT ONE HUNDRED PERCENT. THERE MIGHT HAVE BEEN ONE OR TWO WOMEN WHO STAYED HOME WITH SICK BABIES...
I LAID IT OUT PLAIN AND SQUARE. THEY WERE DISOBEYING ONE FEDERATION DECREE BY SETTLING INSIDE THE QUARANTINE ZONE.
THEY COULD DISOBEY THEM ALL IF THEY FELT LIKE IT. BUT IF THEY WANTED THEIR KIDS TO GO TO FEDERATION COLLEGES, THEY HAD TO MEET EDUCATIONAL STANDARDS, AND THAT MEANT H&MP.
THEY DIDN'T INTERRUPT. THEY DIDN'T ASK ANY QUESTIONS.
HEN MY SPEECH WAS OVER-- IRTY SECONDS AFTER MY TRODUCTION--THEY FILED T QUIETLY, NEVER SPEAK- G A WORD. IT WAS A ESTURE AS ELOQUENT AS N UPRAISED FINGER.
THEIR SILENCE TOLD ME THAT THEY WOULD SUBMIT, AND IT TOLD ME EXACTLY WHAT THEY THOUGHT...
...OF ME AND THE FEDERATION.
I BEGAN TO SENSE THE STRENGTH AND DETERMINATION THAT HAD CARRIED THEM TO THIS BALL OF ROCK. THEY'D MADE IT THIS FAR ON THE STRENGTH OF THEIR BELIEFS.
UNFORTUNATELY, THOSE BELIEFS MAY HAVE LED THEM TO A FATAL MISJUDGMENT.

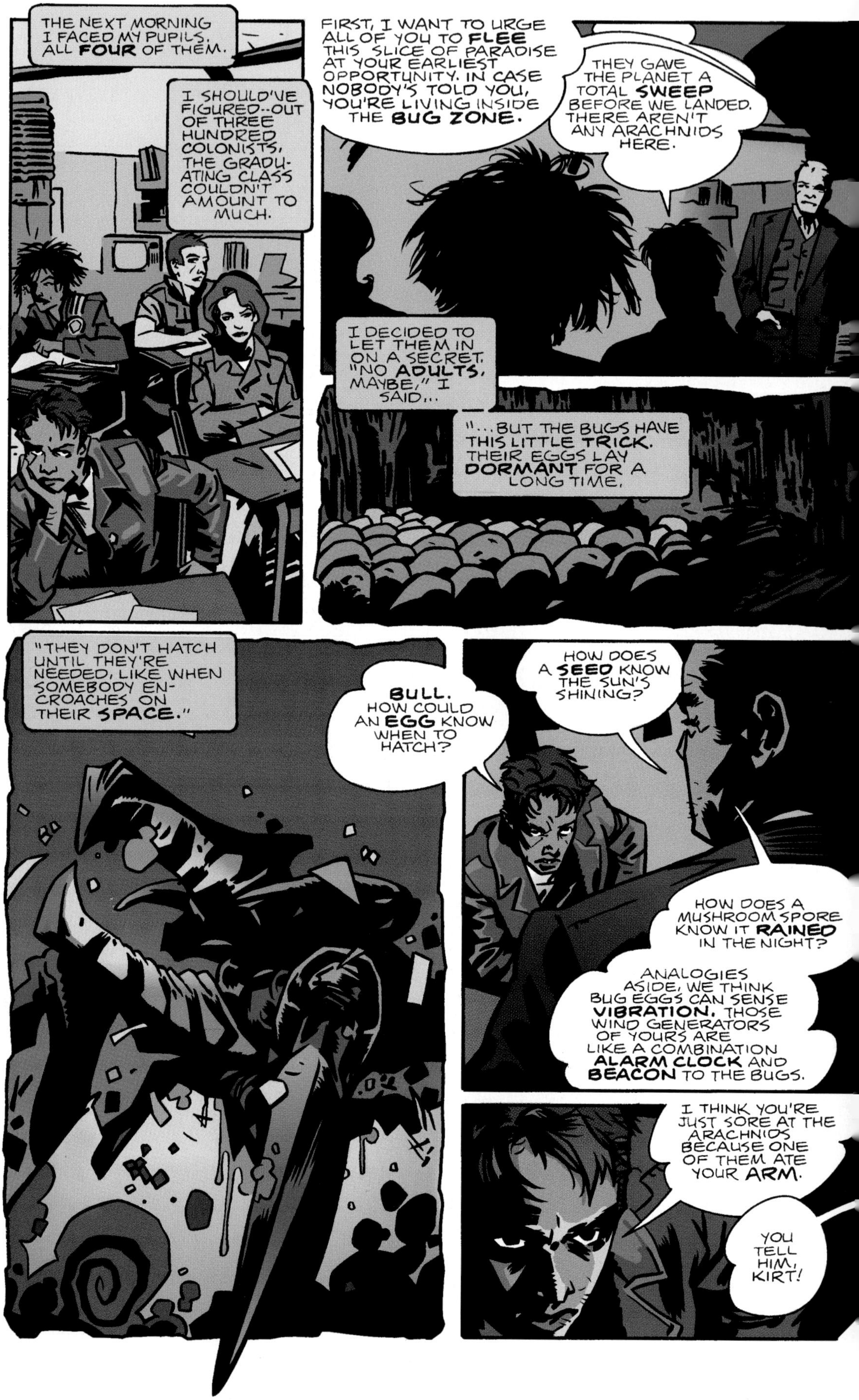
THE NEXT MORNING I FACED MY PUPILS. ALL FOUR OF THEM.
I SHOULD'VE FIGURED--OUT OF THREE HUNDRED COLONISTS, THE GRADUATING CLASS COULDN'T AMOUNT TO MUCH.
FIRST, I WANT TO URGE ALL OF YOU TO FLEE THIS SLICE OF PARADISE AT YOUR EARLIEST OPPORTUNITY. IN CASE NOBODY'S TOLD YOU, YOU'RE LIVING INSIDE THE BUG ZONE.
THEY GAVE THE PLANET A TOTAL SWEEP BEFORE WE LANDED. THERE AREN'T ANY ARACHNIDS HERE.
I DECIDED TO LET THEM IN ON A SECRET. "NO ADULTS, MAYBE," I SAID...
"...BUT THE BUGS HAVE THIS LITTLE TRICK. THEIR EGGS LAY DORMANT FOR A LONG TIME.
"THEY DON'T HATCH UNTIL THEY'RE NEEDED, LIKE WHEN SOMEBODY ENCROACHES ON THEIR SPACE."
BULL. HOW COULD AN EGG KNOW WHEN TO HATCH?
HOW DOES A SEED KNOW THE SUN'S SHINING?
HOW DOES A MUSHROOM SPORE KNOW IT RAINED IN THE NIGHT?
ANALOGIES ASIDE, WE THINK BUG EGGS CAN SENSE VIBRATION. THOSE WIND GENERATORS OF YOURS ARE LIKE A COMBINATION ALARM CLOCK AND BEACON TO THE BUGS.
I THINK YOU'RE JUST SORE AT THE ARACHNIDS BECAUSE ONE OF THEM ATE YOUR ARM.
YOU TELL HIM, KIRT!

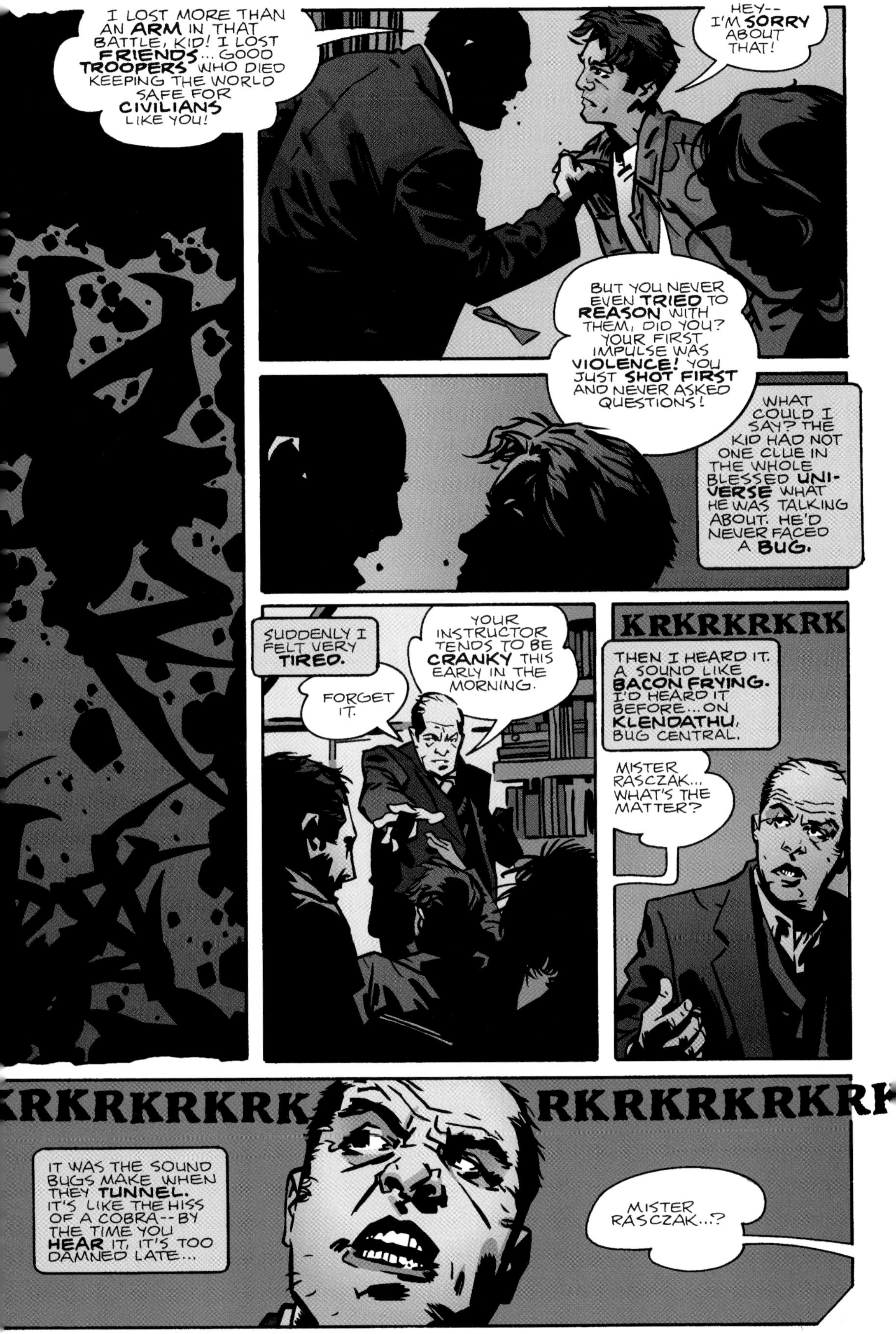
I LOST MORE THAN AN ARM IN THAT BATTLE, KID! I LOST FRIENDS... GOOD TROOPERS WHO DIED KEEPING THE WORLD SAFE FOR CIVILIANS LIKE YOU!
HEY-- I'M SORRY ABOUT THAT!
BUT YOU NEVER EVEN TRIED TO REASON WITH THEM, DID YOU? YOUR FIRST IMPULSE WAS VIOLENCE! YOU JUST SHOT FIRST AND NEVER ASKED QUESTIONS!
WHAT COULD I SAY? THE KID HAD NOT ONE CLUE IN THE WHOLE BLESSED UNIVERSE WHAT HE WAS TALKING ABOUT. HE'D NEVER FACED A BUG.
SUDDENLY I FELT VERY TIRED.
FORGET IT.
YOUR INSTRUCTOR TENDS TO BE CRANKY THIS EARLY IN THE MORNING.
KRKRKRKRKRK
THEN I HEARD IT. A SOUND LIKE BACON FRYING. I'D HEARD IT BEFORE...ON KLENDATHU, BUG CENTRAL.
MISTER RASCZAK... WHAT'S THE MATTER?
KRKRKRKRK RKRKRKRKRK
IT WAS THE SOUND BUGS MAKE WHEN THEY TUNNEL. IT'S LIKE THE HISS OF A COBRA--BY THE TIME YOU HEAR IT, IT'S TOO DAMNED LATE...
MISTER RASCZAK...?

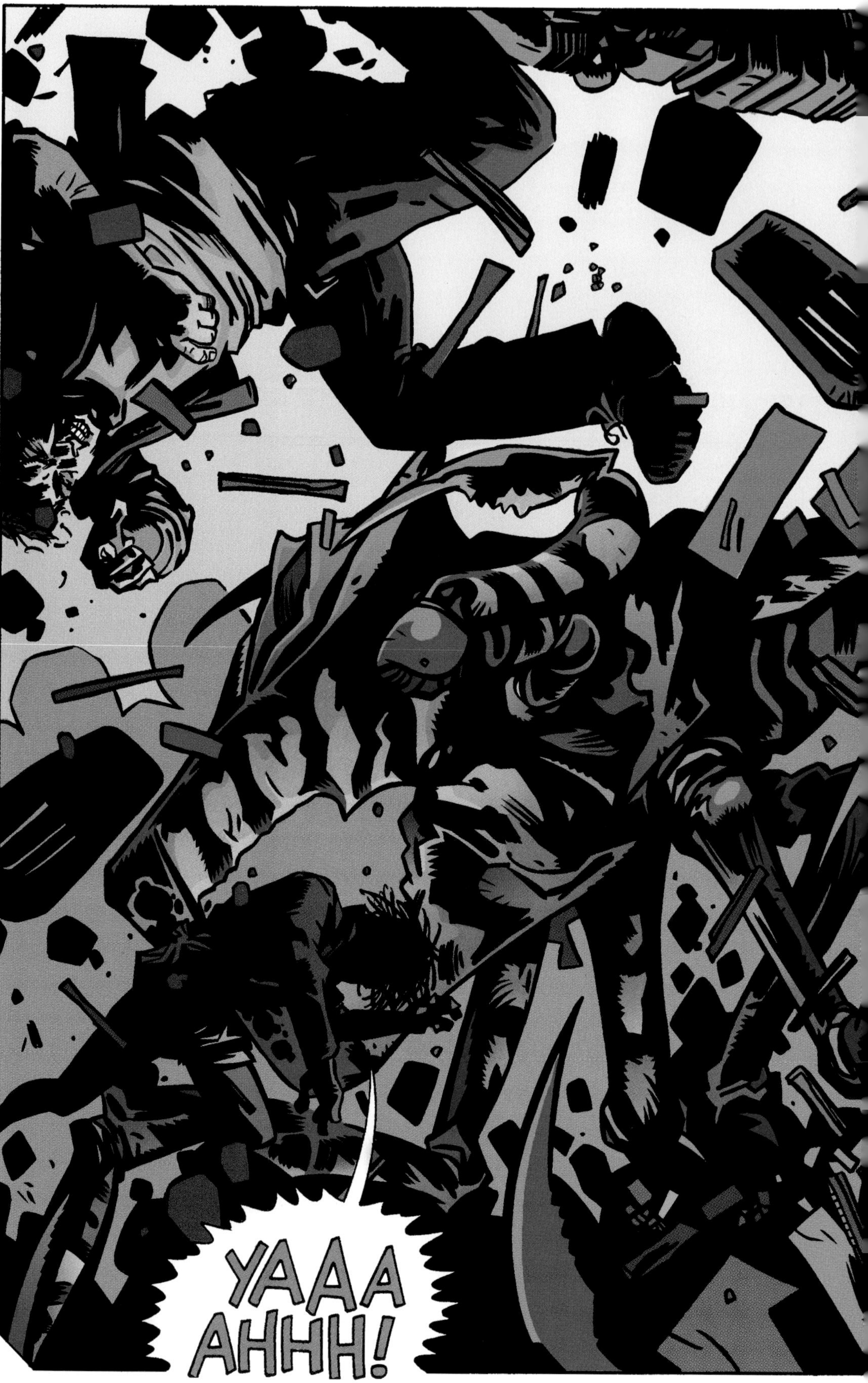
YAAA AHHH!

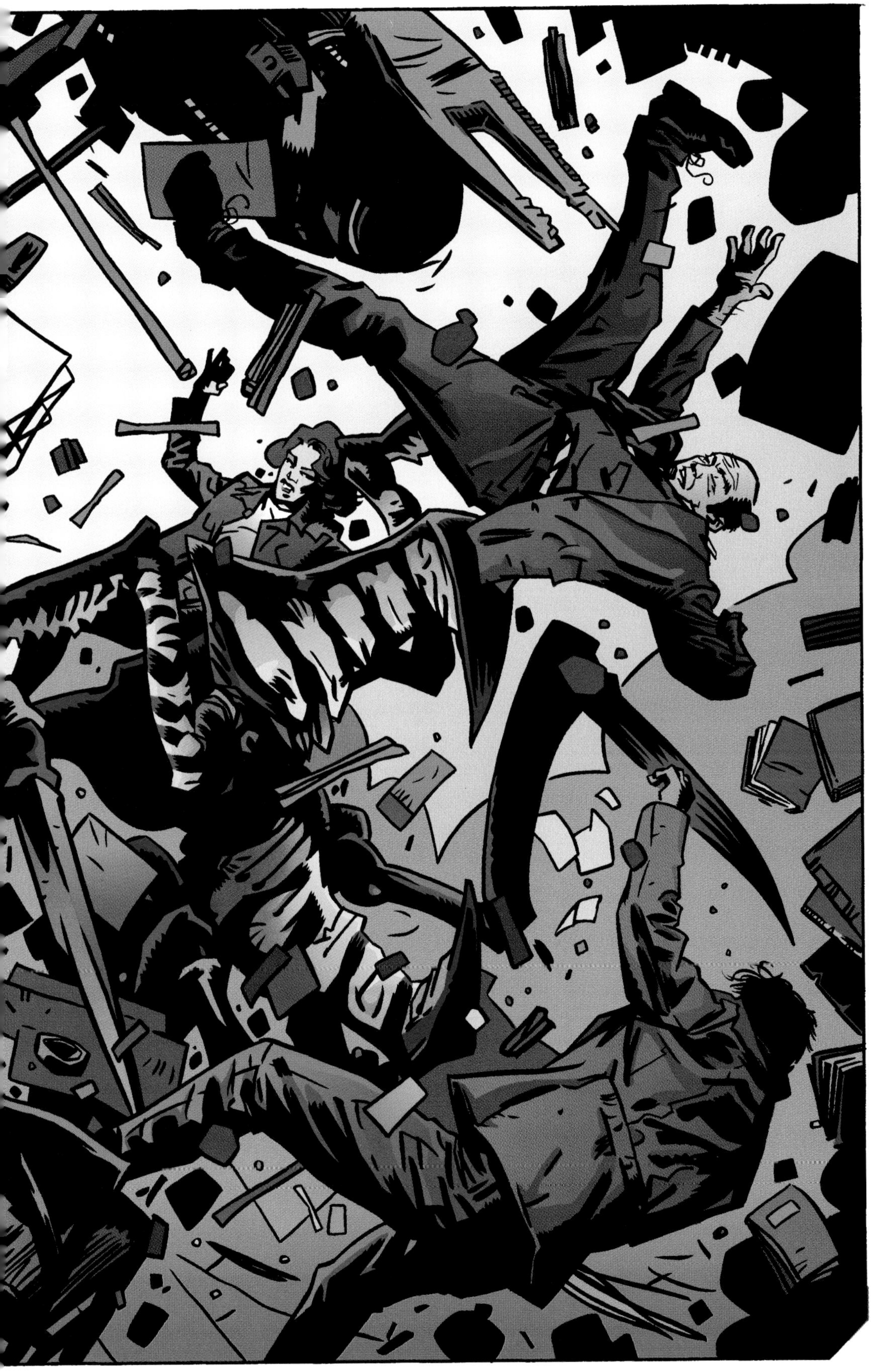

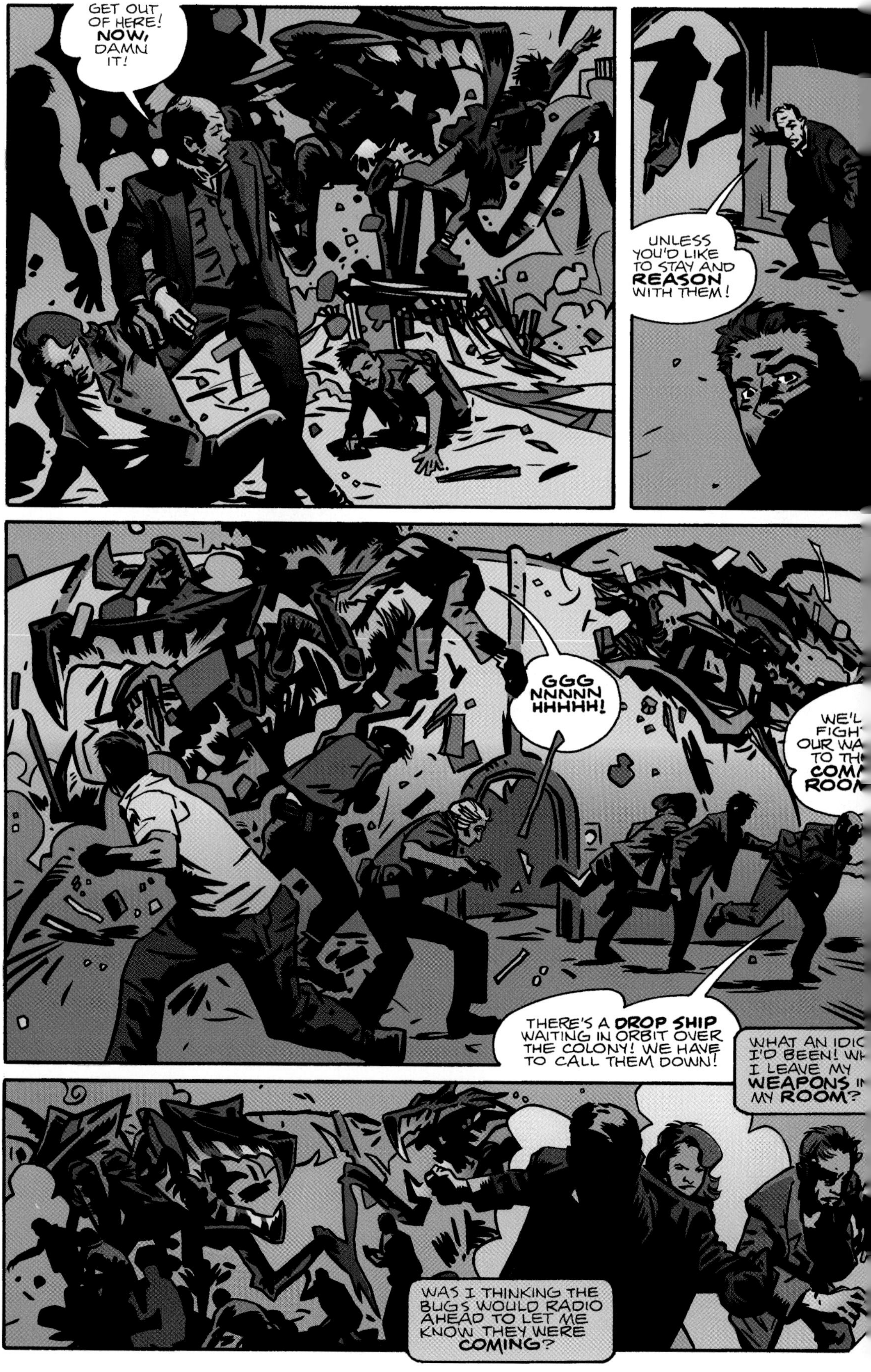
GET OUT OF HERE! NOW, DAMN IT!
UNLESS YOU'D LIKE TO STAY AND REASON WITH THEM!
GGG NNNNN HHHHH!
WE'L FIGH OUR WA TO TH COM ROOM
THERE'S A DROP SHIP WAITING IN ORBIT OVER THE COLONY! WE HAVE TO CALL THEM DOWN!
WHAT AN IDI I'D BEEN! W I LEAVE MY WEAPONS I MY ROOM?
WAS I THINKING THE BUGS WOULD RADIO AHEAD TO LET ME KNOW THEY WERE COMING?

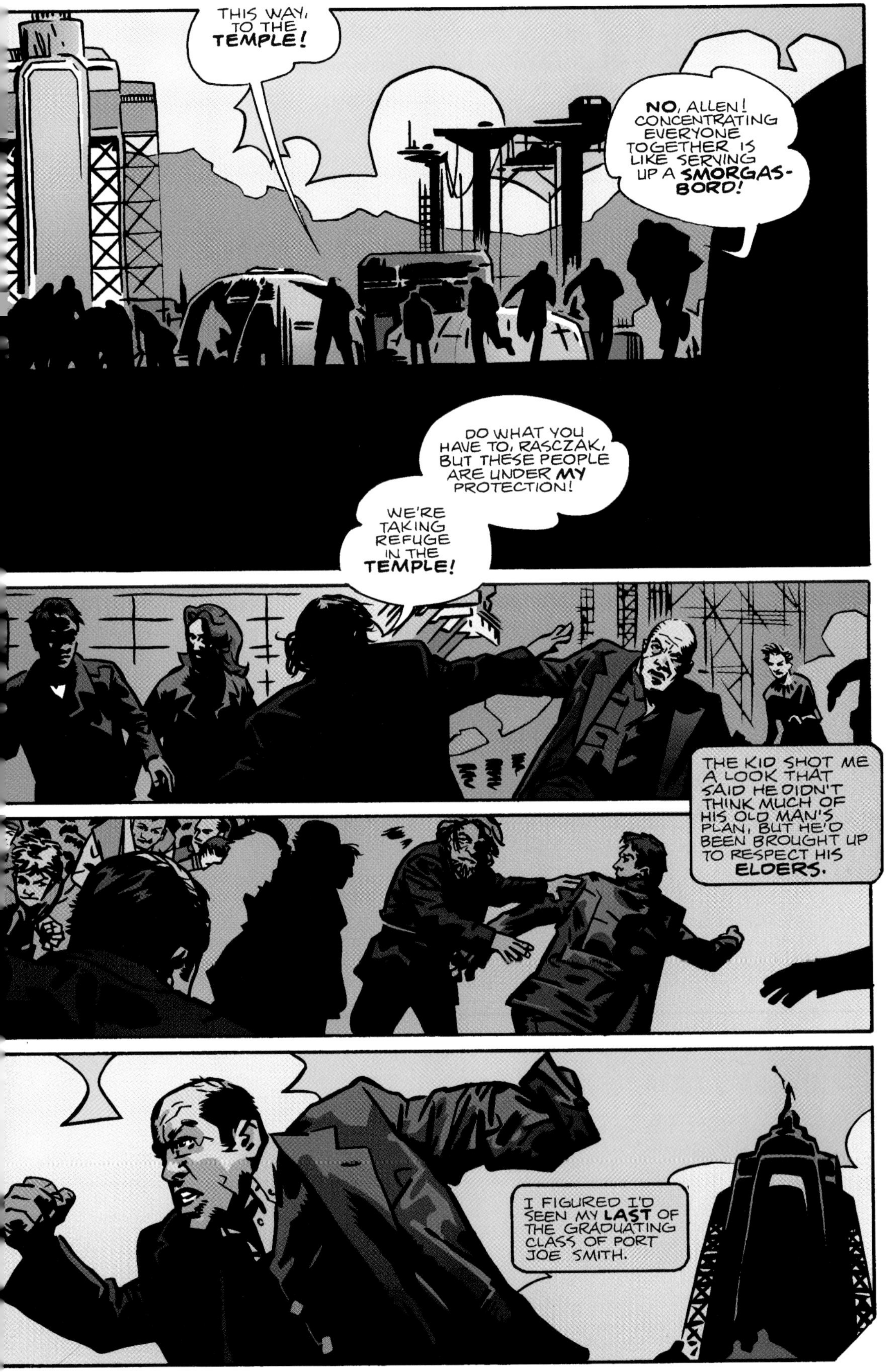
THIS WAY, TO THE TEMPLE!
NO, ALLEN! CONCENTRATING EVERYONE TOGETHER IS LIKE SERVING UP A SMORGASBORD!
DO WHAT YOU HAVE TO, RASCZAK, BUT THESE PEOPLE ARE UNDER MY PROTECTION!
WE'RE TAKING REFUGE IN THE TEMPLE!
THE KID SHOT ME A LOOK THAT SAID HE DIDN'T THINK MUCH OF HIS OLD MAN'S PLAN, BUT HE'D BEEN BROUGHT UP TO RESPECT HIS ELDERS.
I FIGURED I'D SEEN MY LAST OF THE GRADUATING CLASS OF PORT JOE SMITH.

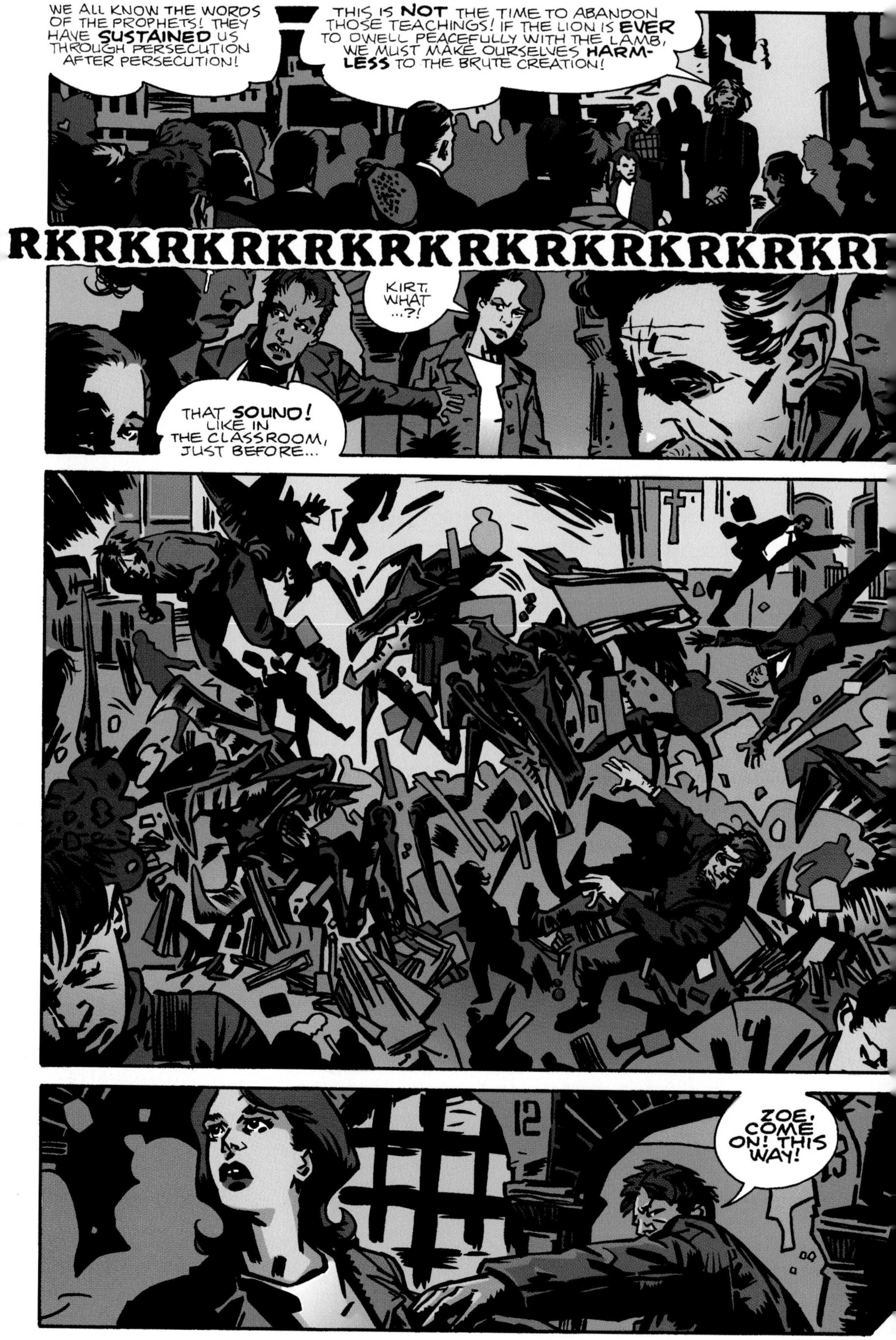
WE ALL KNOW THE WORDS OF THE PROPHETS! THEY HAVE **SUSTAINED** US THROUGH PERSECUTION AFTER PERSECUTION!
THIS IS **NOT** THE TIME TO ABANDON THOSE TEACHINGS! IF THE LION IS **EVER** TO DWELL PEACEFULLY WITH THE LAMB, WE MUST MAKE OURSELVES **HARM-LESS** TO THE BRUTE CREATION!
RKRKRKRKRKRKRKRKRKRKRKRKRKRKRKR
KIRT, WHAT ...?!
THAT **SOUND!** LIKE IN THE CLASSROOM, JUST BEFORE...
ZOE, COME ON! THIS WAY!

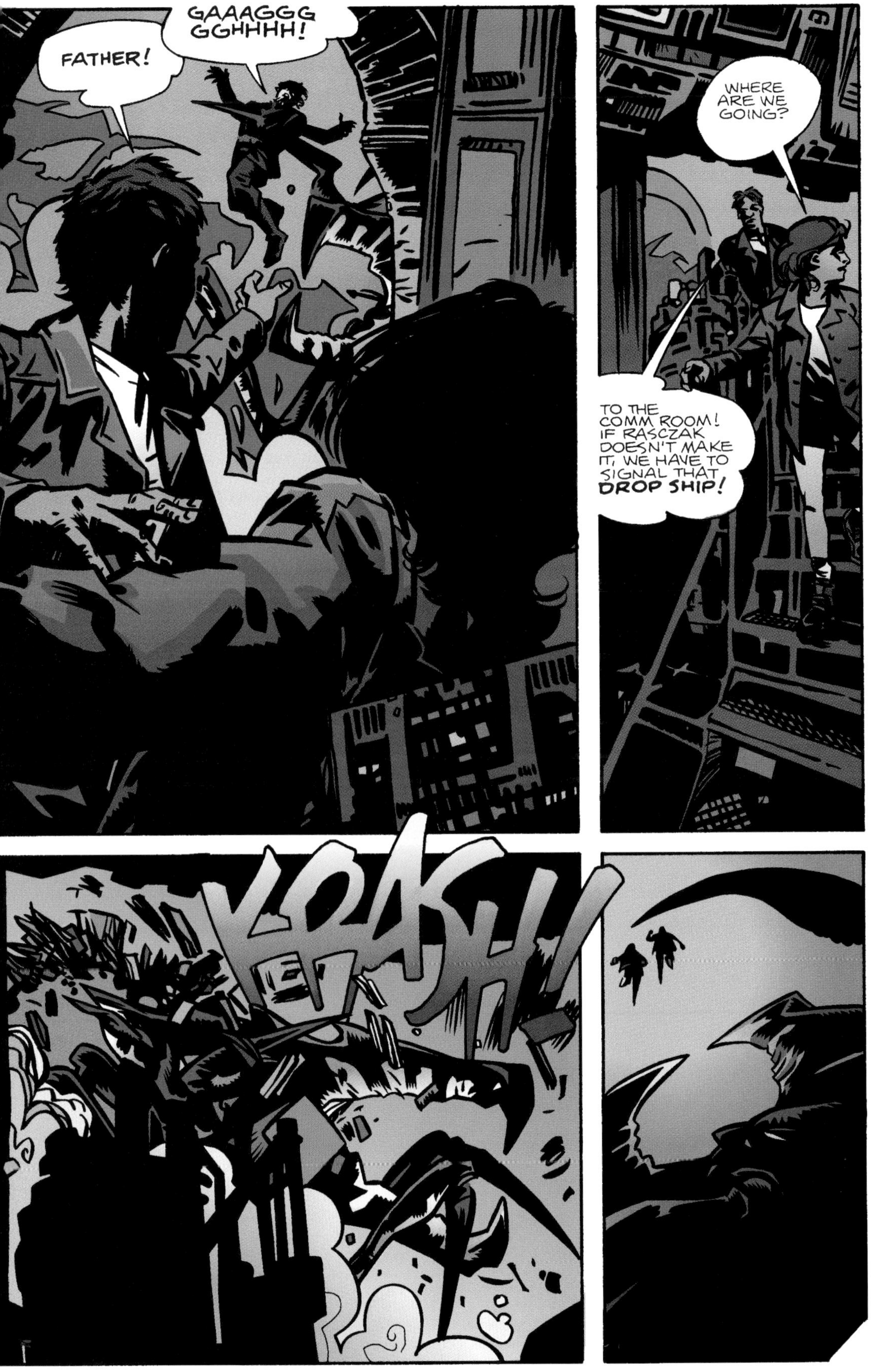

FATHER!
GAAAGGG GGHHHH!
WHERE ARE WE GOING?
TO THE COMM ROOM! IF RASCZAK DOESN'T MAKE IT, WE HAVE TO SIGNAL THAT **DROP SHIP!**
KRASH!

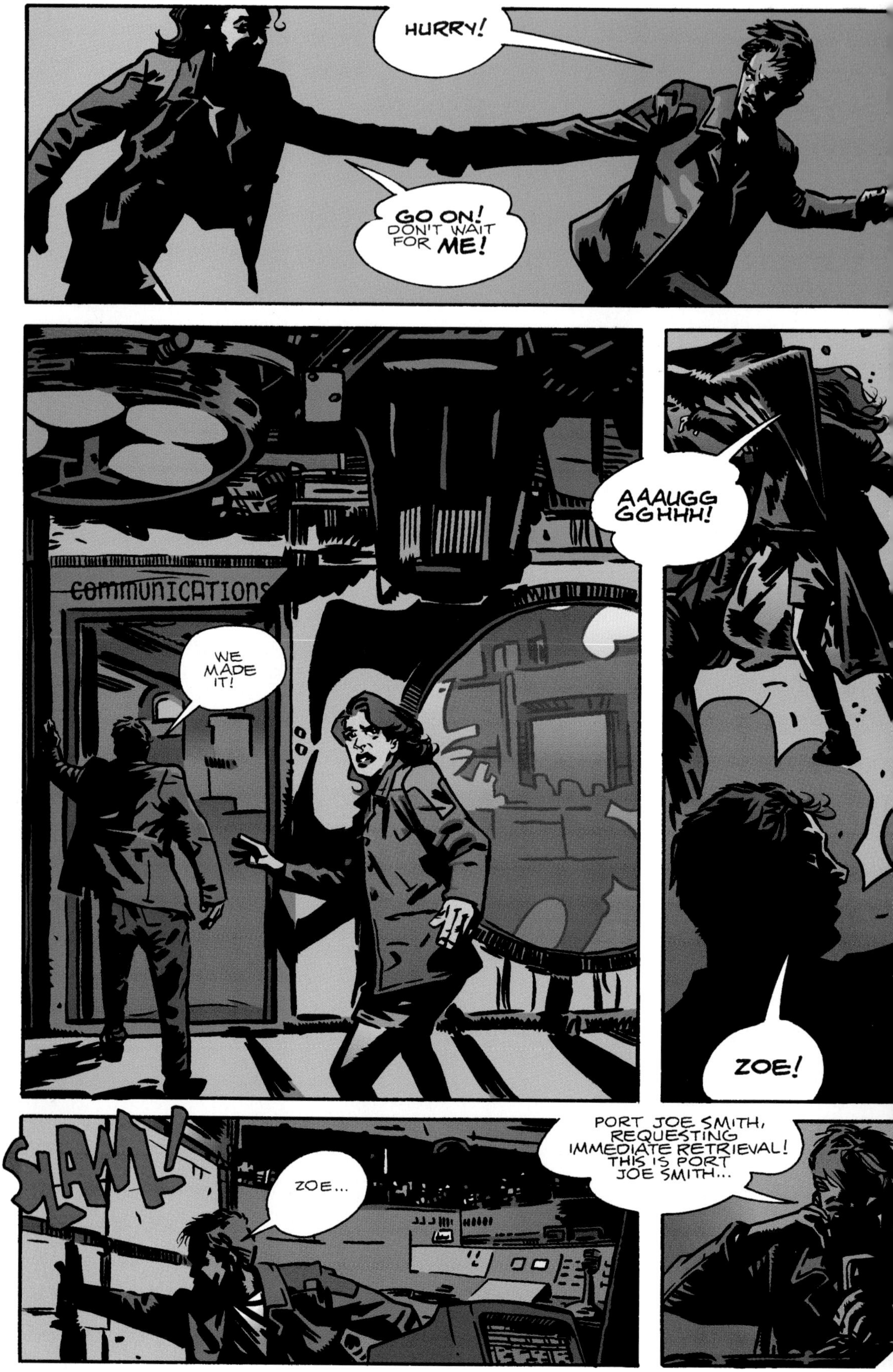
HURRY!
GO ON! DON'T WAIT FOR ME!
COMMUNICATIONS
WE MADE IT!
AAAUGG GGHHH!
ZOE!
SLAM!
ZOE...
PORT JOE SMITH, REQUESTING IMMEDIATE RETRIEVAL! THIS IS PORT JOE SMITH...

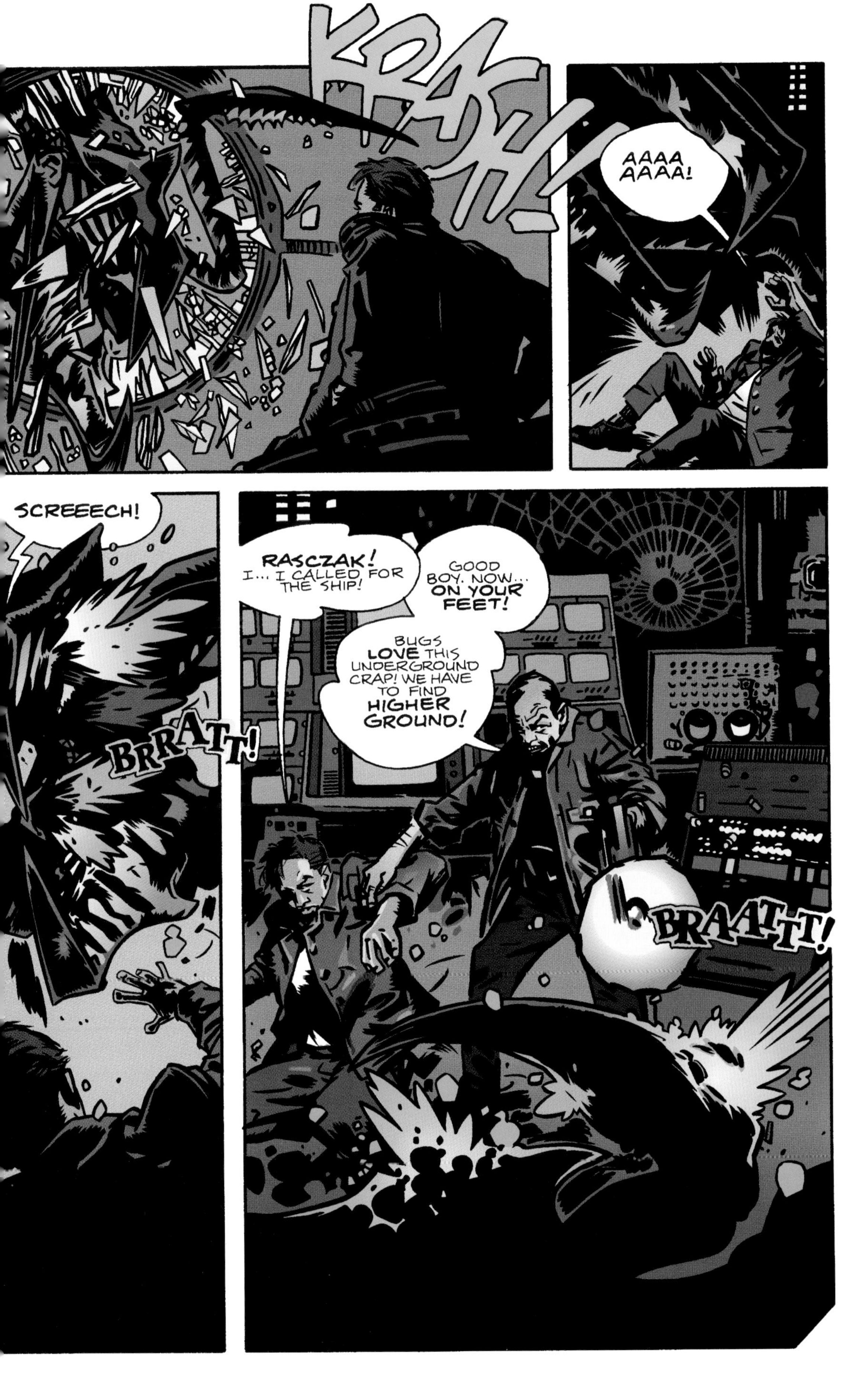
KRASH!
AAAA AAAA!
SCREEECH!
BRRATT!
RASCZAK! I... I CALLED FOR THE SHIP!
GOOD BOY. NOW... ON YOUR FEET!
BUGS LOVE THIS UNDERGROUND CRAP! WE HAVE TO FIND HIGHER GROUND!
BRAATTT!

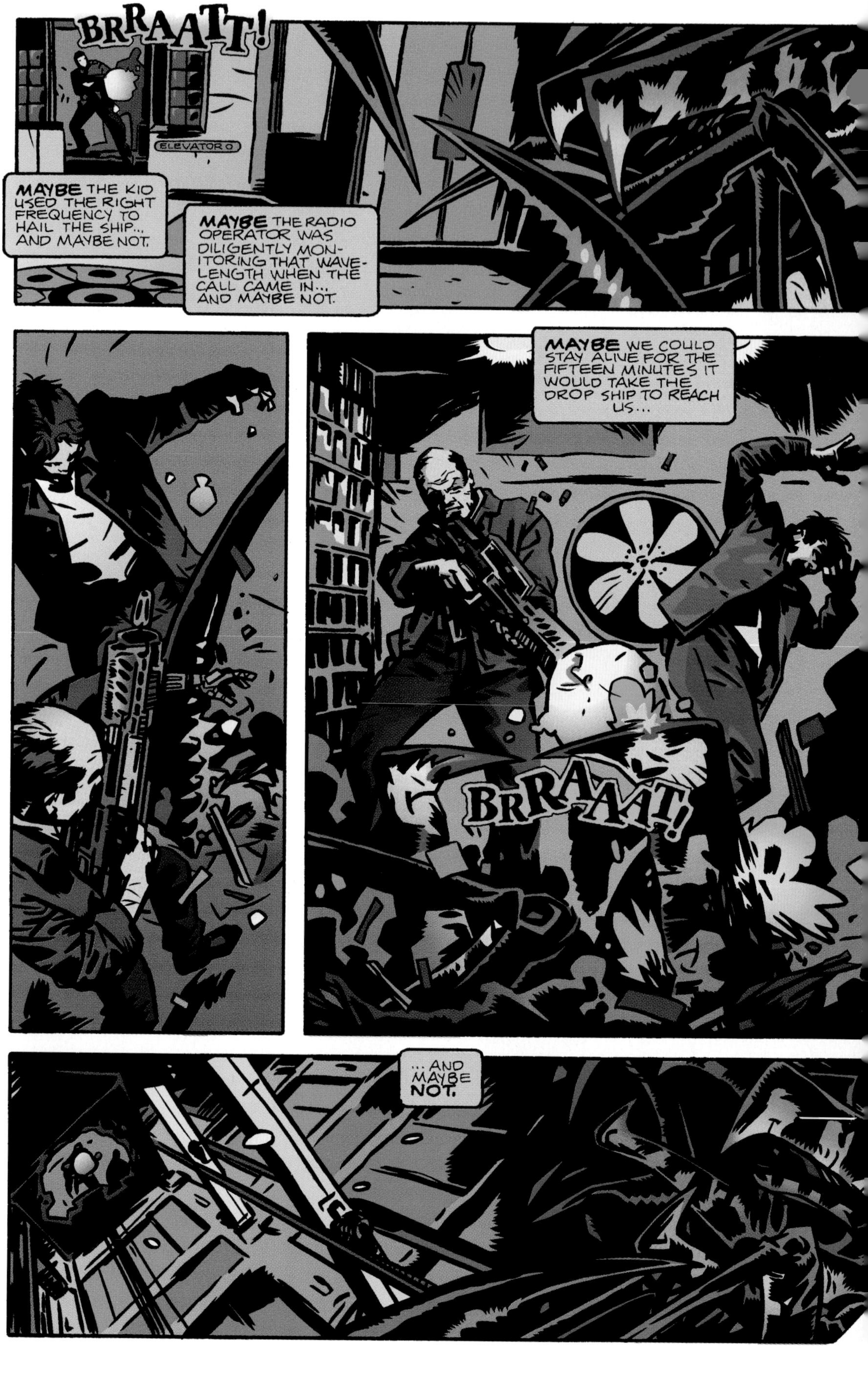
BRRAATT!
ELEVATOR 0
MAYBE THE KID USED THE RIGHT FREQUENCY TO HAIL THE SHIP... AND MAYBE NOT.
MAYBE THE RADIO OPERATOR WAS DILIGENTLY MONITORING THAT WAVELENGTH WHEN THE CALL CAME IN... AND MAYBE NOT.
MAYBE WE COULD STAY ALIVE FOR THE FIFTEEN MINUTES IT WOULD TAKE THE DROP SHIP TO REACH US...
BRRAAAT!
...AND MAYBE NOT.

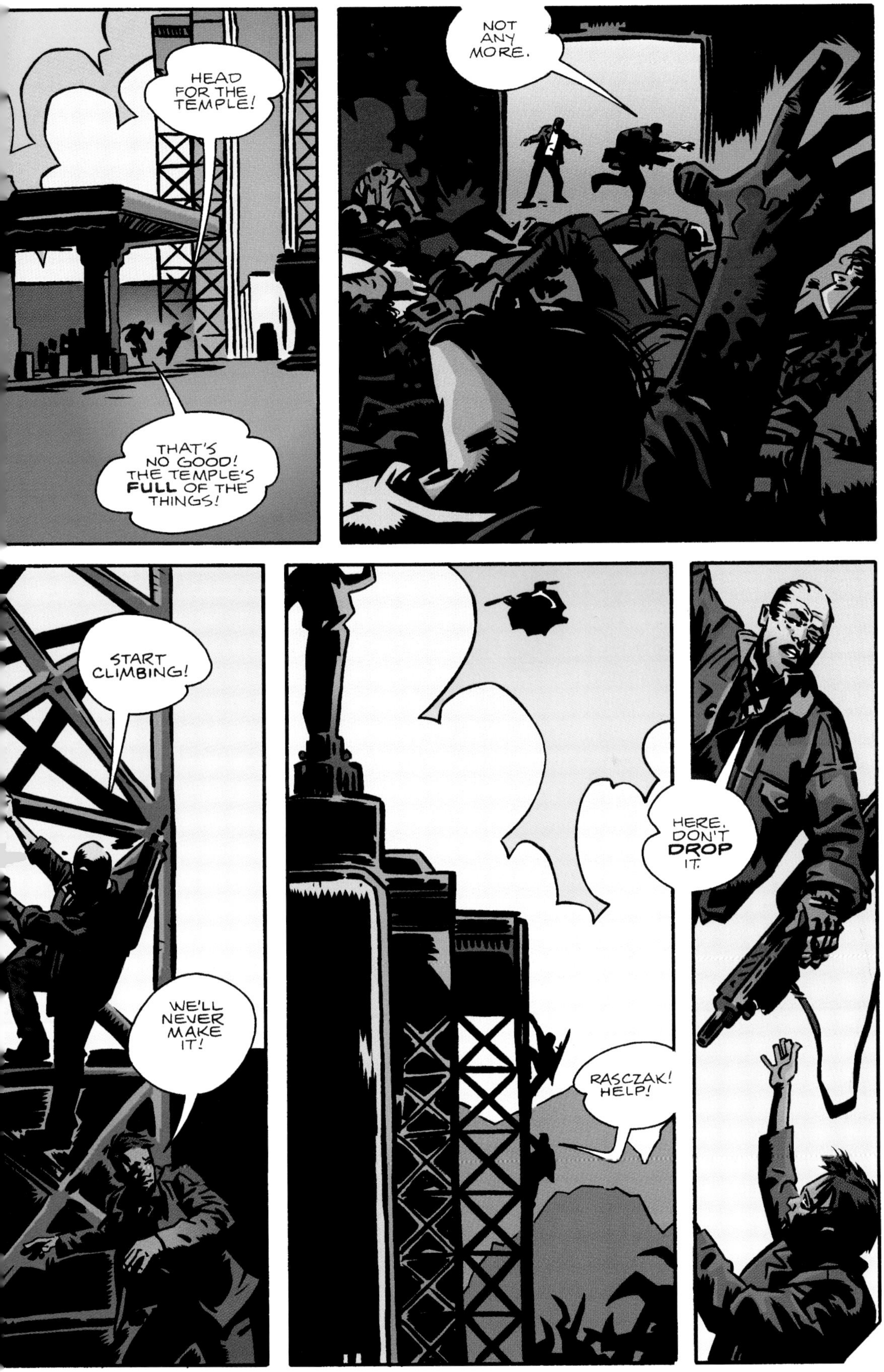
HEAD FOR THE TEMPLE!
THAT'S NO GOOD! THE TEMPLE'S **FULL** OF THE THINGS!
NOT ANY MORE.
START CLIMBING!
WE'LL NEVER MAKE IT!
RASCZAK! HELP!
HERE. DON'T **DROP** IT.

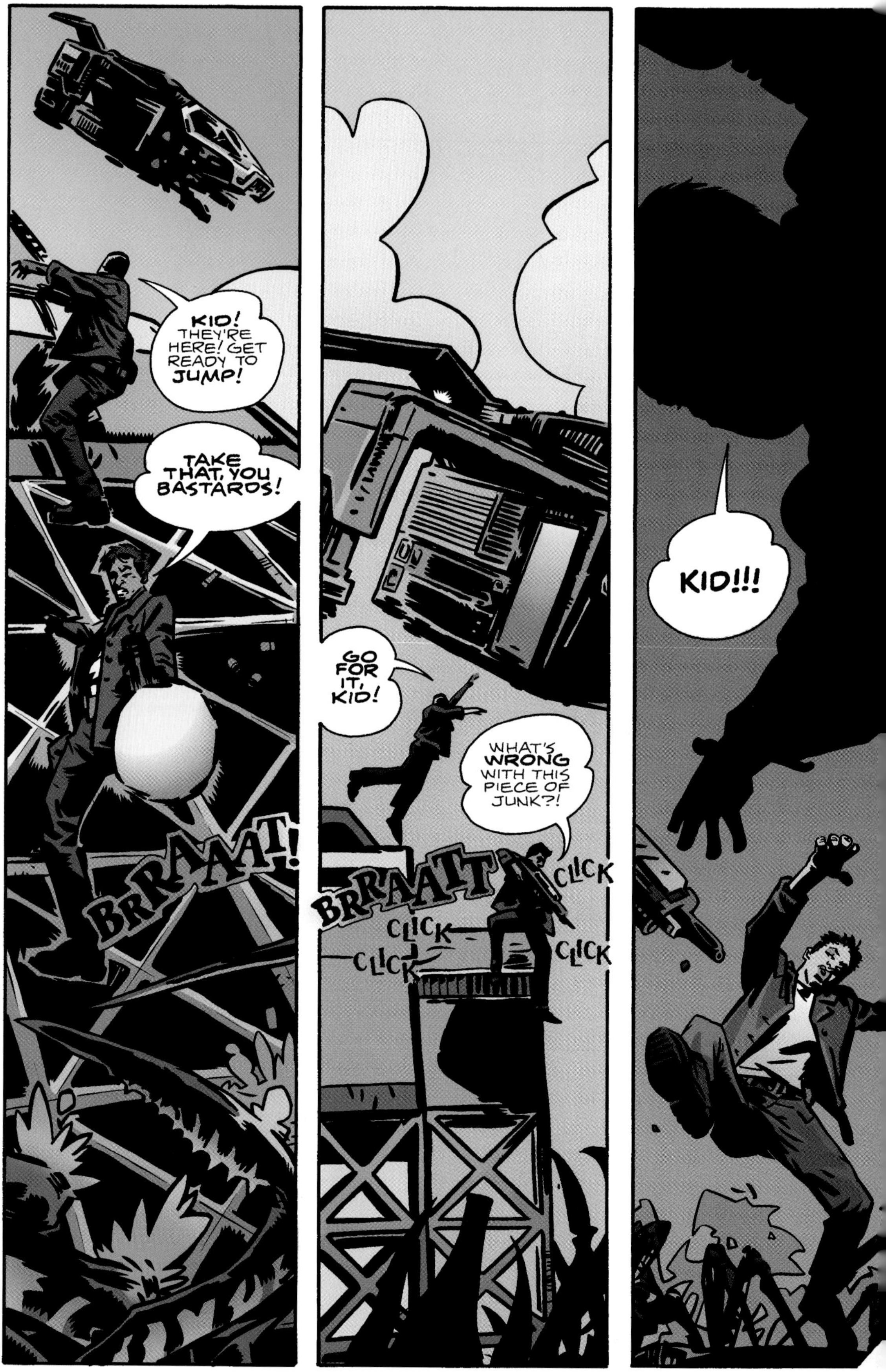
KID! THEY'RE HERE! GET READY TO JUMP!
TAKE THAT, YOU BASTARDS!
BRRAAAT!
GO FOR IT, KID!
WHAT'S WRONG WITH THIS PIECE OF JUNK?!
BRRAATT
CLICK
CLICK
CLICK
CLICK
KID!!!

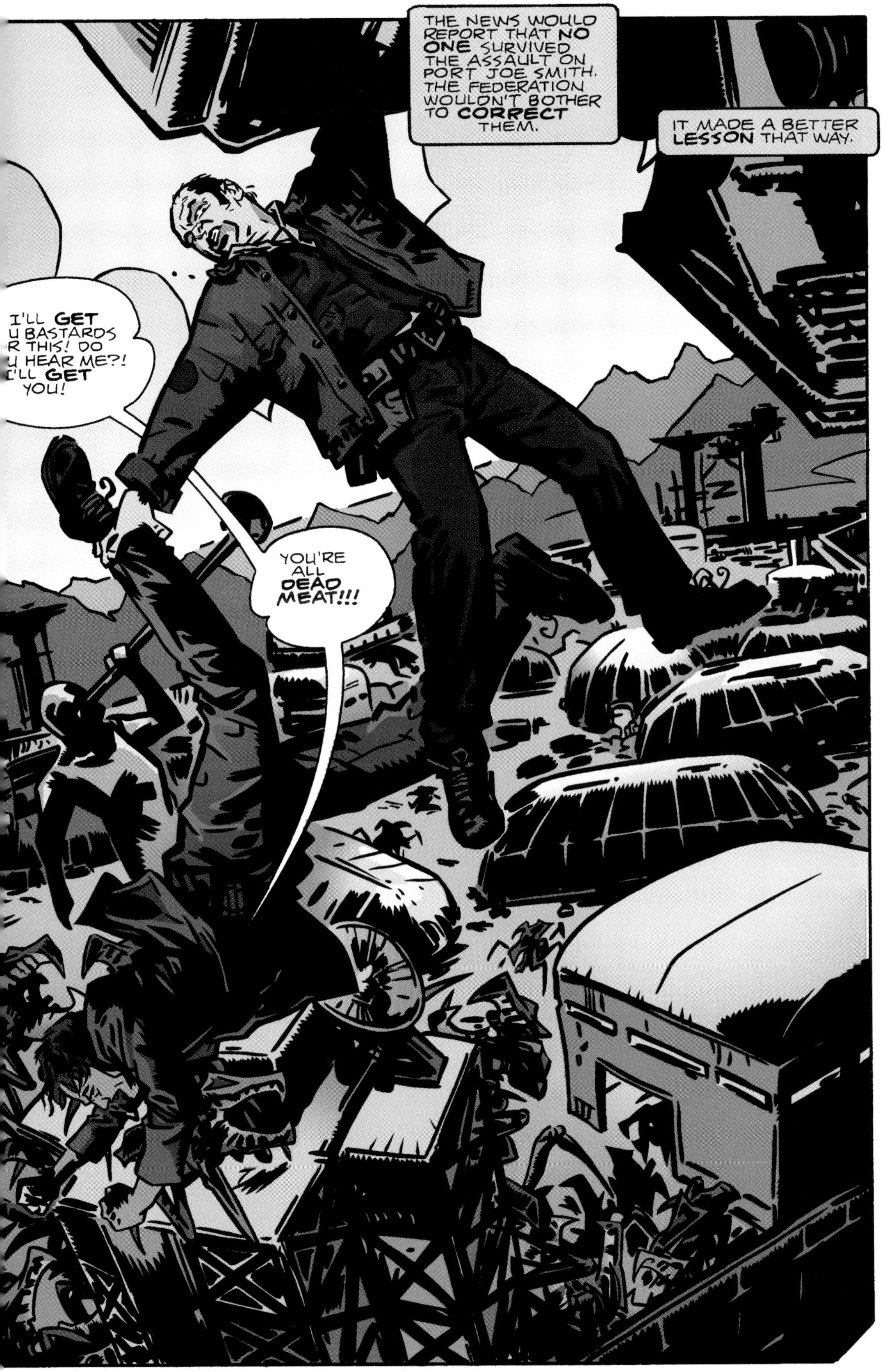
THE NEWS WOULD REPORT THAT NO ONE SURVIVED THE ASSAULT ON PORT JOE SMITH. THE FEDERATION WOULDN'T BOTHER TO CORRECT THEM.
IT MADE A BETTER LESSON THAT WAY.
I'LL GET U BASTARDS R THIS! DO U HEAR ME?! I'LL GET YOU!
YOU'RE ALL DEAD MEAT!!!

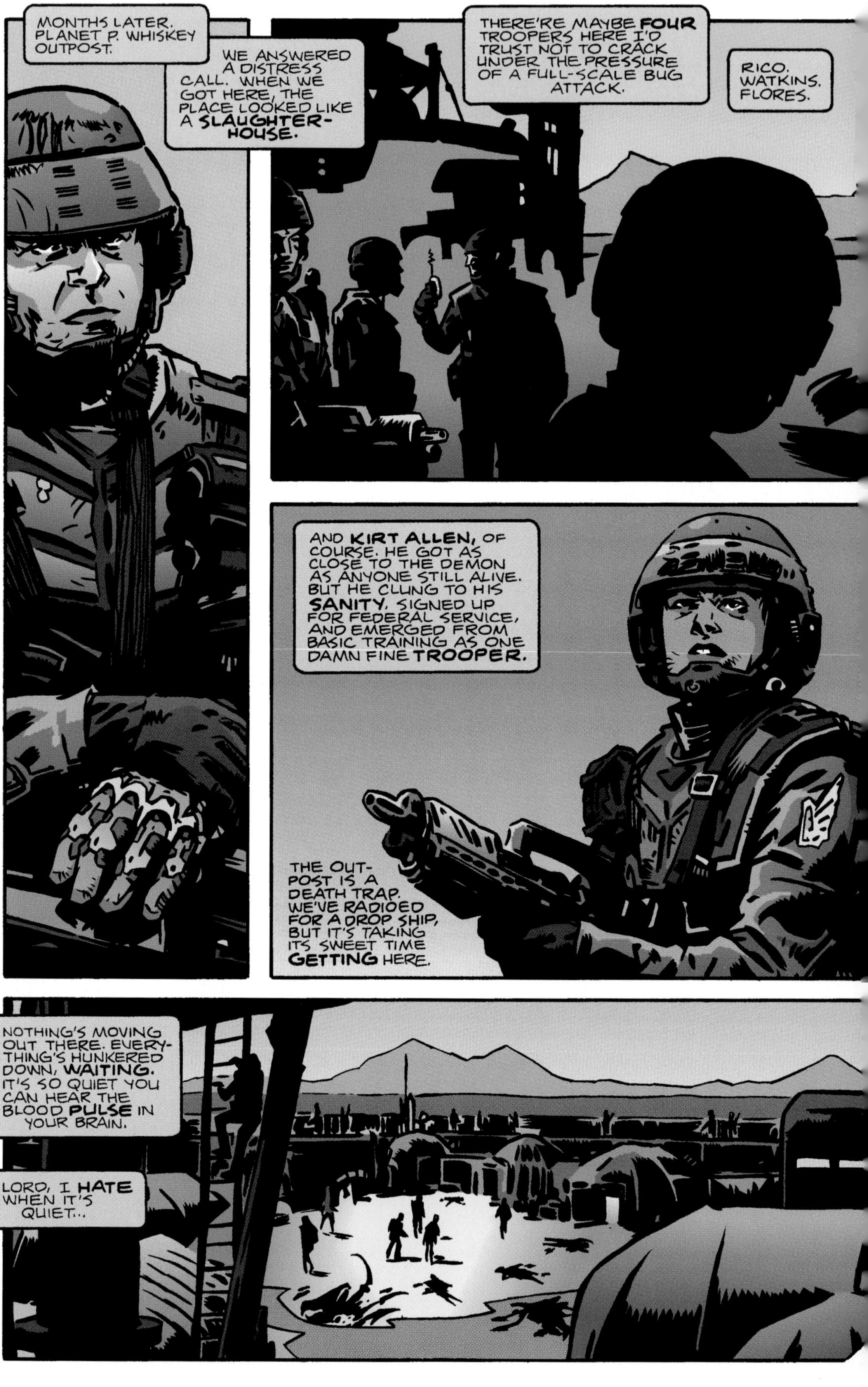

MONTHS LATER. PLANET P. WHISKEY OUTPOST.
WE ANSWERED A DISTRESS CALL. WHEN WE GOT HERE, THE PLACE LOOKED LIKE A **SLAUGHTER-HOUSE.**
THERE'RE MAYBE **FOUR** TROOPERS HERE I'D TRUST NOT TO CRACK UNDER THE PRESSURE OF A FULL-SCALE BUG ATTACK.
RICO. WATKINS. FLORES.
AND **KIRT ALLEN,** OF COURSE. HE GOT AS CLOSE TO THE DEMON AS ANYONE STILL ALIVE. BUT HE CLUNG TO HIS **SANITY.** SIGNED UP FOR FEDERAL SERVICE, AND EMERGED FROM BASIC TRAINING AS ONE DAMN FINE **TROOPER.**
THE OUT-POST IS A DEATH TRAP. WE'VE RADIOED FOR A DROP SHIP, BUT IT'S TAKING ITS SWEET TIME **GETTING** HERE.
NOTHING'S MOVING OUT THERE. EVERY-THING'S HUNKERED DOWN, **WAITING.** IT'S SO QUIET YOU CAN HEAR THE BLOOD **PULSE** IN YOUR BRAIN.
LORD, I **HATE** WHEN IT'S QUIET...

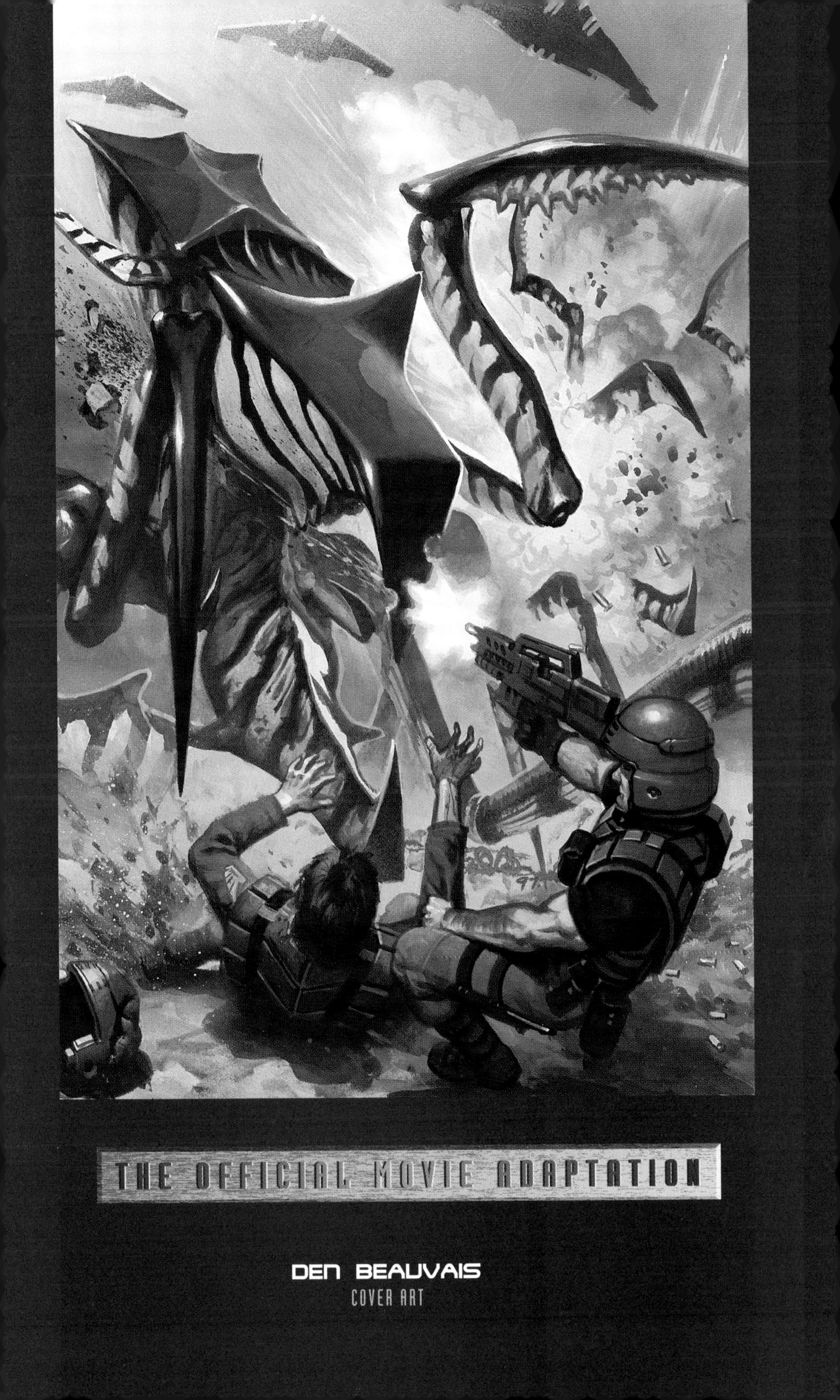

THE OFFICIAL MOVIE ADAPTATION

DEN BEAUVAIS
COVER ART

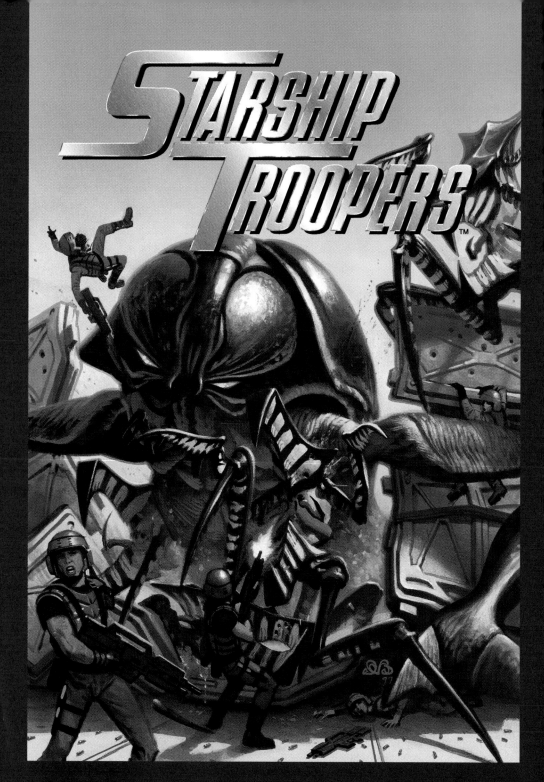

TriStar Pictures and Touchstone Pictures present a Jon Davison production a Paul Verhoeven film 'Starship Troopers'

Casper Van Dien Dina Meyer Denise Richards Jake Busey Neil Patrick Harris Patrick Muldoon and Michael Ironside Music by Basil Poledouris Creature Visual Effects Supervisor Phil Tip

Spaceship Visual Effects Supervisor Scott E. Anderson Visual Effects by Amalgamated Dynamics, Inc. Kevin Yagher Based on the Book by Robert A. Heinlein Screenplay by Ed Neumeier Produced by Alan Marshall Jon Da

Touchstone Pictures | DISTRIBUTED THROUGH SONY PICTURES RELEASING www.sony.com READ THE BERKLEY BOOK Directed by Paul Verhoeven | SDDS | DOLBY | TRI STAR

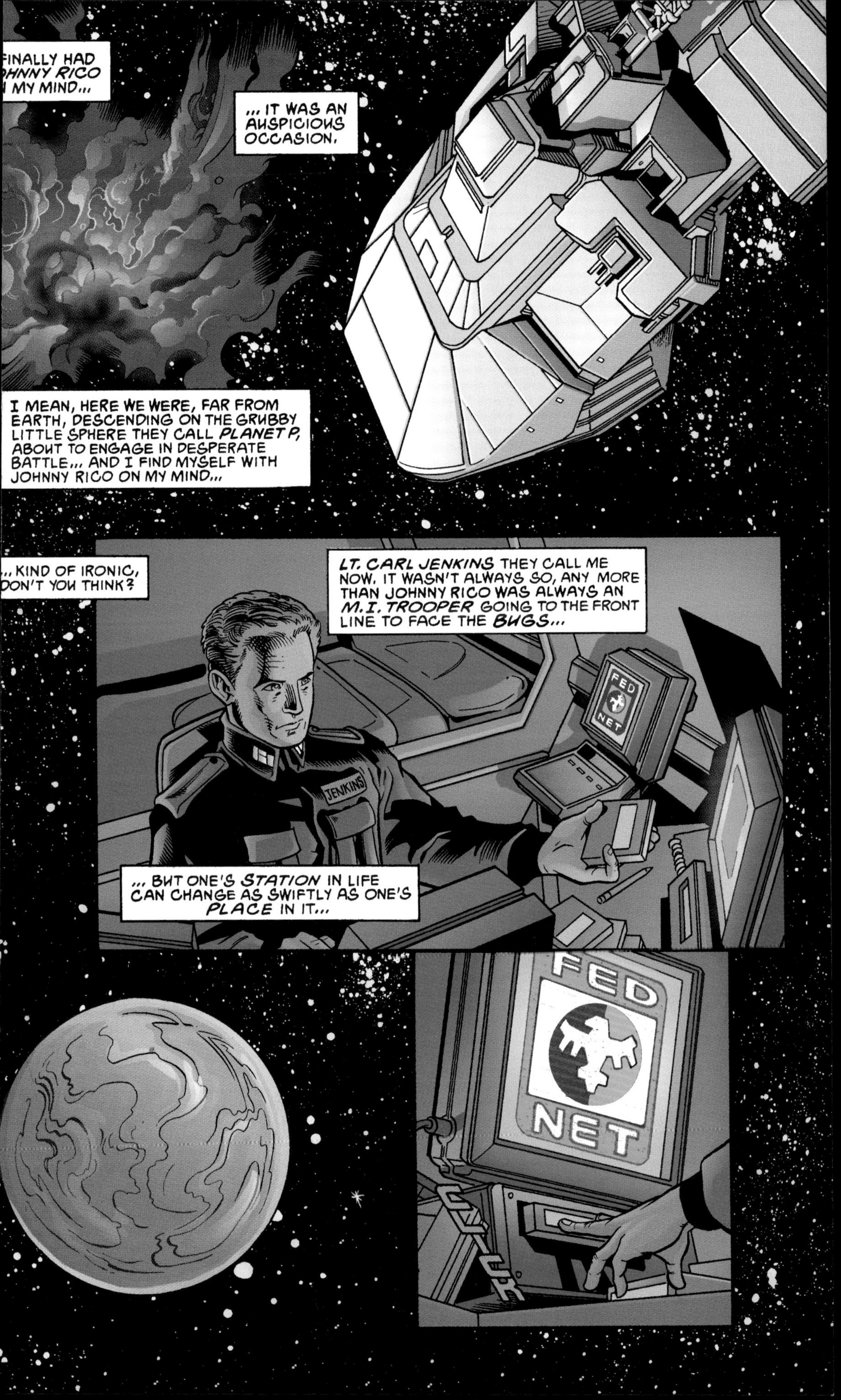
FINALLY HAD
JOHNNY RICO
IN MY MIND...
...IT WAS AN AUSPICIOUS OCCASION.
I MEAN, HERE WE WERE, FAR FROM EARTH, DESCENDING ON THE GRUBBY LITTLE SPHERE THEY CALL PLANET P, ABOUT TO ENGAGE IN DESPERATE BATTLE... AND I FIND MYSELF WITH JOHNNY RICO ON MY MIND...
...KIND OF IRONIC, DON'T YOU THINK?
LT. CARL JENKINS THEY CALL ME NOW. IT WASN'T ALWAYS SO, ANY MORE THAN JOHNNY RICO WAS ALWAYS AN M.I. TROOPER GOING TO THE FRONT LINE TO FACE THE BUGS...
FED NET
JENKINS
...BUT ONE'S STATION IN LIFE CAN CHANGE AS SWIFTLY AS ONE'S PLACE IN IT...
FED NET

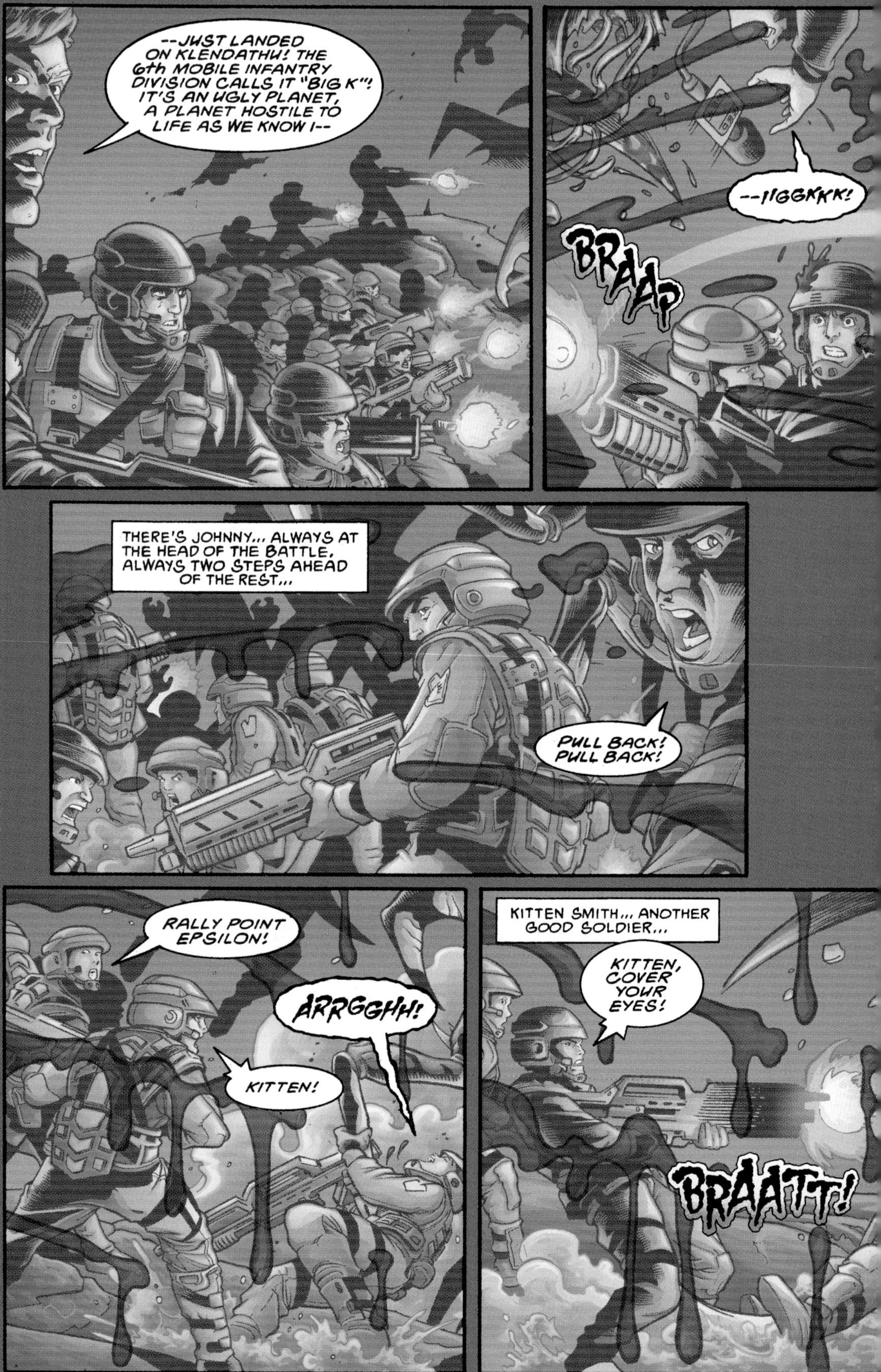
--JUST LANDED ON KLENDATHU! THE 6th MOBILE INFANTRY DIVISION CALLS IT "BIG K"! IT'S AN UGLY PLANET, A PLANET HOSTILE TO LIFE AS WE KNOW I--
--IIGGKKK!
BRAAP
THERE'S JOHNNY... ALWAYS AT THE HEAD OF THE BATTLE, ALWAYS TWO STEPS AHEAD OF THE REST...
PULL BACK! PULL BACK!
RALLY POINT EPSILON!
ARRGGHH!
KITTEN!
KITTEN SMITH... ANOTHER GOOD SOLDIER...
KITTEN, COVER YOUR EYES!
BRAATT!

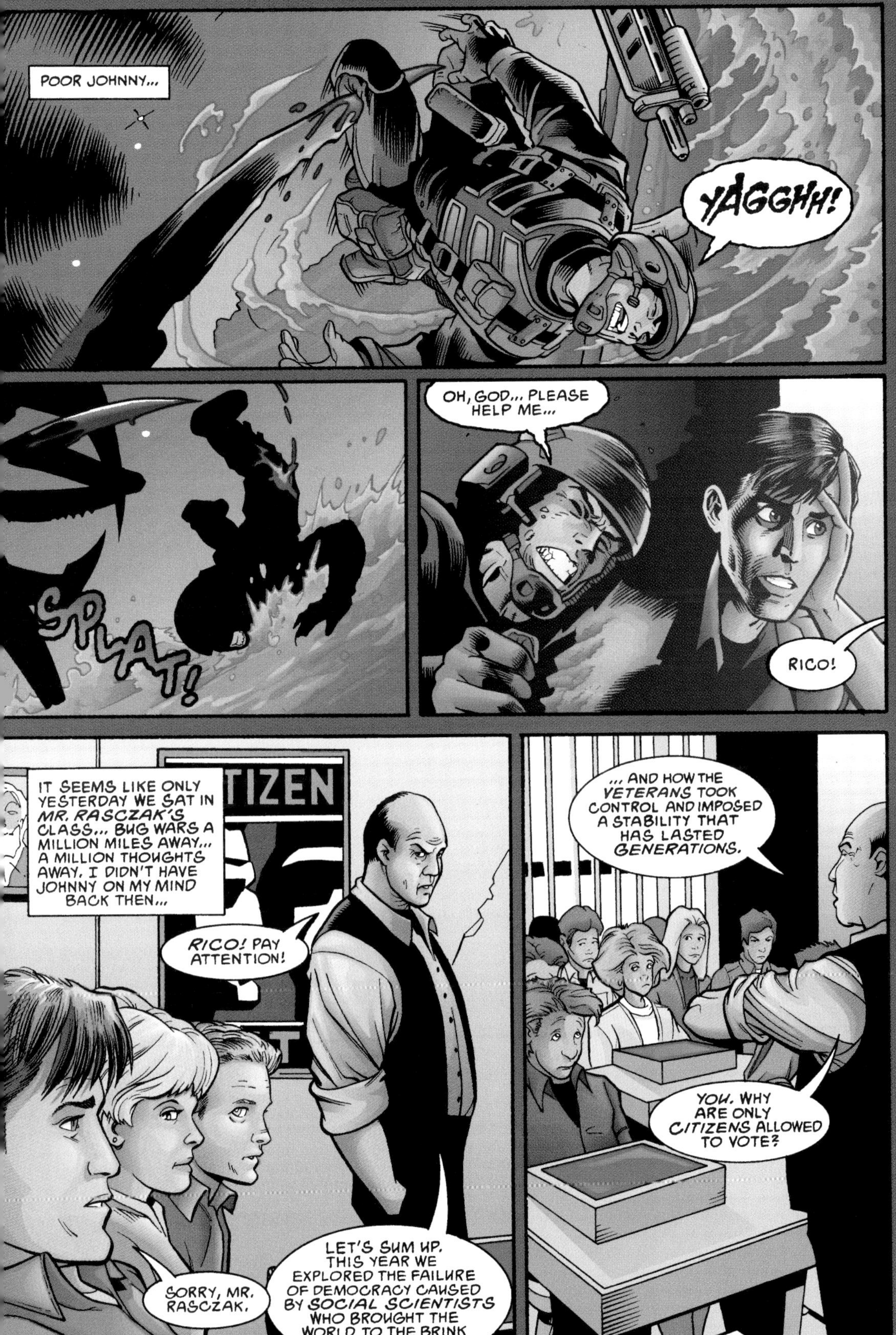
POOR JOHNNY...
YAGGHH!
SPLAT!
OH, GOD... PLEASE HELP ME...
RICO!
IT SEEMS LIKE ONLY YESTERDAY WE SAT IN MR. RASCZAK'S CLASS... BUG WARS A MILLION MILES AWAY... A MILLION THOUGHTS AWAY. I DIDN'T HAVE JOHNNY ON MY MIND BACK THEN...
TIZEN
RICO! PAY ATTENTION!
SORRY, MR. RASCZAK.
LET'S SUM UP. THIS YEAR WE EXPLORED THE FAILURE OF DEMOCRACY CAUSED BY SOCIAL SCIENTISTS WHO BROUGHT THE WORLD TO THE BRINK OF CHAOS...
...AND HOW THE VETERANS TOOK CONTROL AND IMPOSED A STABILITY THAT HAS LASTED GENERATIONS.
YOU. WHY ARE ONLY CITIZENS ALLOWED TO VOTE?

IT'S A REWARD, WHAT THE FEDERATION GIVES YOU FOR DOING FEDERAL SERVICE.

WRONG! WHEN YOU VOTE, YOU'RE EXERCISING POLITICAL AUTHORITY. YOU'RE USING FORCE!

FORCE IS VIOLENCE-- THE SUPREME AUTHORITY! POLITICAL AUTHORITY IS VIOLENCE BY DECREE.

CITIZENS HAVE EARNED THE RIGHT TO USE IT.

HOW YOUNG WE WERE BACK THEN IN THAT BUENOS AIRES HIGH SCHOOL... HOW INEXPERIENCED. EVEN ME...

GEE, WE ALWAYS THOUGHT YOU WERE THE SUPREME AUTHOR, MR. RASCZAK!

BRRiiiNG

VERY FUNNY, JENKINS.

THERE'S THE BELL. END OF ANOTHER SCHOOL YEAR. HAVE A NICE LIFE.

HEY! YOU WITH THE LEGS...

CARMEN IBANEZ, MAYBE I DIDN'T HAVE JOHNNY ON MY MIND BACK THEN, BUT HE CERTAINLY HAD CARMEN ON HIS... CONSTANTLY.

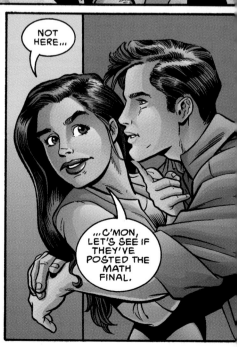

NOT HERE...

...C'MON, LET'S SEE IF THEY'VE POSTED THE MATH FINAL.

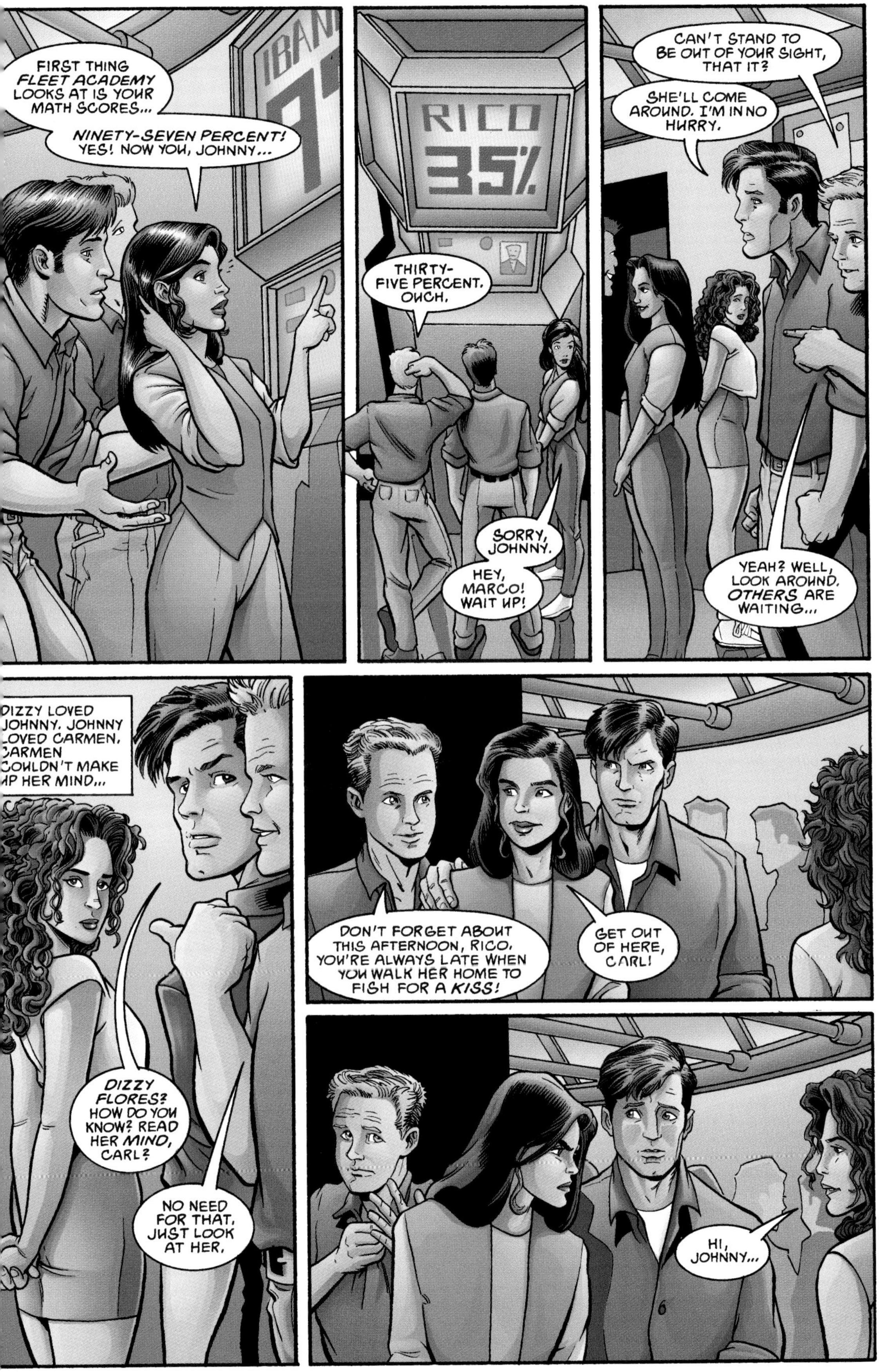
FIRST THING FLEET ACADEMY LOOKS AT IS YOUR MATH SCORES...
NINETY-SEVEN PERCENT! YES! NOW YOU, JOHNNY...
RICO 35%
THIRTY-FIVE PERCENT. OUCH.
SORRY, JOHNNY.
HEY, MARCO! WAIT UP!
CAN'T STAND TO BE OUT OF YOUR SIGHT, THAT IT?
SHE'LL COME AROUND. I'M IN NO HURRY.
YEAH? WELL, LOOK AROUND. OTHERS ARE WAITING...
DIZZY LOVED JOHNNY. JOHNNY LOVED CARMEN. CARMEN COULDN'T MAKE UP HER MIND...
DIZZY FLORES? HOW DO YOU KNOW? READ HER MIND, CARL?
NO NEED FOR THAT. JUST LOOK AT HER.
DON'T FORGET ABOUT THIS AFTERNOON, RICO. YOU'RE ALWAYS LATE WHEN YOU WALK HER HOME TO FISH FOR A KISS!
GET OUT OF HERE, CARL!
HI, JOHNNY...

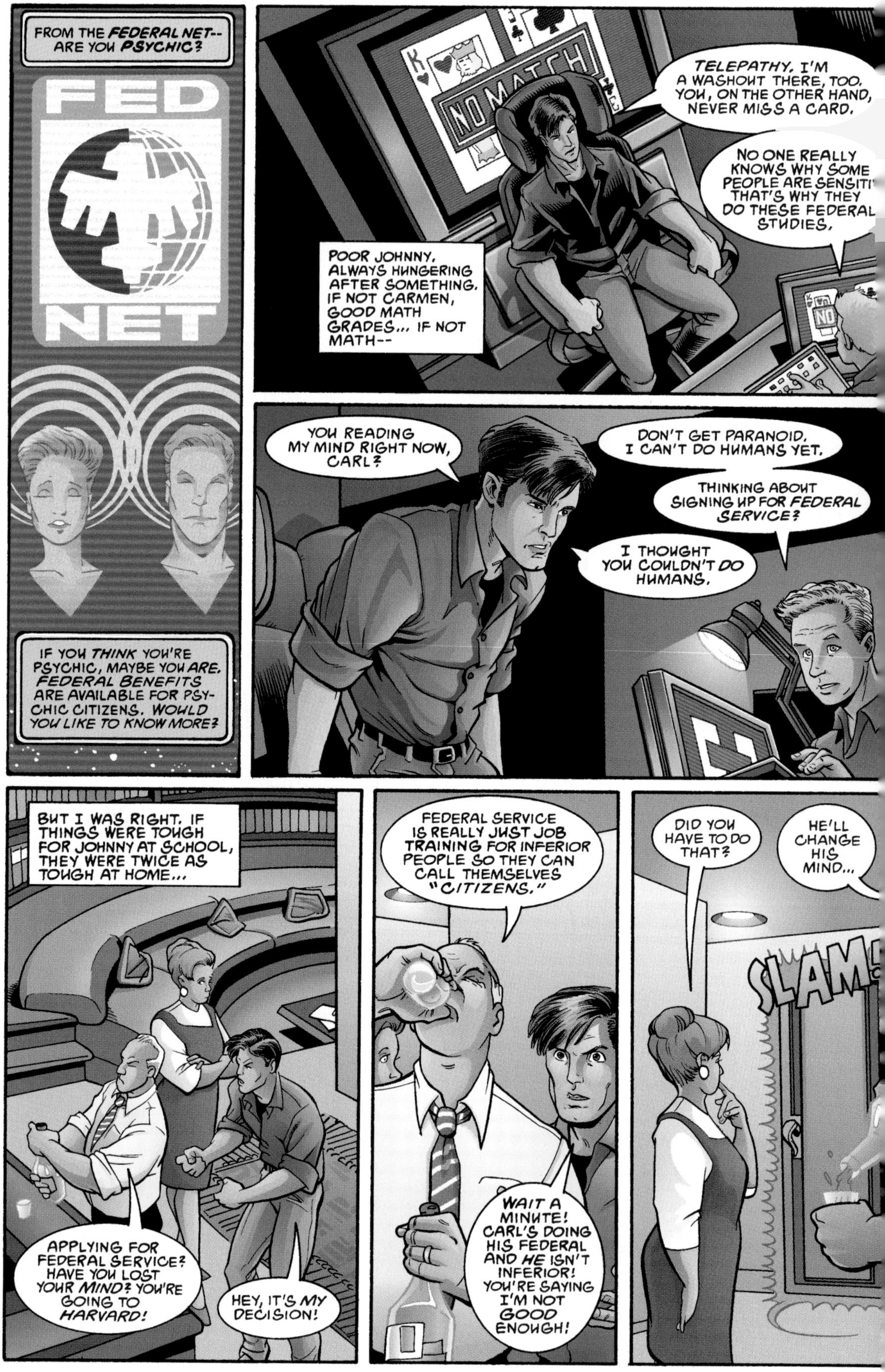

FROM THE FEDERAL NET-- ARE YOU PSYCHIC?
FED NET
IF YOU THINK YOU'RE PSYCHIC, MAYBE YOU ARE. FEDERAL BENEFITS ARE AVAILABLE FOR PSYCHIC CITIZENS. WOULD YOU LIKE TO KNOW MORE?
NO MATCH
TELEPATHY. I'M A WASHOUT THERE, TOO. YOU, ON THE OTHER HAND, NEVER MISS A CARD.
NO ONE REALLY KNOWS WHY SOME PEOPLE ARE SENSITI THAT'S WHY THEY DO THESE FEDERAL STUDIES.
POOR JOHNNY, ALWAYS HUNGERING AFTER SOMETHING. IF NOT CARMEN, GOOD MATH GRADES... IF NOT MATH--
YOU READING MY MIND RIGHT NOW, CARL?
DON'T GET PARANOID. I CAN'T DO HUMANS YET.
THINKING ABOUT SIGNING UP FOR FEDERAL SERVICE?
I THOUGHT YOU COULDN'T DO HUMANS.
BUT I WAS RIGHT. IF THINGS WERE TOUGH FOR JOHNNY AT SCHOOL, THEY WERE TWICE AS TOUGH AT HOME...
APPLYING FOR FEDERAL SERVICE? HAVE YOU LOST YOUR MIND? YOU'RE GOING TO HARVARD!
HEY, IT'S MY DECISION!
FEDERAL SERVICE IS REALLY JUST JOB TRAINING FOR INFERIOR PEOPLE SO THEY CAN CALL THEMSELVES "CITIZENS."
WAIT A MINUTE! CARL'S DOING HIS FEDERAL AND HE ISN'T INFERIOR! YOU'RE SAYING I'M NOT GOOD ENOUGH!
DID YOU HAVE TO DO THAT?
HE'LL CHANGE HIS MIND...
SLAM

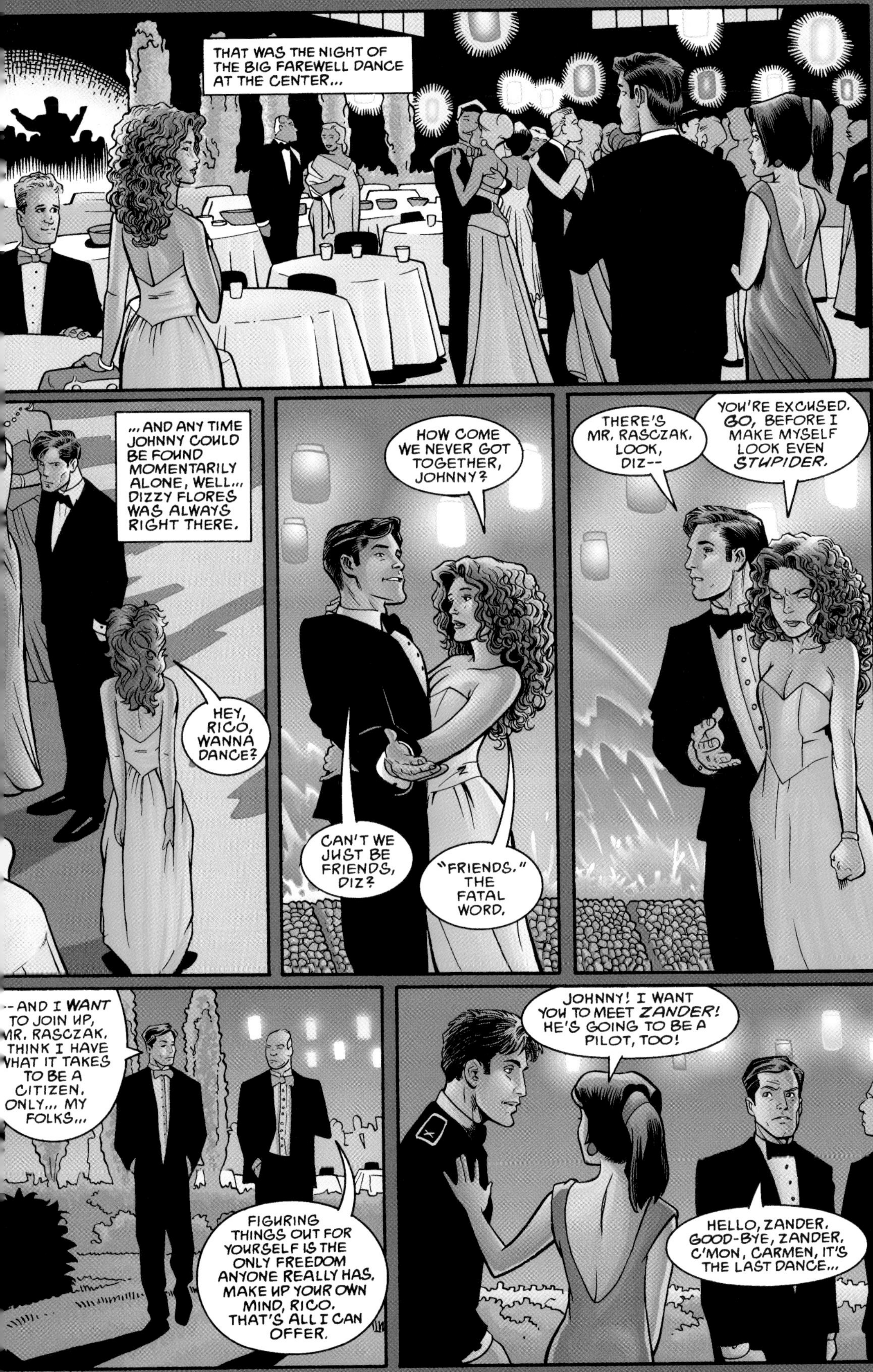
THAT WAS THE NIGHT OF THE BIG FAREWELL DANCE AT THE CENTER...
...AND ANY TIME JOHNNY COULD BE FOUND MOMENTARILY ALONE, WELL... DIZZY FLORES WAS ALWAYS RIGHT THERE.
HEY, RICO, WANNA DANCE?
HOW COME WE NEVER GOT TOGETHER, JOHNNY?
CAN'T WE JUST BE FRIENDS, DIZ?
"FRIENDS." THE FATAL WORD.
THERE'S MR. RASCZAK. LOOK, DIZ--
YOU'RE EXCUSED. GO, BEFORE I MAKE MYSELF LOOK EVEN STUPIDER.
--AND I WANT TO JOIN UP, MR. RASCZAK. THINK I HAVE WHAT IT TAKES TO BE A CITIZEN. ONLY... MY FOLKS...
FIGURING THINGS OUT FOR YOURSELF IS THE ONLY FREEDOM ANYONE REALLY HAS. MAKE UP YOUR OWN MIND, RICO. THAT'S ALL I CAN OFFER.
JOHNNY! I WANT YOU TO MEET ZANDER! HE'S GOING TO BE A PILOT, TOO!
HELLO, ZANDER. GOOD-BYE, ZANDER. C'MON, CARMEN, IT'S THE LAST DANCE...

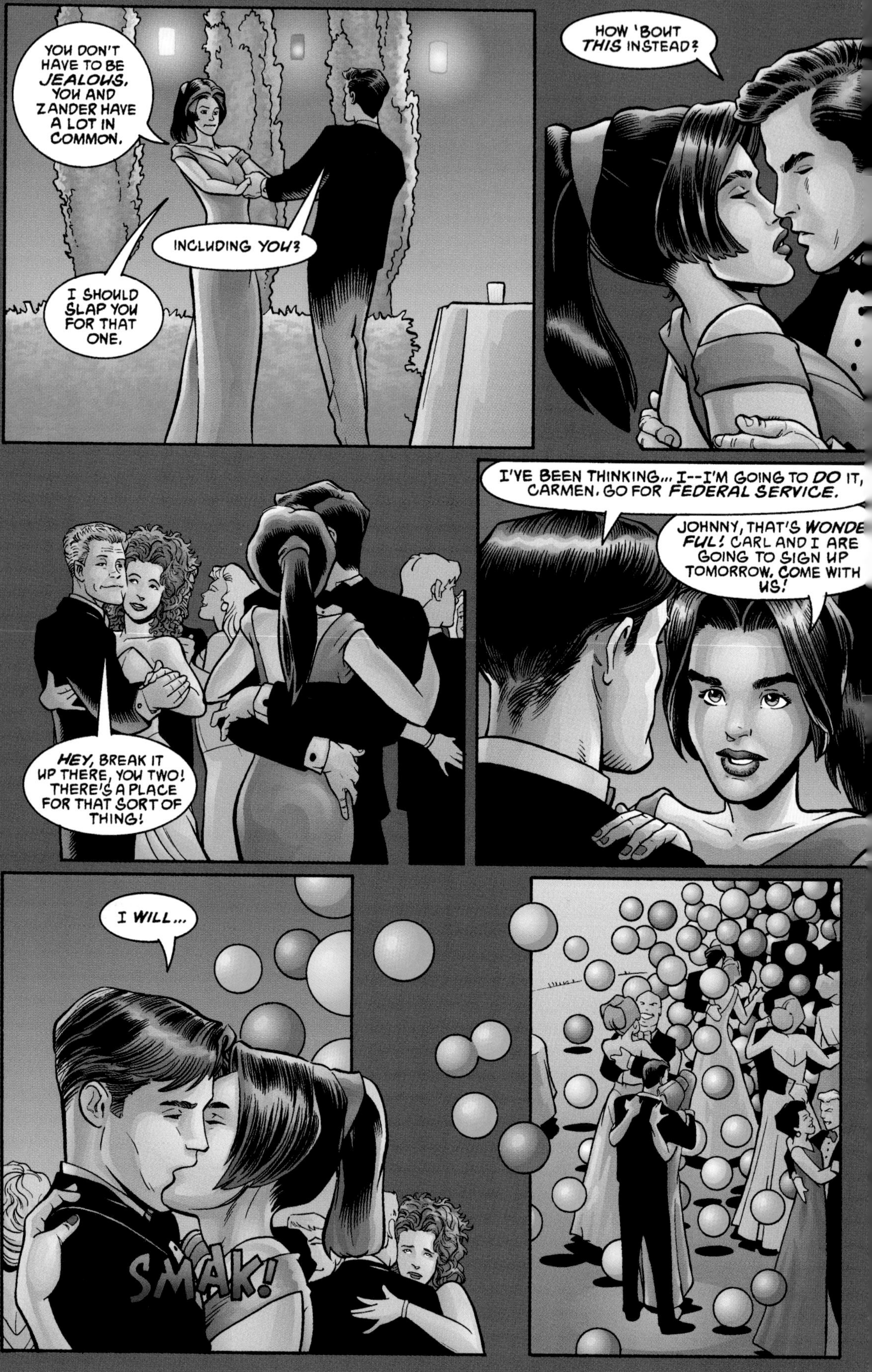
YOU DON'T HAVE TO BE JEALOUS. YOU AND ZANDER HAVE A LOT IN COMMON.
INCLUDING YOU?
I SHOULD SLAP YOU FOR THAT ONE.
HOW 'BOUT THIS INSTEAD?
HEY, BREAK IT UP THERE, YOU TWO! THERE'S A PLACE FOR THAT SORT OF THING!
I'VE BEEN THINKING... I--I'M GOING TO DO IT, CARMEN. GO FOR FEDERAL SERVICE.
JOHNNY, THAT'S WONDE FUL! CARL AND I ARE GOING TO SIGN UP TOMORROW. COME WITH US!
I WILL...
SMAK!

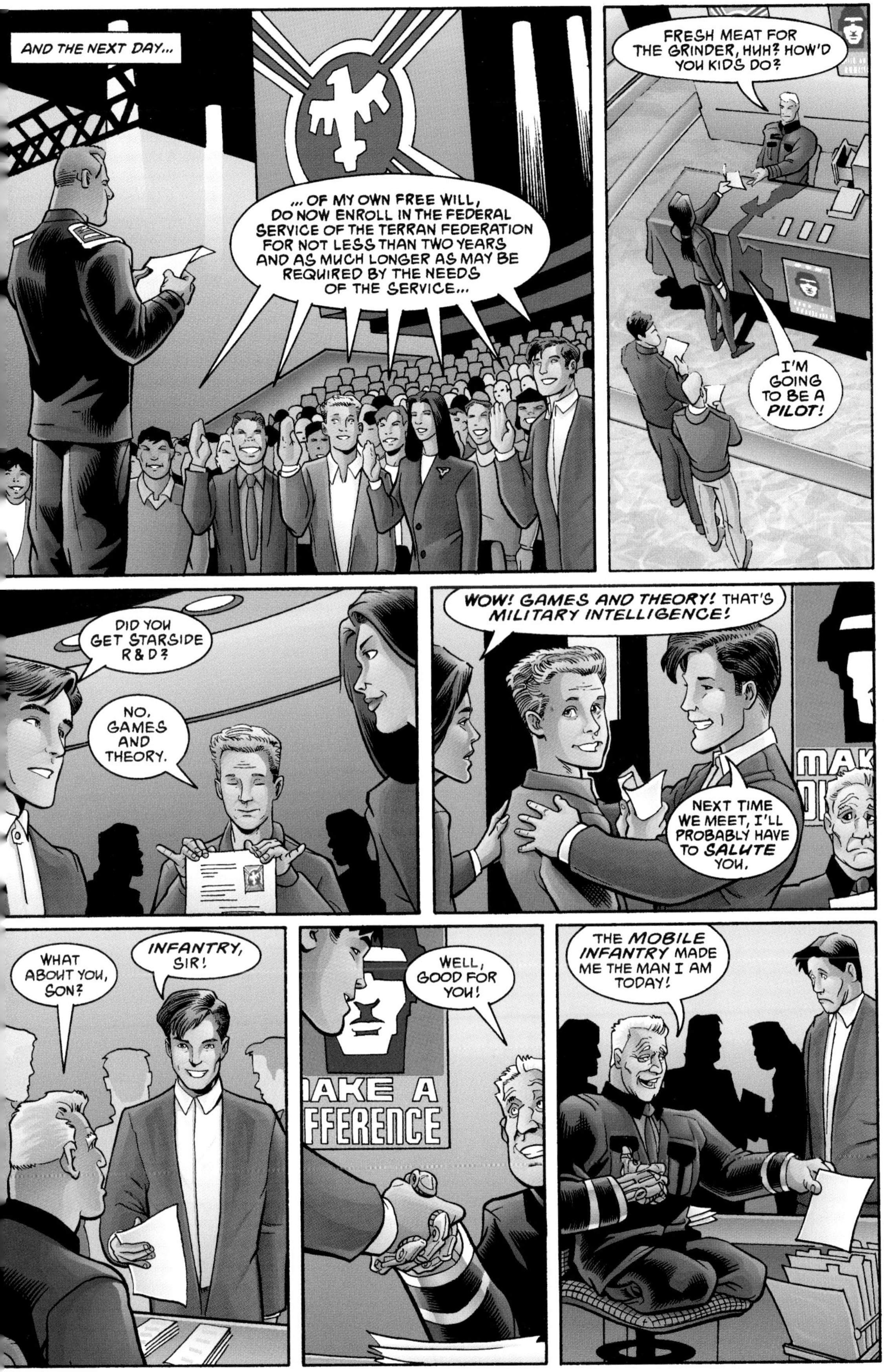

AND THE NEXT DAY...
...OF MY OWN FREE WILL, DO NOW ENROLL IN THE FEDERAL SERVICE OF THE TERRAN FEDERATION FOR NOT LESS THAN TWO YEARS AND AS MUCH LONGER AS MAY BE REQUIRED BY THE NEEDS OF THE SERVICE...
FRESH MEAT FOR THE GRINDER, HUH? HOW'D YOU KIDS DO?
I'M GOING TO BE A PILOT!
DID YOU GET STARSIDE R & D?
NO, GAMES AND THEORY.
WOW! GAMES AND THEORY! THAT'S MILITARY INTELLIGENCE!
NEXT TIME WE MEET, I'LL PROBABLY HAVE TO SALUTE YOU.
WHAT ABOUT YOU, SON?
INFANTRY, SIR!
WELL, GOOD FOR YOU!
IAKE A
FFERENCE
THE MOBILE INFANTRY MADE ME THE MAN I AM TODAY!

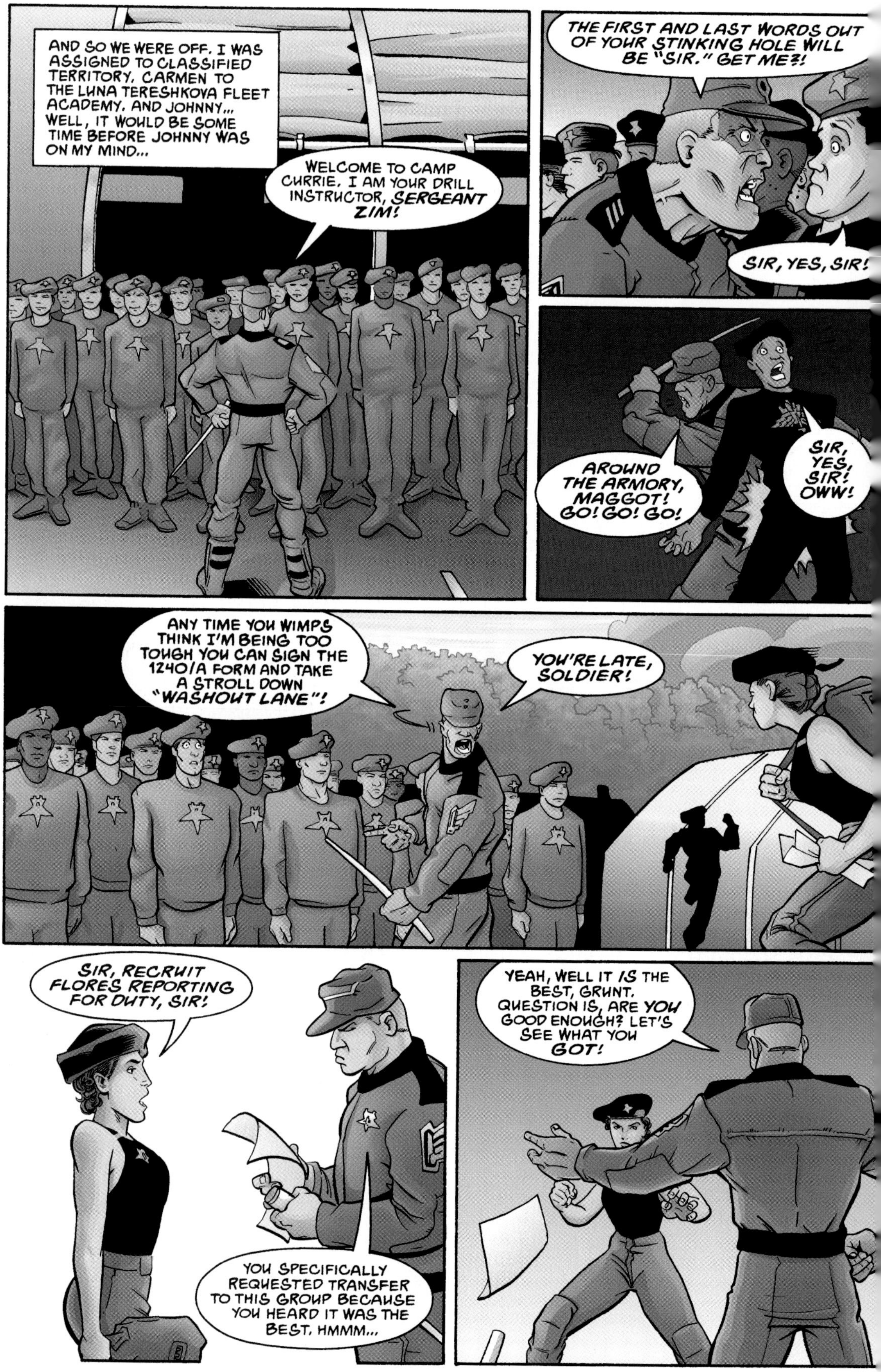
AND SO WE WERE OFF. I WAS ASSIGNED TO CLASSIFIED TERRITORY, CARMEN TO THE LUNA TERESHKOVA FLEET ACADEMY. AND JOHNNY... WELL, IT WOULD BE SOME TIME BEFORE JOHNNY WAS ON MY MIND...
WELCOME TO CAMP CURRIE. I AM YOUR DRILL INSTRUCTOR, SERGEANT ZIM!
THE FIRST AND LAST WORDS OUT OF YOUR STINKING HOLE WILL BE "SIR." GET ME?!
SIR, YES, SIR!
AROUND THE ARMORY, MAGGOT! GO! GO! GO!
SIR, YES, SIR! OWW!
ANY TIME YOU WIMPS THINK I'M BEING TOO TOUGH YOU CAN SIGN THE 1240/A FORM AND TAKE A STROLL DOWN "WASHOUT LANE"!
YOU'RE LATE, SOLDIER!
SIR, RECRUIT FLORES REPORTING FOR DUTY, SIR!
YOU SPECIFICALLY REQUESTED TRANSFER TO THIS GROUP BECAUSE YOU HEARD IT WAS THE BEST. HMMM...
YEAH, WELL IT IS THE BEST, GRUNT. QUESTION IS, ARE YOU GOOD ENOUGH? LET'S SEE WHAT YOU GOT!

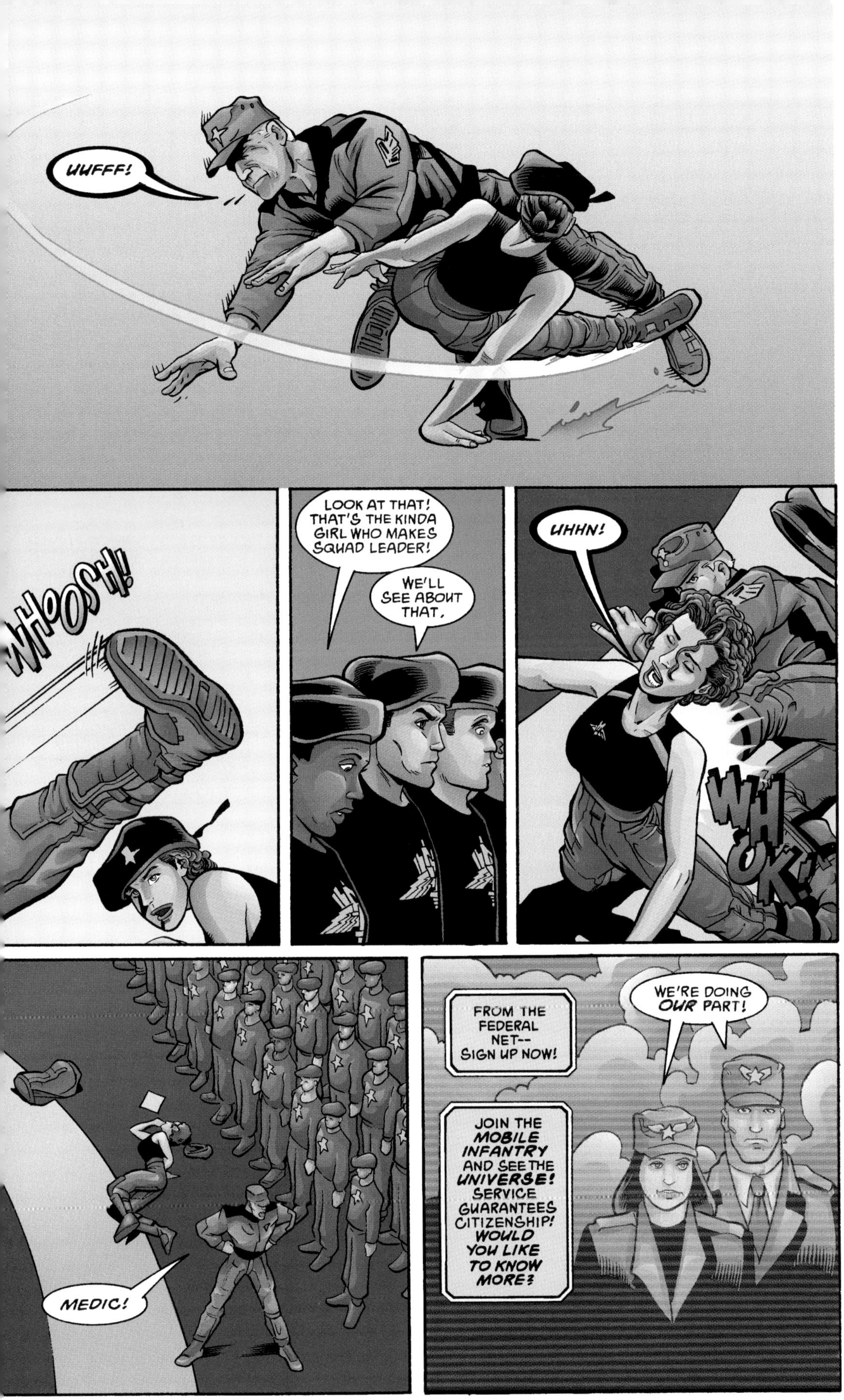
UUFFF!
WHOOSH!
LOOK AT THAT! THAT'S THE KINDA GIRL WHO MAKES SQUAD LEADER!
WE'LL SEE ABOUT THAT.
UHHN!
WHOK!
MEDIC!
FROM THE FEDERAL NET-- SIGN UP NOW!
WE'RE DOING OUR PART!
JOIN THE MOBILE INFANTRY AND SEE THE UNIVERSE! SERVICE GUARANTEES CITIZENSHIP! WOULD YOU LIKE TO KNOW MORE?

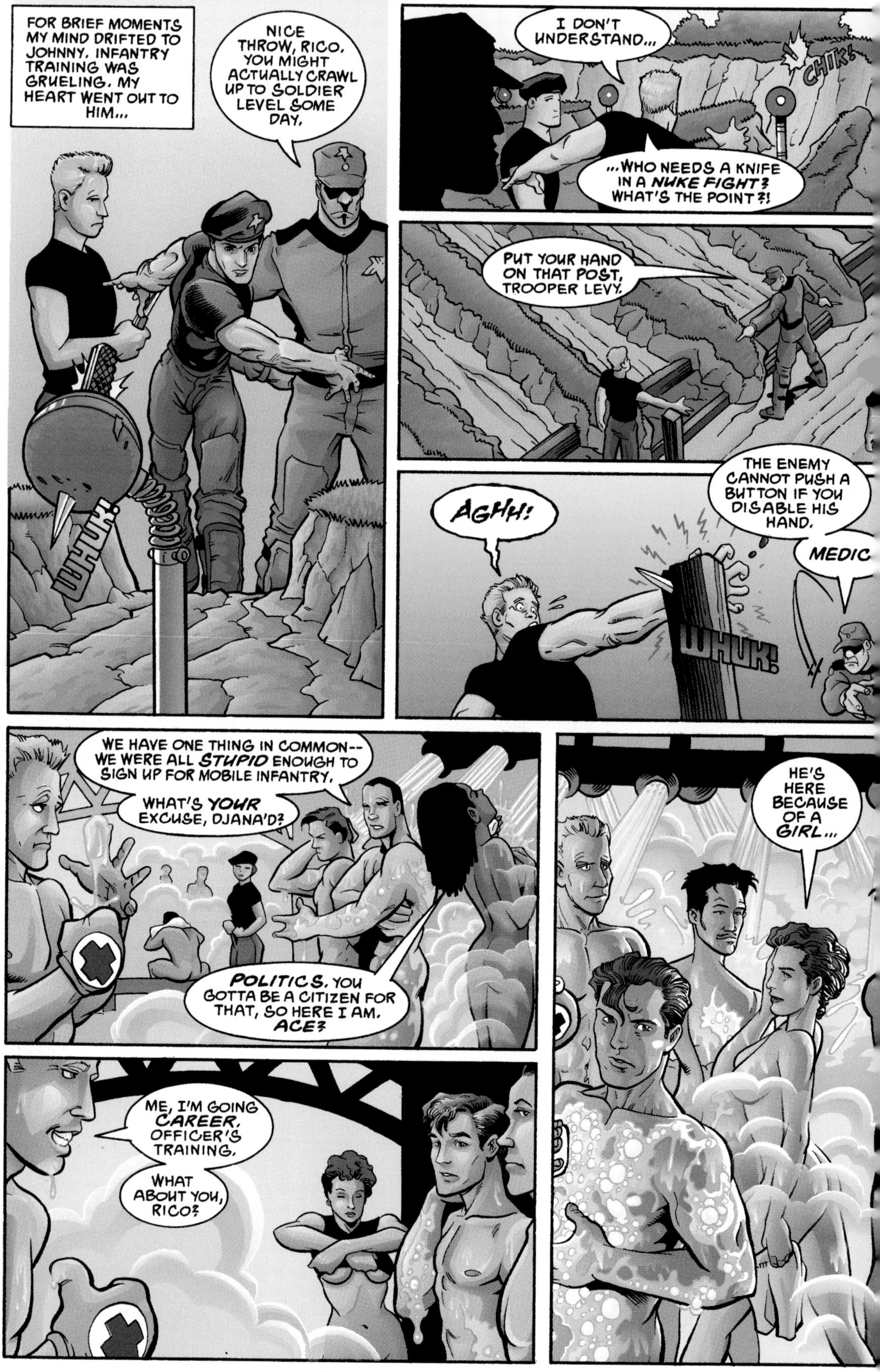
FOR BRIEF MOMENTS MY MIND DRIFTED TO JOHNNY. INFANTRY TRAINING WAS GRUELING. MY HEART WENT OUT TO HIM...
NICE THROW, RICO. YOU MIGHT ACTUALLY CRAWL UP TO SOLDIER LEVEL SOME DAY.
WHUK!
I DON'T UNDERSTAND...
CHIK!
...WHO NEEDS A KNIFE IN A NUKE FIGHT? WHAT'S THE POINT?!
PUT YOUR HAND ON THAT POST, TROOPER LEVY.
AGHH!
THE ENEMY CANNOT PUSH A BUTTON IF YOU DISABLE HIS HAND.
MEDIC
WHUK!
WE HAVE ONE THING IN COMMON-- WE WERE ALL STUPID ENOUGH TO SIGN UP FOR MOBILE INFANTRY.
WHAT'S YOUR EXCUSE, DJANA'D?
POLITICS. YOU GOTTA BE A CITIZEN FOR THAT, SO HERE I AM. ACE?
ME, I'M GOING CAREER. OFFICER'S TRAINING.
WHAT ABOUT YOU, RICO?
HE'S HERE BECAUSE OF A GIRL...

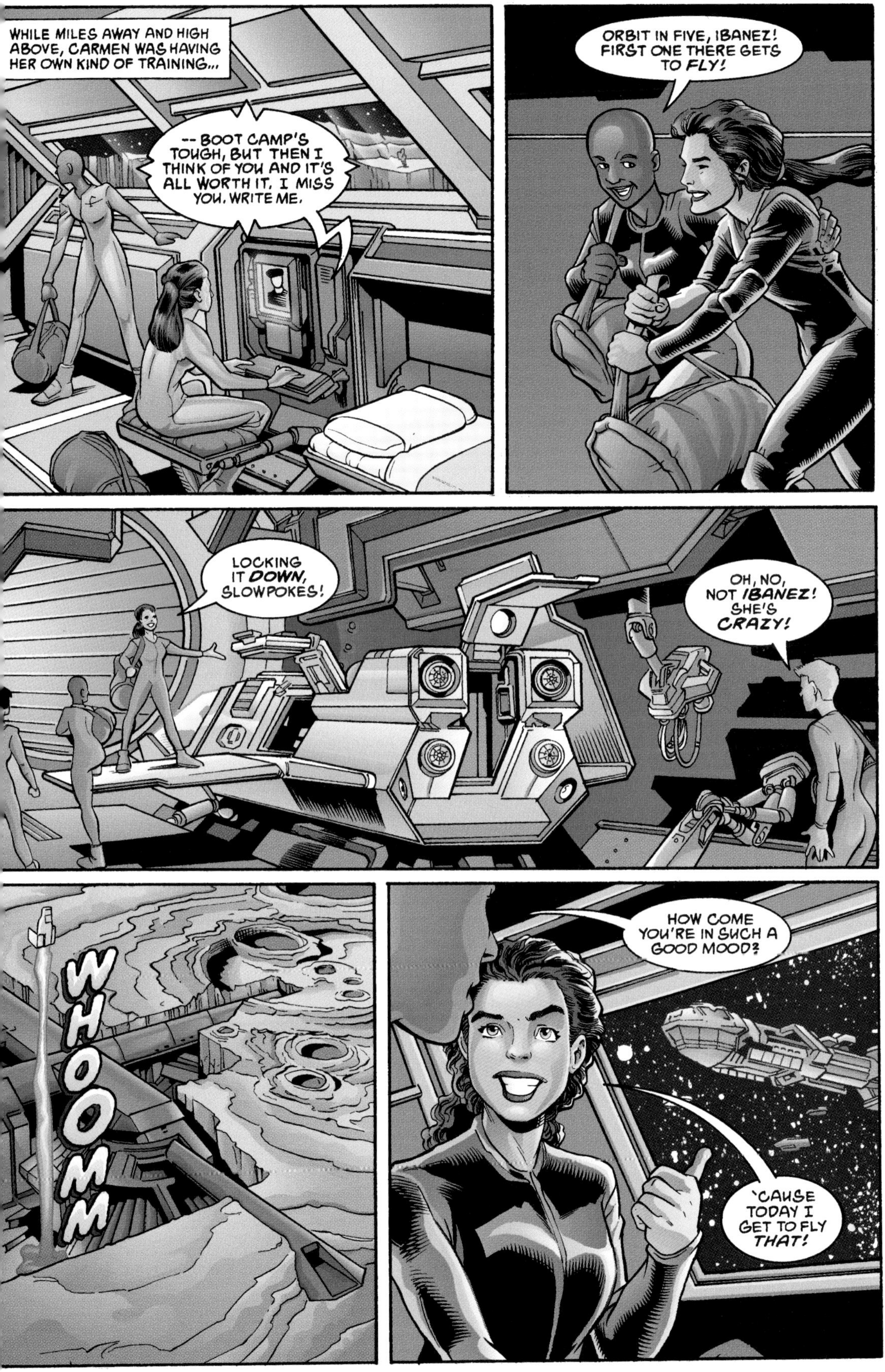
WHILE MILES AWAY AND HIGH ABOVE, CARMEN WAS HAVING HER OWN KIND OF TRAINING...
-- BOOT CAMP'S TOUGH, BUT THEN I THINK OF YOU AND IT'S ALL WORTH IT. I MISS YOU. WRITE ME.
ORBIT IN FIVE, IBANEZ! FIRST ONE THERE GETS TO *FLY!*
LOCKING IT *DOWN*, SLOWPOKES!
OH, NO, NOT *IBANEZ!* SHE'S *CRAZY!*
WHOOMM
HOW COME YOU'RE IN SUCH A GOOD MOOD?
'CAUSE TODAY I GET TO FLY *THAT!*

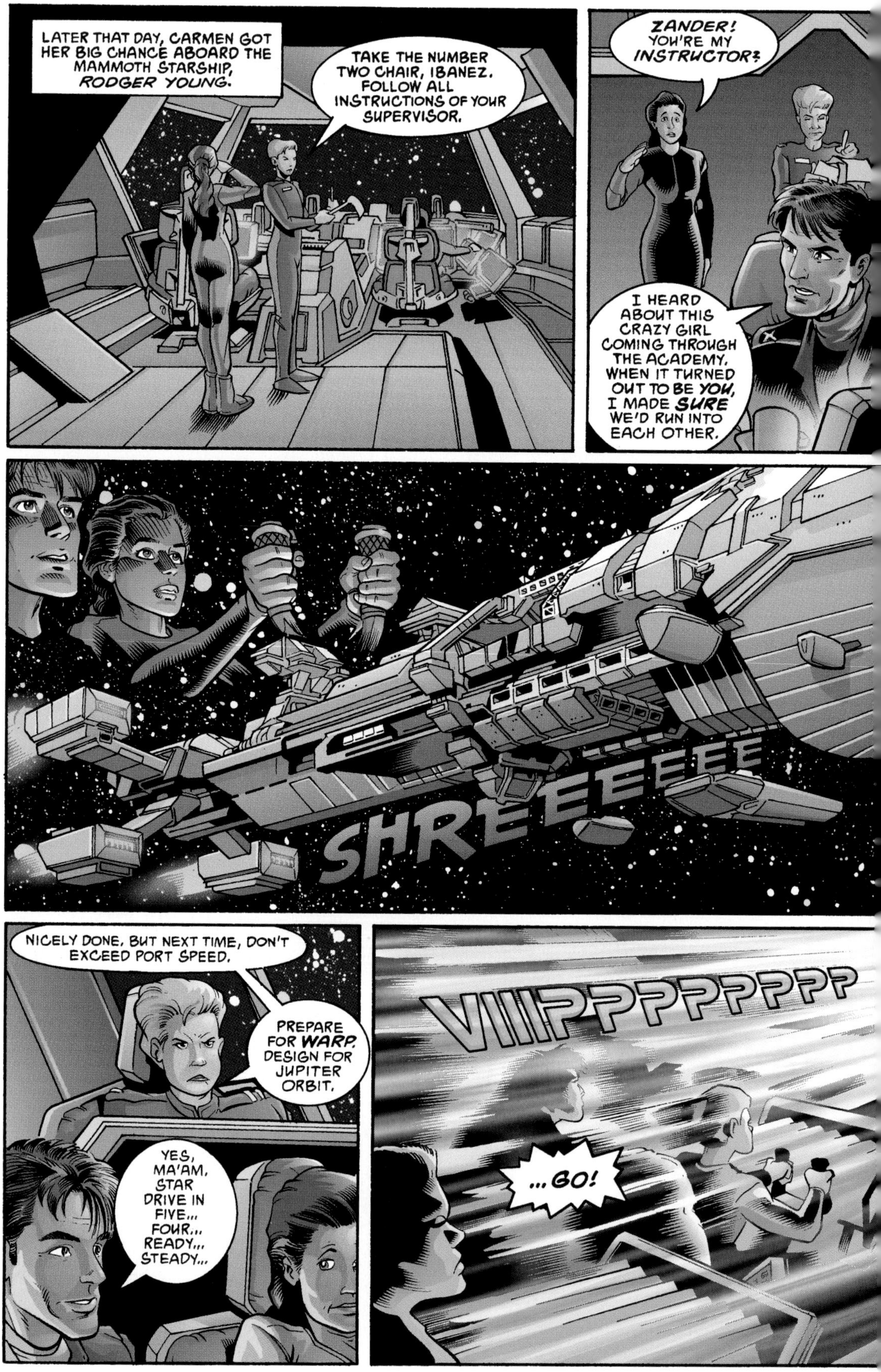
LATER THAT DAY, CARMEN GOT HER BIG CHANCE ABOARD THE MAMMOTH STARSHIP, RODGER YOUNG.
TAKE THE NUMBER TWO CHAIR, IBANEZ. FOLLOW ALL INSTRUCTIONS OF YOUR SUPERVISOR.
ZANDER! YOU'RE MY INSTRUCTOR?
I HEARD ABOUT THIS CRAZY GIRL COMING THROUGH THE ACADEMY. WHEN IT TURNED OUT TO BE YOU, I MADE SURE WE'D RUN INTO EACH OTHER.
SHREEEEEEE
NICELY DONE, BUT NEXT TIME, DON'T EXCEED PORT SPEED.
PREPARE FOR WARP. DESIGN FOR JUPITER ORBIT.
YES, MA'AM, STAR DRIVE IN FIVE... FOUR... READY... STEADY...
VIIIPPPPPPPP
...GO!

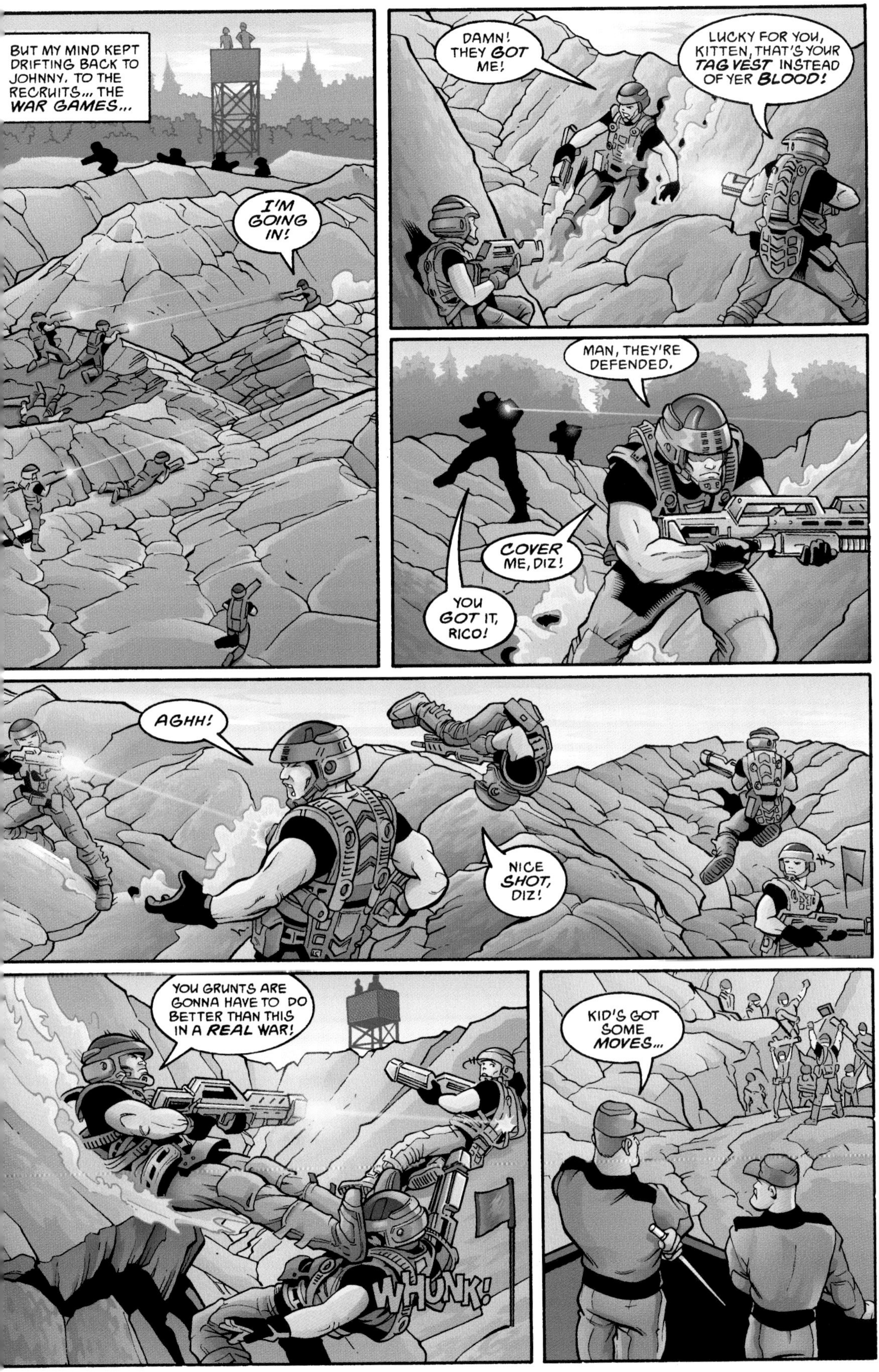

BUT MY MIND KEPT DRIFTING BACK TO JOHNNY. TO THE RECRUITS... THE WAR GAMES...
I'M GOING IN!
DAMN! THEY GOT ME!
LUCKY FOR YOU, KITTEN, THAT'S YOUR TAG VEST INSTEAD OF YER BLOOD!
MAN, THEY'RE DEFENDED.
COVER ME, DIZ!
YOU GOT IT, RICO!
AGHH!
NICE SHOT, DIZ!
YOU GRUNTS ARE GONNA HAVE TO DO BETTER THAN THIS IN A REAL WAR!
WHUNK!
KID'S GOT SOME MOVES...

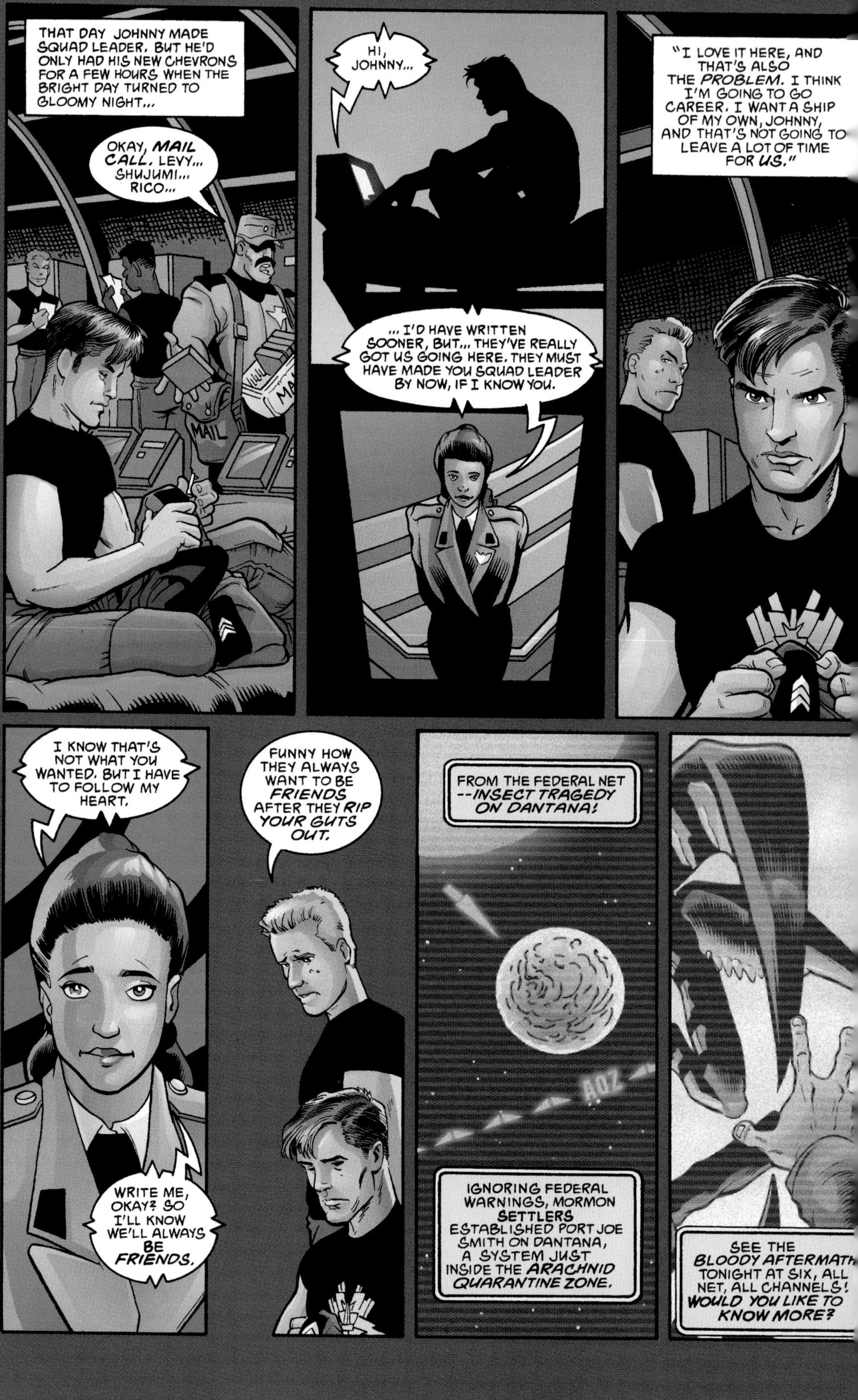
THAT DAY JOHNNY MADE SQUAD LEADER. BUT HE'D ONLY HAD HIS NEW CHEVRONS FOR A FEW HOURS WHEN THE BRIGHT DAY TURNED TO GLOOMY NIGHT...
OKAY, MAIL CALL. LEVY... SHUJUMI... RICO...
MAIL
MAIL
HI, JOHNNY...
... I'D HAVE WRITTEN SOONER, BUT... THEY'VE REALLY GOT US GOING HERE. THEY MUST HAVE MADE YOU SQUAD LEADER BY NOW, IF I KNOW YOU.
"I LOVE IT HERE, AND THAT'S ALSO THE PROBLEM. I THINK I'M GOING TO GO CAREER. I WANT A SHIP OF MY OWN, JOHNNY, AND THAT'S NOT GOING TO LEAVE A LOT OF TIME FOR US."
I KNOW THAT'S NOT WHAT YOU WANTED. BUT I HAVE TO FOLLOW MY HEART.
WRITE ME, OKAY? SO I'LL KNOW WE'LL ALWAYS BE FRIENDS.
FUNNY HOW THEY ALWAYS WANT TO BE FRIENDS AFTER THEY RIP YOUR GUTS OUT.
FROM THE FEDERAL NET --INSECT TRAGEDY ON DANTANA!
AQZ
IGNORING FEDERAL WARNINGS, MORMON SETTLERS ESTABLISHED PORT JOE SMITH ON DANTANA, A SYSTEM JUST INSIDE THE ARACHNID QUARANTINE ZONE.
SEE THE BLOODY AFTERMATH TONIGHT AT SIX, ALL NET, ALL CHANNELS! WOULD YOU LIKE TO KNOW MORE?

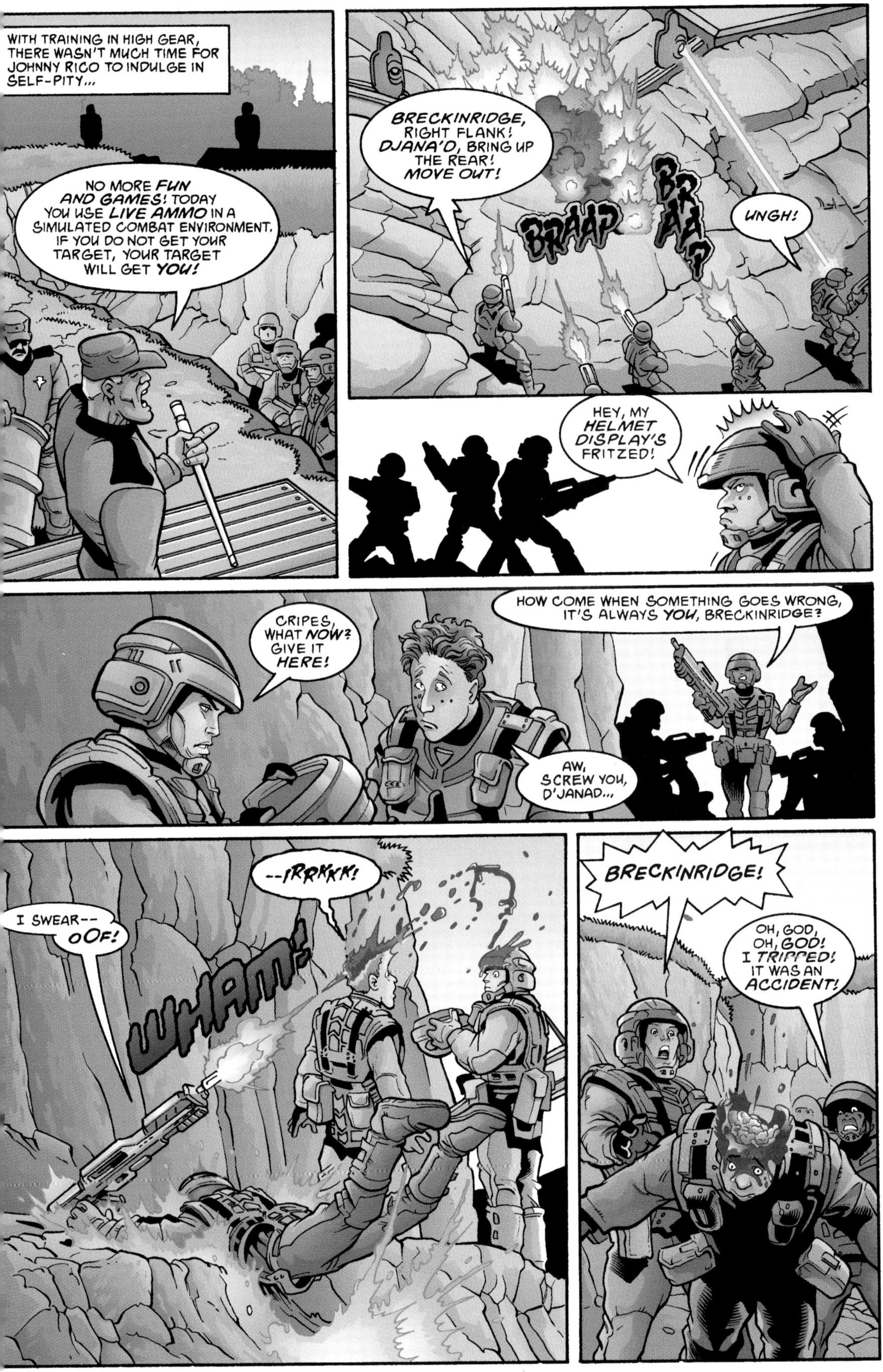
WITH TRAINING IN HIGH GEAR, THERE WASN'T MUCH TIME FOR JOHNNY RICO TO INDULGE IN SELF-PITY...
NO MORE FUN AND GAMES! TODAY YOU USE LIVE AMMO IN A SIMULATED COMBAT ENVIRONMENT. IF YOU DO NOT GET YOUR TARGET, YOUR TARGET WILL GET YOU!
BRECKINRIDGE, RIGHT FLANK! DJANA'D, BRING UP THE REAR! MOVE OUT!
BRAAP
BRAAP
UNGH!
HEY, MY HELMET DISPLAY'S FRITZED!
CRIPES, WHAT NOW? GIVE IT HERE!
HOW COME WHEN SOMETHING GOES WRONG, IT'S ALWAYS YOU, BRECKINRIDGE?
AW, SCREW YOU, D'JANAD...
I SWEAR-- OOF!
WHAM!
--IRRKKK!
BRECKINRIDGE!
OH, GOD, OH, GOD! I TRIPPED! IT WAS AN ACCIDENT!

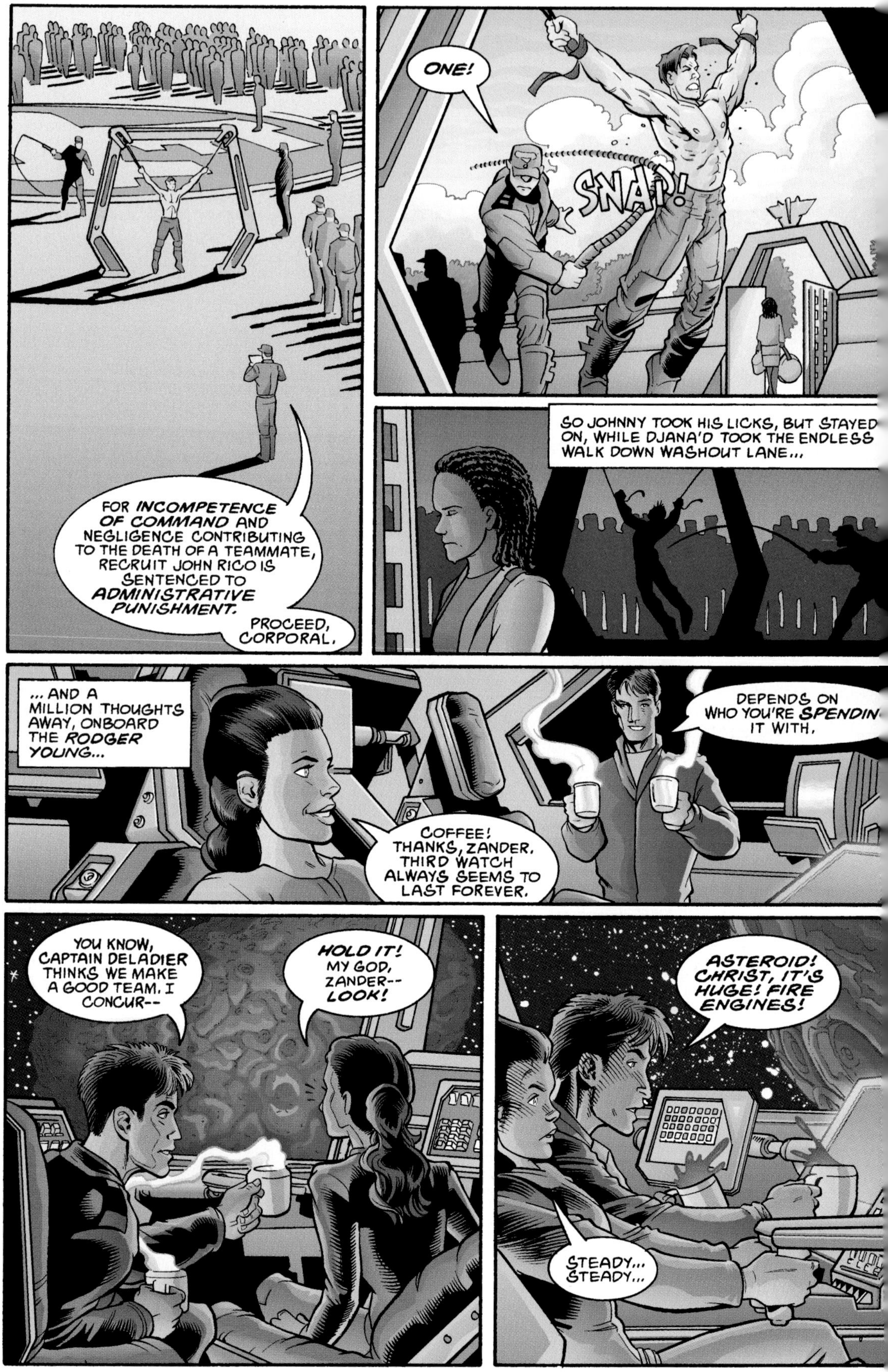
ONE!
SNAP!
FOR INCOMPETENCE OF COMMAND AND NEGLIGENCE CONTRIBUTING TO THE DEATH OF A TEAMMATE, RECRUIT JOHN RICO IS SENTENCED TO ADMINISTRATIVE PUNISHMENT.
PROCEED, CORPORAL.
SO JOHNNY TOOK HIS LICKS, BUT STAYED ON, WHILE DJANA'D TOOK THE ENDLESS WALK DOWN WASHOUT LANE...
...AND A MILLION THOUGHTS AWAY, ONBOARD THE RODGER YOUNG...
COFFEE! THANKS, ZANDER. THIRD WATCH ALWAYS SEEMS TO LAST FOREVER.
DEPENDS ON WHO YOU'RE SPENDIN IT WITH.
YOU KNOW, CAPTAIN DELADIER THINKS WE MAKE A GOOD TEAM. I CONCUR--
HOLD IT! MY GOD, ZANDER-- LOOK!
ASTEROID! CHRIST, IT'S HUGE! FIRE ENGINES!
STEADY... STEADY...

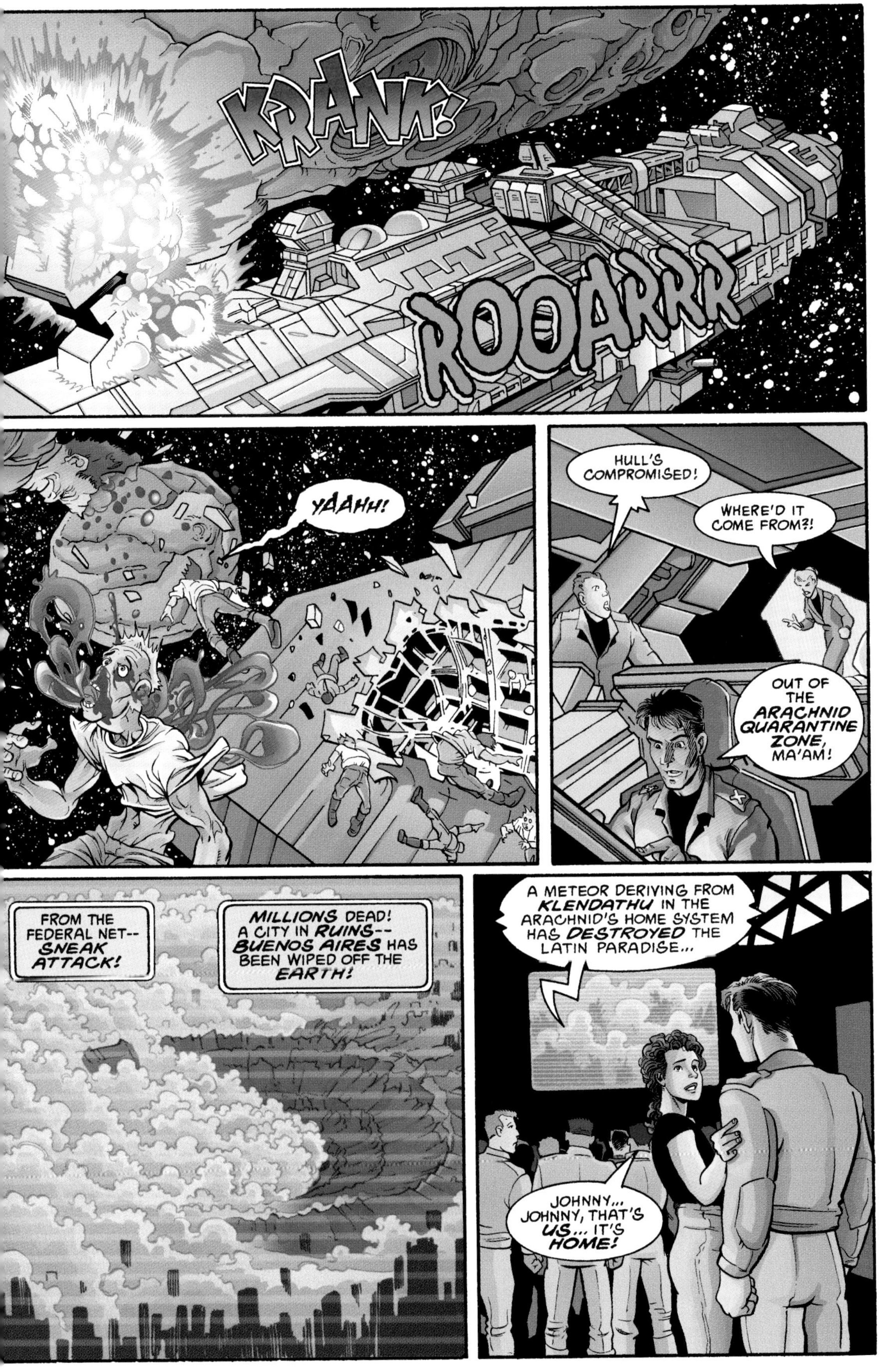
KRANK!
ROOARRR
YAAHH!
HULL'S COMPROMISED!
WHERE'D IT COME FROM?!
OUT OF THE ARACHNID QUARANTINE ZONE, MA'AM!
FROM THE FEDERAL NET-- SNEAK ATTACK!
MILLIONS DEAD! A CITY IN RUINS-- BUENOS AIRES HAS BEEN WIPED OFF THE EARTH!
A METEOR DERIVING FROM KLENDATHU IN THE ARACHNID'S HOME SYSTEM HAS DESTROYED THE LATIN PARADISE...
JOHNNY... JOHNNY, THAT'S US... IT'S HOME!

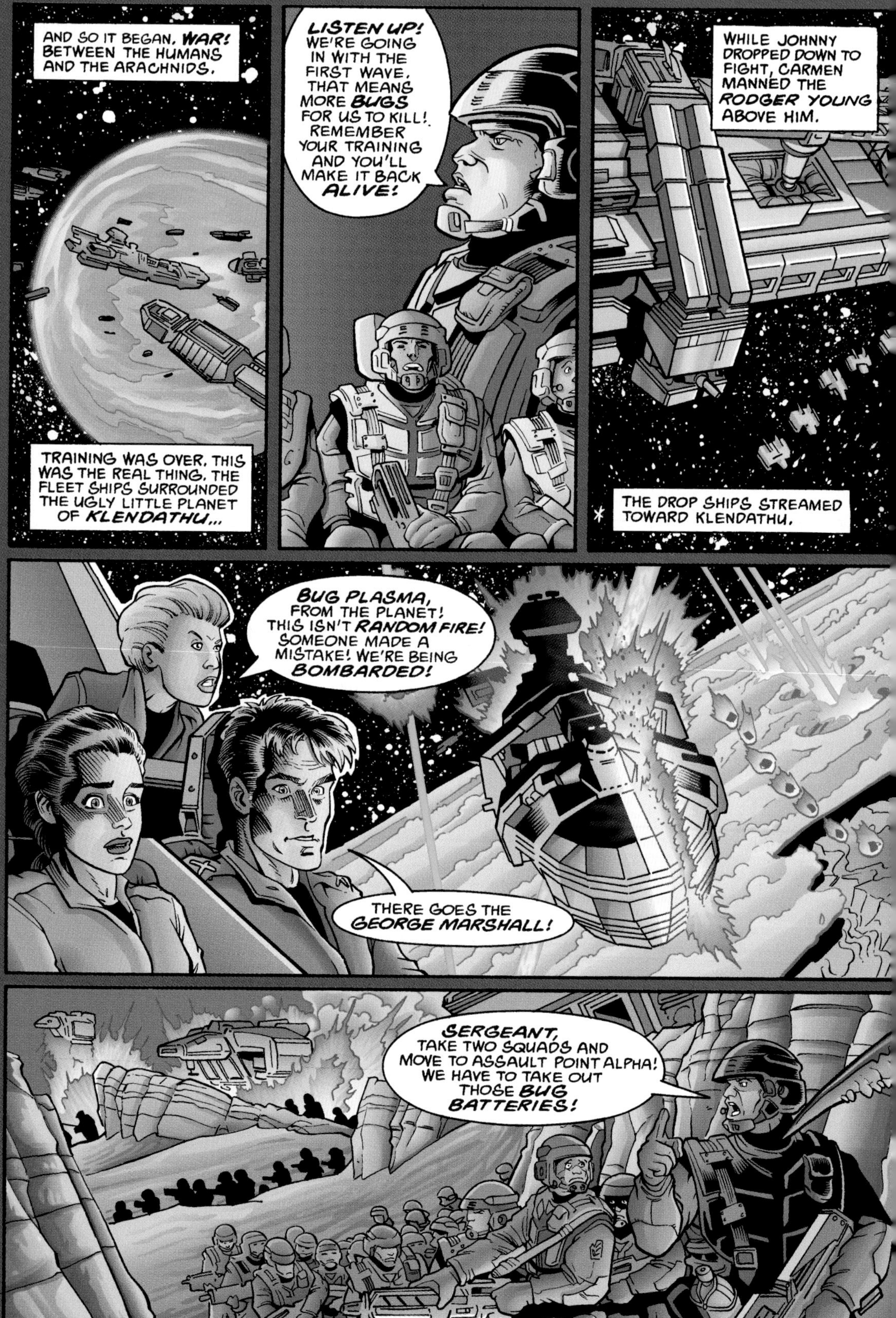
AND SO IT BEGAN. WAR! BETWEEN THE HUMANS AND THE ARACHNIDS.
TRAINING WAS OVER. THIS WAS THE REAL THING. THE FLEET SHIPS SURROUNDED THE UGLY LITTLE PLANET OF KLENDATHU...
LISTEN UP! WE'RE GOING IN WITH THE FIRST WAVE. THAT MEANS MORE BUGS FOR US TO KILL! REMEMBER YOUR TRAINING AND YOU'LL MAKE IT BACK ALIVE!
WHILE JOHNNY DROPPED DOWN TO FIGHT, CARMEN MANNED THE RODGER YOUNG ABOVE HIM.
THE DROP SHIPS STREAMED TOWARD KLENDATHU.
BUG PLASMA, FROM THE PLANET! THIS ISN'T RANDOM FIRE! SOMEONE MADE A MISTAKE! WE'RE BEING BOMBARDED!
THERE GOES THE GEORGE MARSHALL!
SERGEANT, TAKE TWO SQUADS AND MOVE TO ASSAULT POINT ALPHA! WE HAVE TO TAKE OUT THOSE BUG BATTERIES!

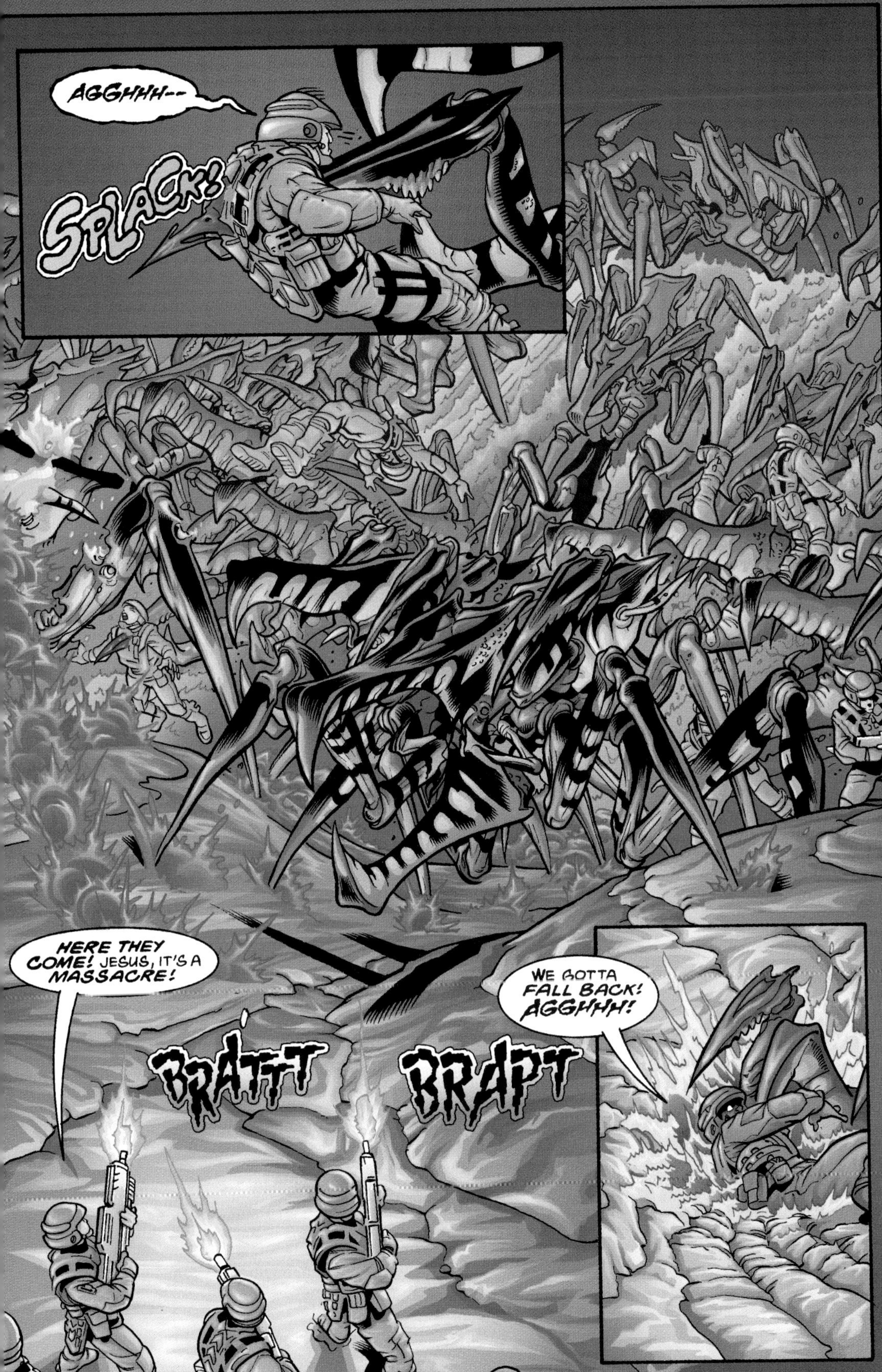
AGGHHH--
SPLACK!
HERE THEY COME! JESUS, IT'S A MASSACRE!
BRATTT
BRAPT
WE GOTTA FALL BACK! AGGHHH!

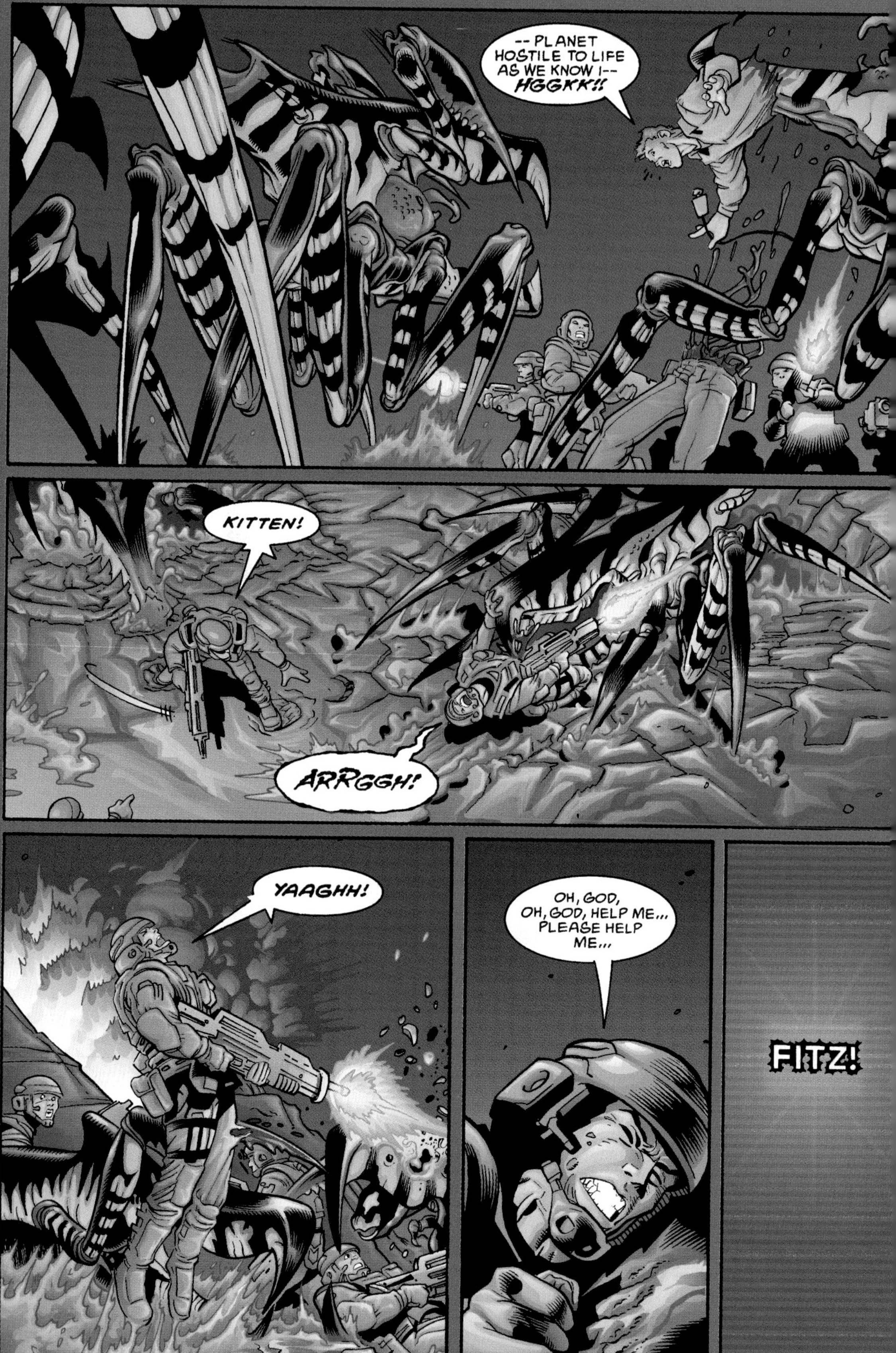
-- PLANET HOSTILE TO LIFE AS WE KNOW I-- HGGKK!!
KITTEN!
ARRGGH!
YAAGHH!
OH, GOD, OH, GOD, HELP ME... PLEASE HELP ME...
FITZ!

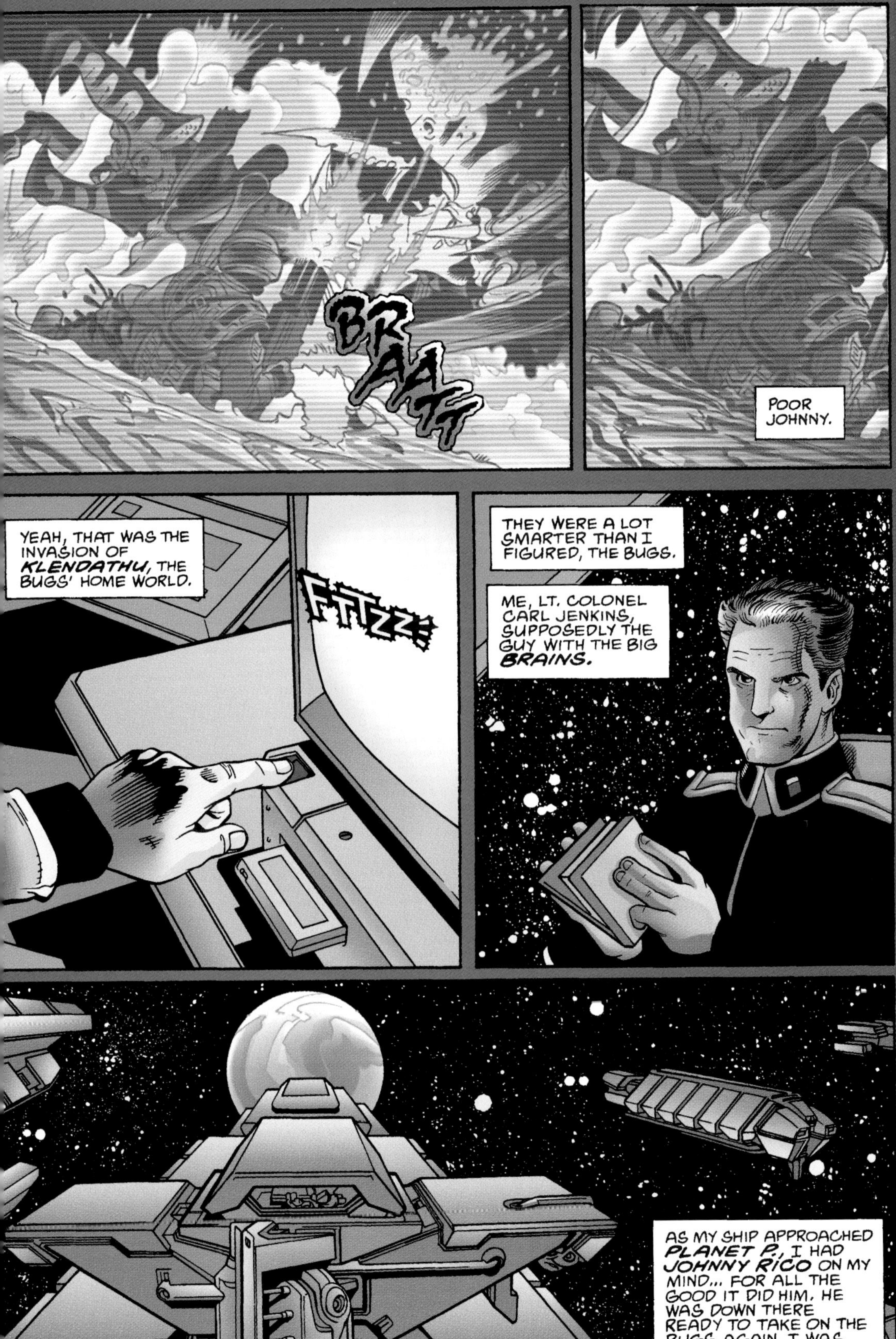
BRAAAT
POOR JOHNNY.
YEAH, THAT WAS THE INVASION OF KLENDATHU, THE BUGS' HOME WORLD.
FTTZZ
THEY WERE A LOT SMARTER THAN I FIGURED, THE BUGS.
ME, LT. COLONEL CARL JENKINS, SUPPOSEDLY THE GUY WITH THE BIG BRAINS.
AS MY SHIP APPROACHED PLANET P., I HAD JOHNNY RICO ON MY MIND... FOR ALL THE GOOD IT DID HIM. HE WAS DOWN THERE READY TO TAKE ON THE BUGS AGAIN, I WAS UP HERE.

JOHNNY'S OLD FLAME *CARMEN* AND HIS RIVAL *ZANDER* HAD BEEN ABOARD THE RODGER YOUNG DURING THE INVASION OF KLENDATHU.

THE STARSHIP DOCKED AT BATTLE STATION *TICONDEROGA* FOR REPAIRS.

YOU KNOW, FLEET ENCOURAGES MARRIAGE AMONG FLIGHT OFFICERS. I WAS THINKING...

UH, CARMEN...?

GOOD GOD, ZANDER, LOOK AT THE CASUALTIES...

BUGS DON'T TAKE PRISONERS.

OH, *NO*...

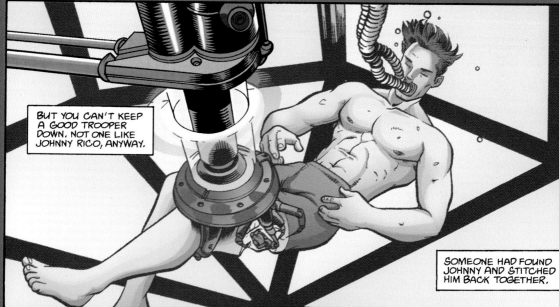

BUT YOU CAN'T KEEP A GOOD TROOPER DOWN. NOT ONE LIKE JOHNNY RICO, ANYWAY.

SOMEONE HAD FOUND JOHNNY AND STITCHED HIM BACK TOGETHER.

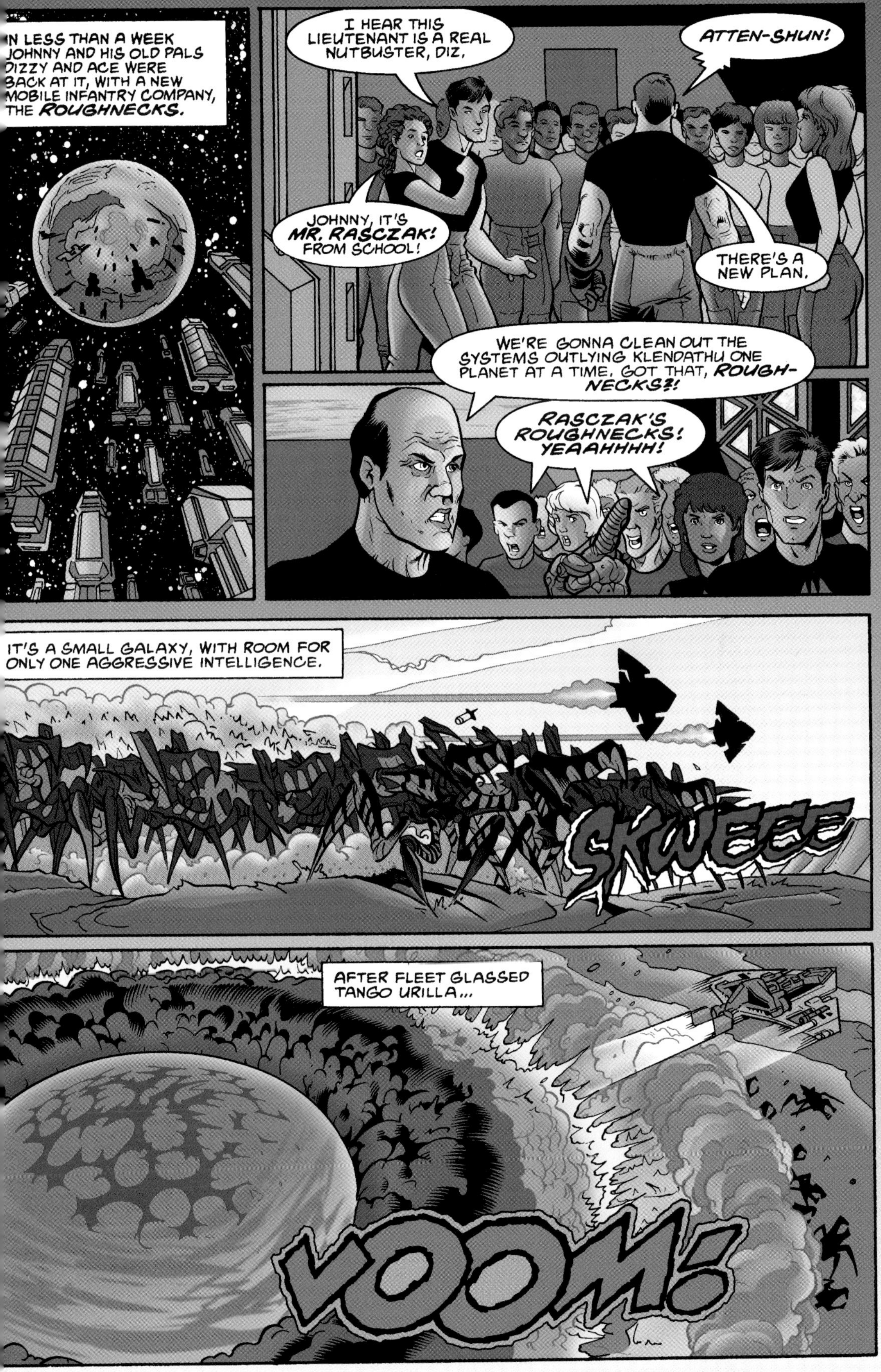

IN LESS THAN A WEEK JOHNNY AND HIS OLD PALS DIZZY AND ACE WERE BACK AT IT, WITH A NEW MOBILE INFANTRY COMPANY, THE ROUGHNECKS.
I HEAR THIS LIEUTENANT IS A REAL NUTBUSTER, DIZ.
ATTEN-SHUN!
JOHNNY, IT'S MR. RASCZAK! FROM SCHOOL!
THERE'S A NEW PLAN.
WE'RE GONNA CLEAN OUT THE SYSTEMS OUTLYING KLENDATHU ONE PLANET AT A TIME. GOT THAT, ROUGHNECKS?!
RASCZAK'S ROUGHNECKS! YEAAHHHH!
IT'S A SMALL GALAXY, WITH ROOM FOR ONLY ONE AGGRESSIVE INTELLIGENCE.
SKWEEE
AFTER FLEET GLASSED TANGO URILLA...
VOOM!

... THE ROUGHNECKS MOPPED UP.

SPREAD OUT. WHEN YOU LOCATE A BUG HOLE, NUKE IT!

THERE'S THE HOLE! C'MON, SUGAR LET'S BLOW IT!

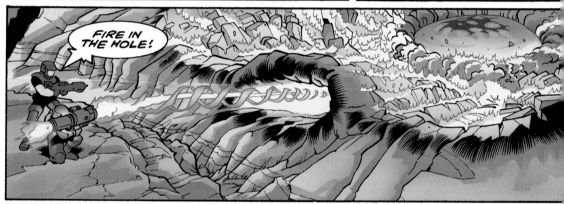

FIRE IN THE HOLE!

LOOKS LIKE WE WOKE 'EM UP!

HEADS UP! TANKER BUG!

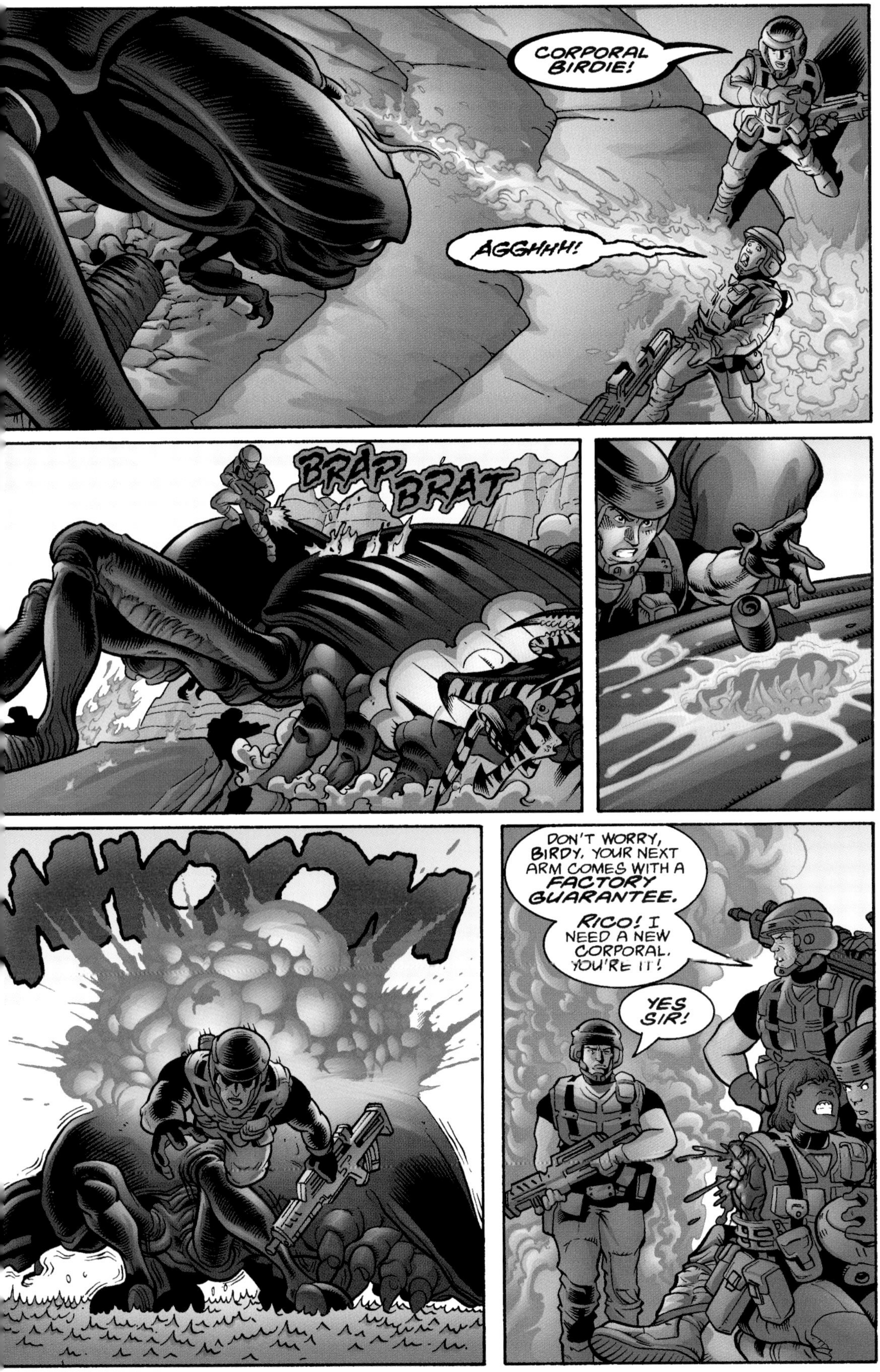
CORPORAL BIRDIE!
AGGHHH!
BRAP BRAT
WHOOM
DON'T WORRY, BIRDY. YOUR NEXT ARM COMES WITH A FACTORY GUARANTEE.
RICO! I NEED A NEW CORPORAL. YOU'RE IT!
YES SIR!

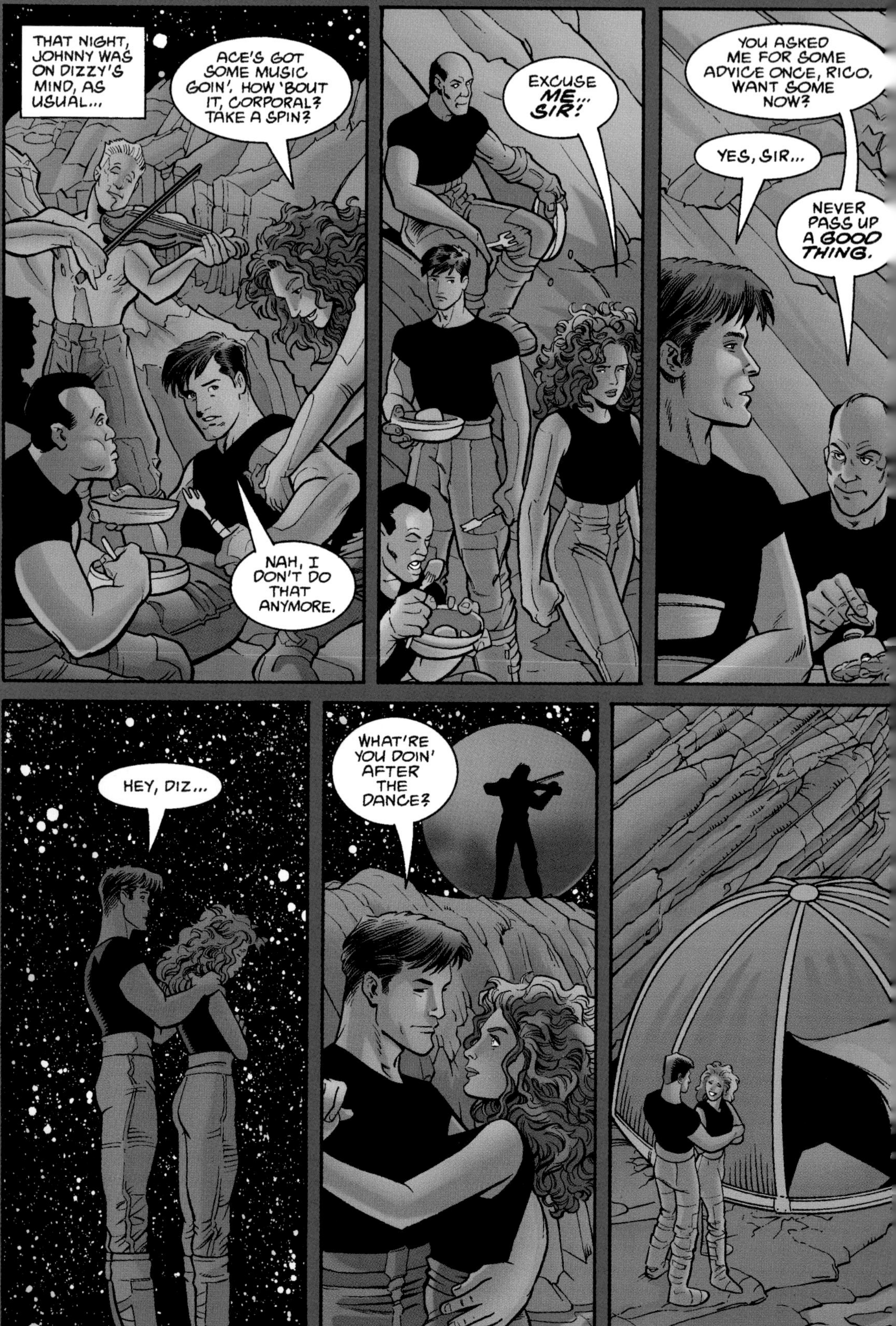
THAT NIGHT, JOHNNY WAS ON DIZZY'S MIND, AS USUAL...
ACE'S GOT SOME MUSIC GOIN'. HOW 'BOUT IT, CORPORAL? TAKE A SPIN?
NAH, I DON'T DO THAT ANYMORE.
EXCUSE ME... SIR!
YOU ASKED ME FOR SOME ADVICE ONCE, RICO. WANT SOME NOW?
YES, SIR...
NEVER PASS UP A GOOD THING.
HEY, DIZ...
WHAT'RE YOU DOIN' AFTER THE DANCE?

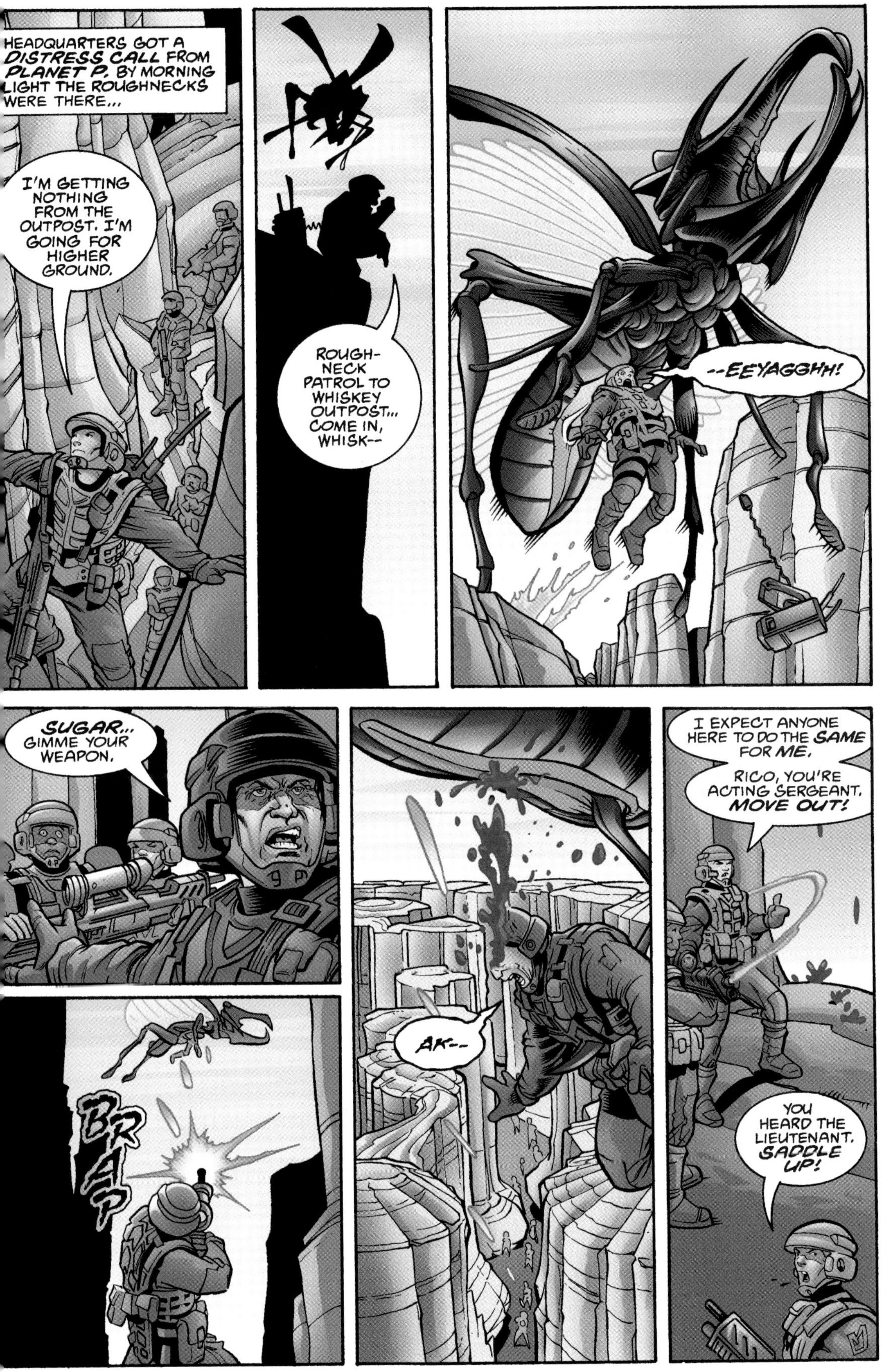
HEADQUARTERS GOT A DISTRESS CALL FROM PLANET P. BY MORNING LIGHT THE ROUGHNECKS WERE THERE...
I'M GETTING NOTHING FROM THE OUTPOST. I'M GOING FOR HIGHER GROUND.
ROUGH-NECK PATROL TO WHISKEY OUTPOST... COME IN, WHISK--
--EEYAGGHH!
SUGAR... GIMME YOUR WEAPON.
BRAP
AK--
I EXPECT ANYONE HERE TO DO THE SAME FOR ME.
RICO, YOU'RE ACTING SERGEANT. MOVE OUT!
YOU HEARD THE LIEUTENANT. SADDLE UP!

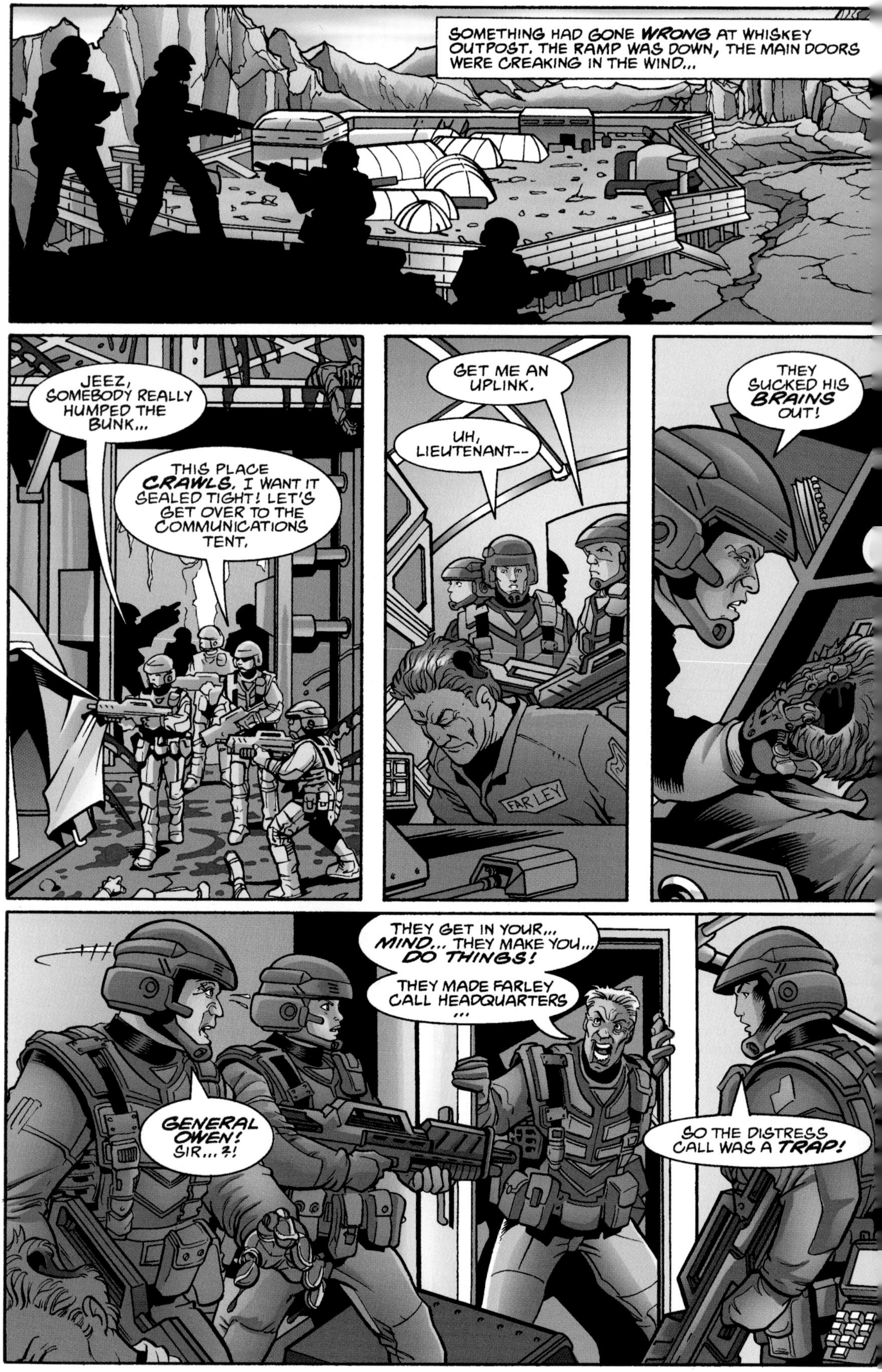

SOMETHING HAD GONE WRONG AT WHISKEY OUTPOST. THE RAMP WAS DOWN, THE MAIN DOORS WERE CREAKING IN THE WIND...
JEEZ, SOMEBODY REALLY HUMPED THE BUNK...
THIS PLACE CRAWLS. I WANT IT SEALED TIGHT! LET'S GET OVER TO THE COMMUNICATIONS TENT.
GET ME AN UPLINK.
UH, LIEUTENANT--
FARLEY
THEY SUCKED HIS BRAINS OUT!
THEY GET IN YOUR... MIND... THEY MAKE YOU... DO THINGS!
THEY MADE FARLEY CALL HEADQUARTERS...
GENERAL OWEN! SIR...?!
SO THE DISTRESS CALL WAS A TRAP!

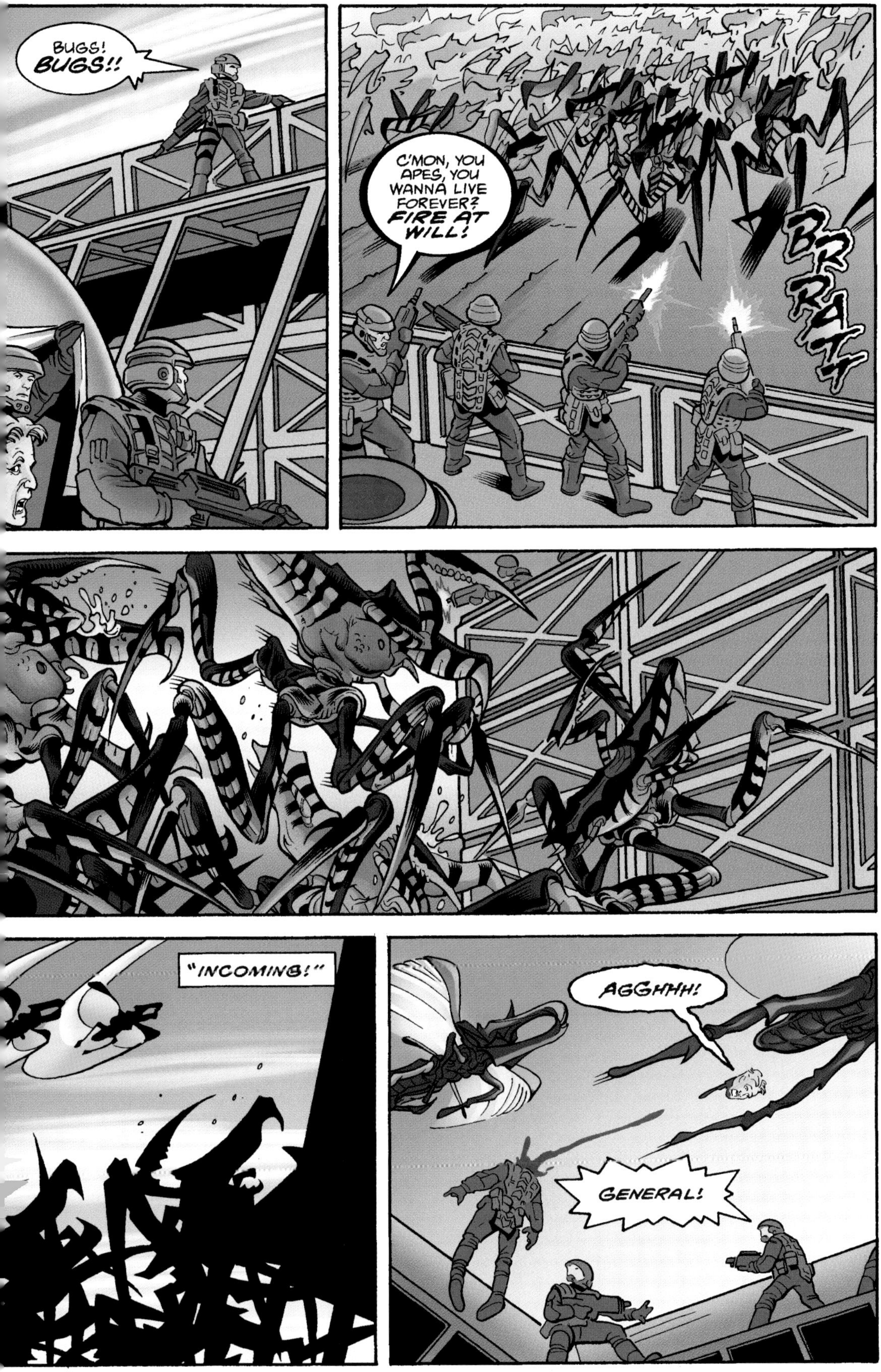
BUGS! BUGS!!
C'MON, YOU APES, YOU WANNA LIVE FOREVER? FIRE AT WILL!
BRRAAK
"INCOMING!"
AGGHHH!
GENERAL!

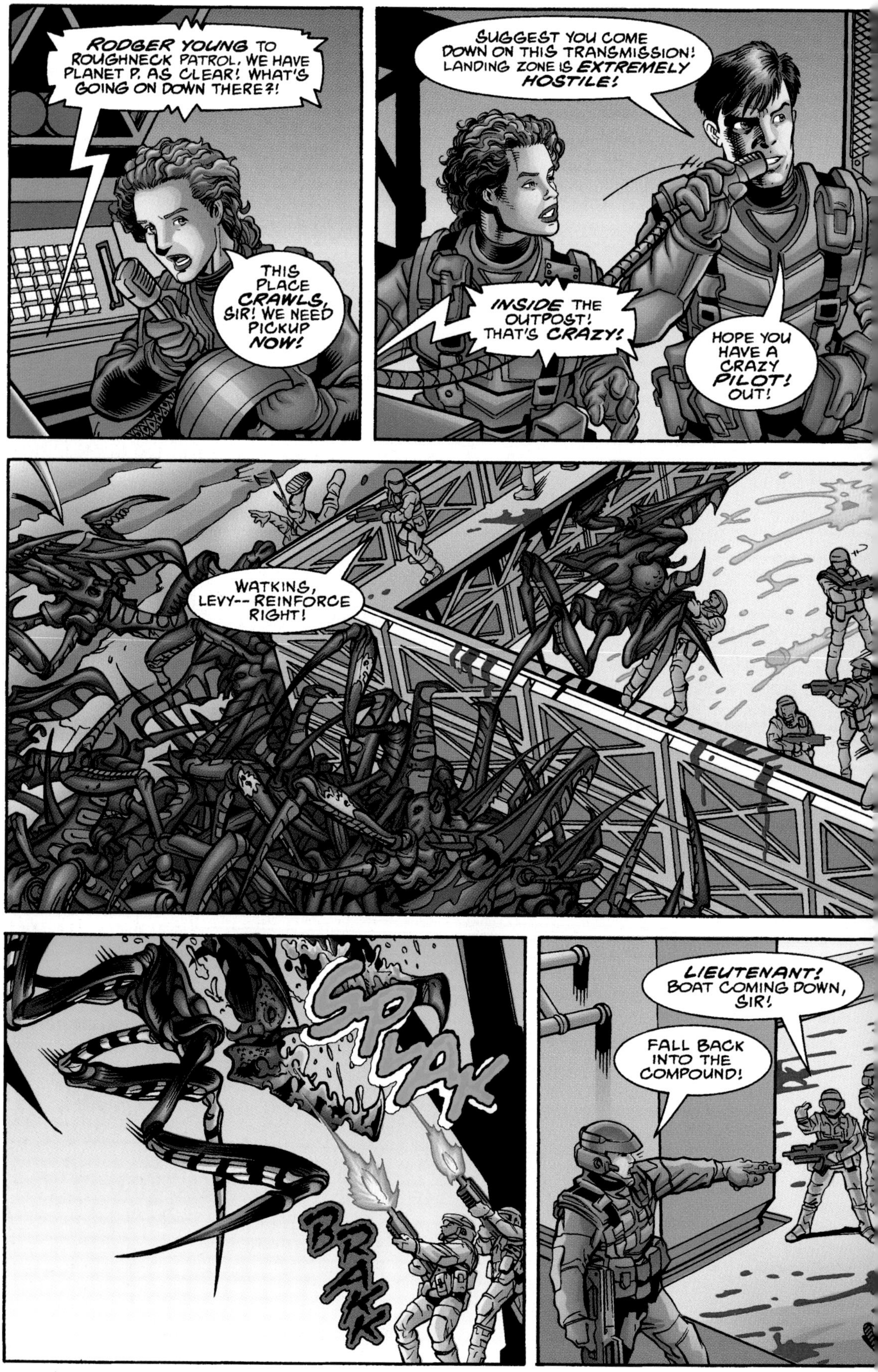
RODGER YOUNG TO ROUGHNECK PATROL. WE HAVE PLANET P. AS CLEAR! WHAT'S GOING ON DOWN THERE?!
THIS PLACE CRAWLS, SIR! WE NEED PICKUP NOW!
SUGGEST YOU COME DOWN ON THIS TRANSMISSION! LANDING ZONE IS EXTREMELY HOSTILE!
INSIDE THE OUTPOST! THAT'S CRAZY!
HOPE YOU HAVE A CRAZY PILOT! OUT!
WATKINS, LEVY-- REINFORCE RIGHT!
SPLAK
BRAKK
LIEUTENANT! BOAT COMING DOWN, SIR!
FALL BACK INTO THE COMPOUND!

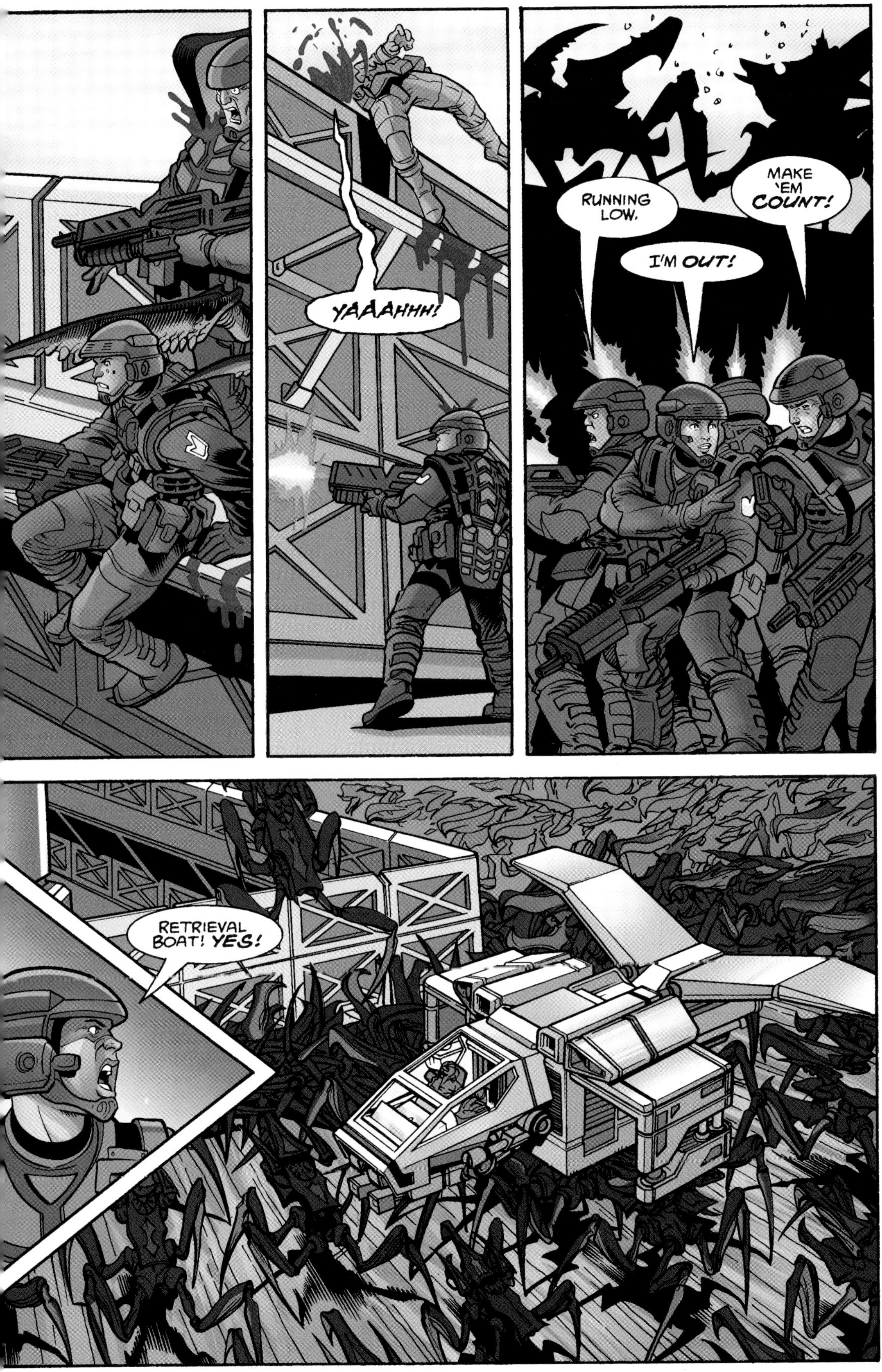
YAAAHHH!
RUNNING LOW.
I'M OUT!
MAKE 'EM COUNT!
RETRIEVAL BOAT! YES!

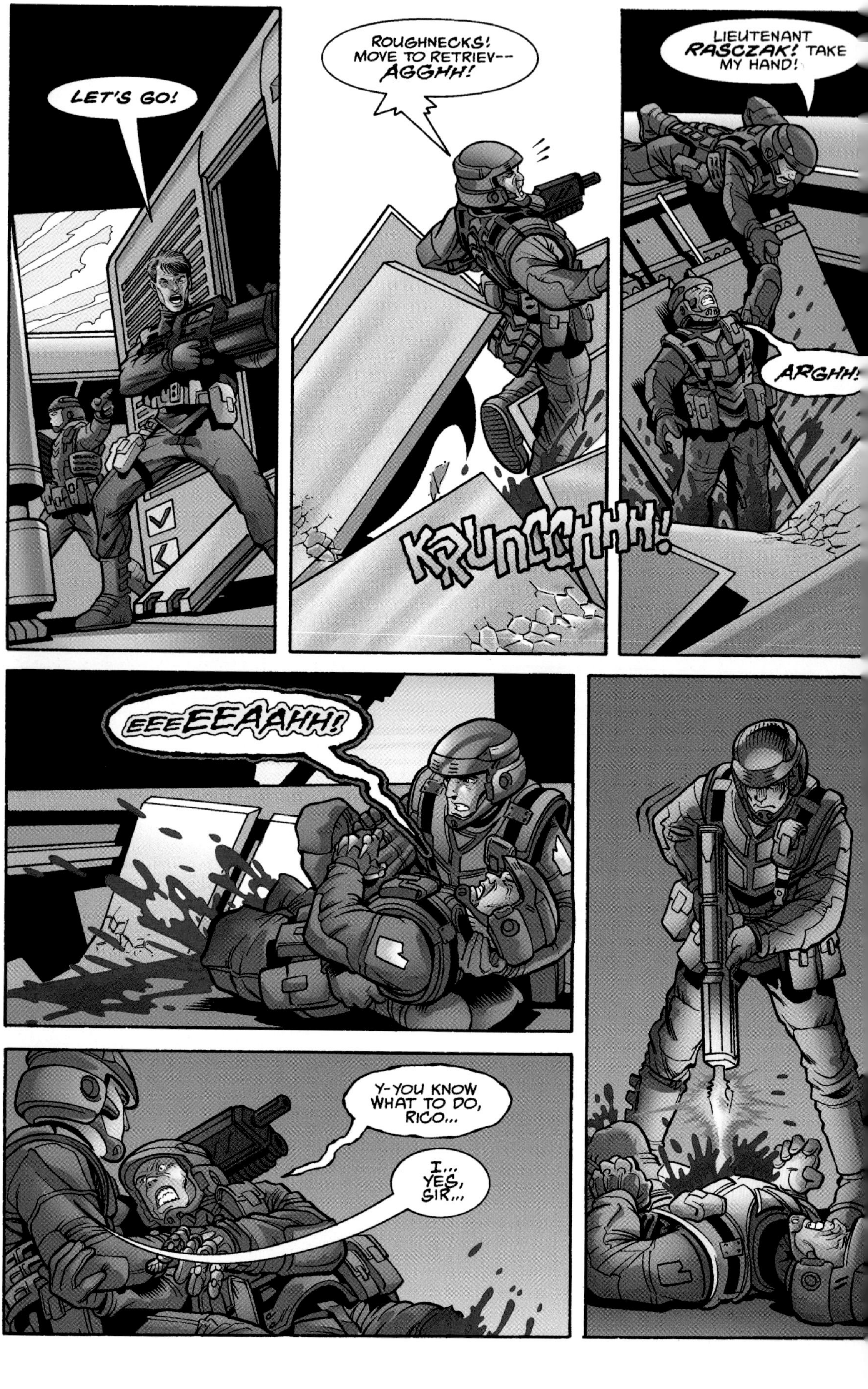
LET'S GO!
ROUGHNECKS! MOVE TO RETRIEV-- AGGHH!
KRUNCCHHH!
LIEUTENANT RASCZAK! TAKE MY HAND!
ARGHH!
EEEEEAAHH!
Y-YOU KNOW WHAT TO DO, RICO...
I... YES, SIR...

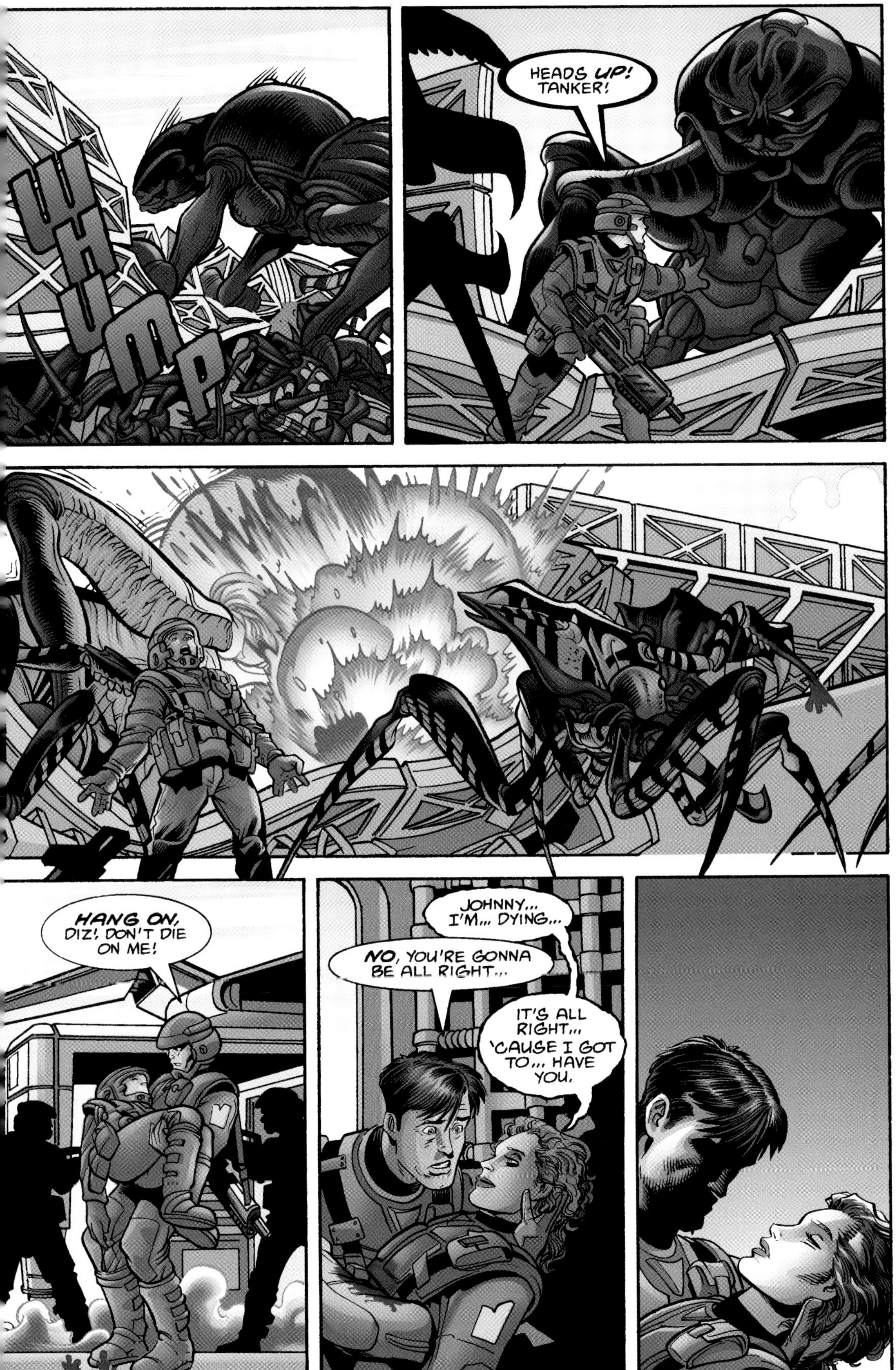
WHUMP
HEADS UP! TANKER!
HANG ON, DIZ! DON'T DIE ON ME!
JOHNNY... I'M... DYING...
NO, YOU'RE GONNA BE ALL RIGHT...
IT'S ALL RIGHT... 'CAUSE I GOT TO... HAVE YOU.

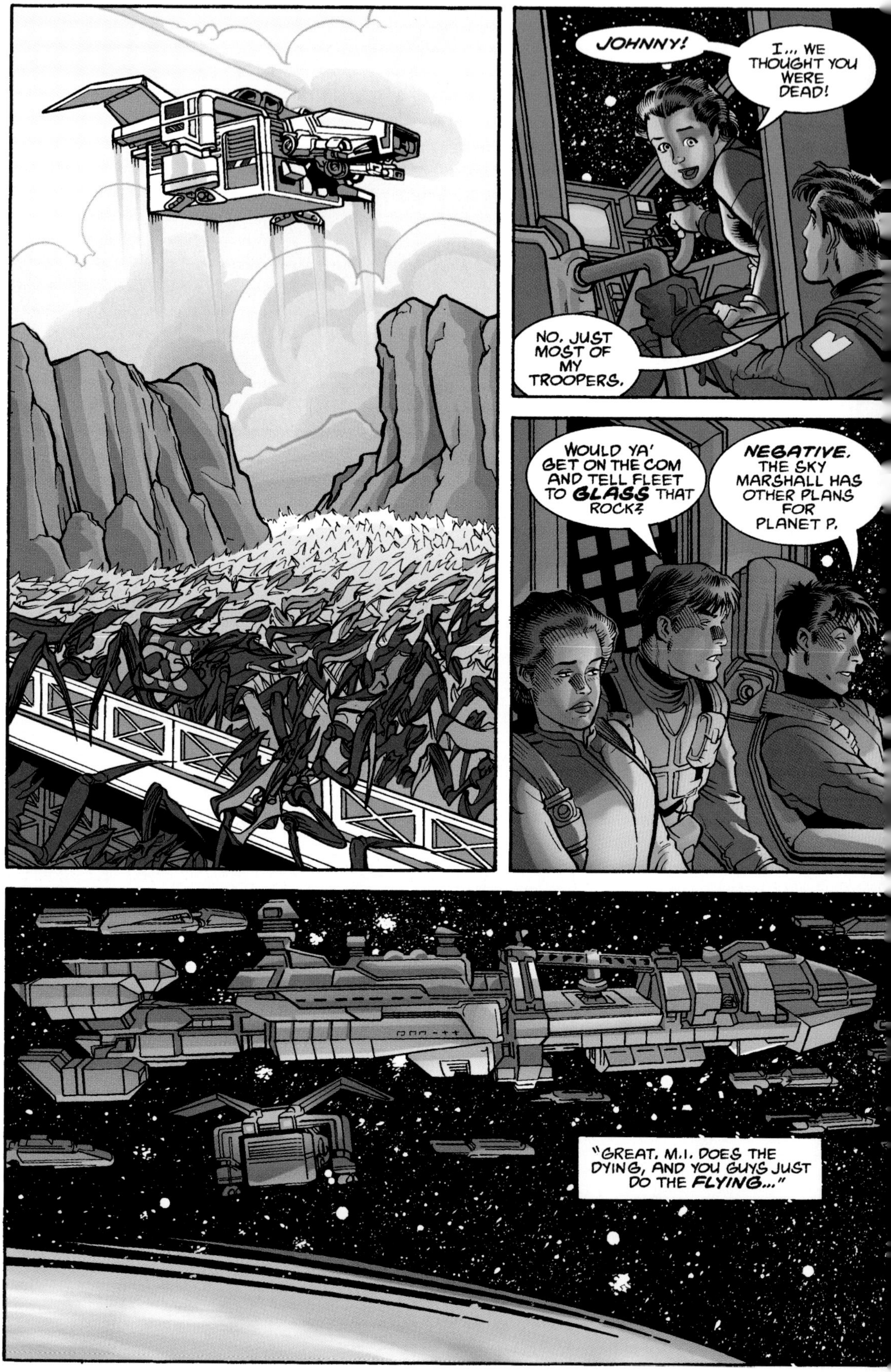
JOHNNY!
I... WE THOUGHT YOU WERE DEAD!
NO. JUST MOST OF MY TROOPERS.
WOULD YA' GET ON THE COM AND TELL FLEET TO GLASS THAT ROCK?
NEGATIVE. THE SKY MARSHALL HAS OTHER PLANS FOR PLANET P.
"GREAT. M.I. DOES THE DYING, AND YOU GUYS JUST DO THE FLYING..."

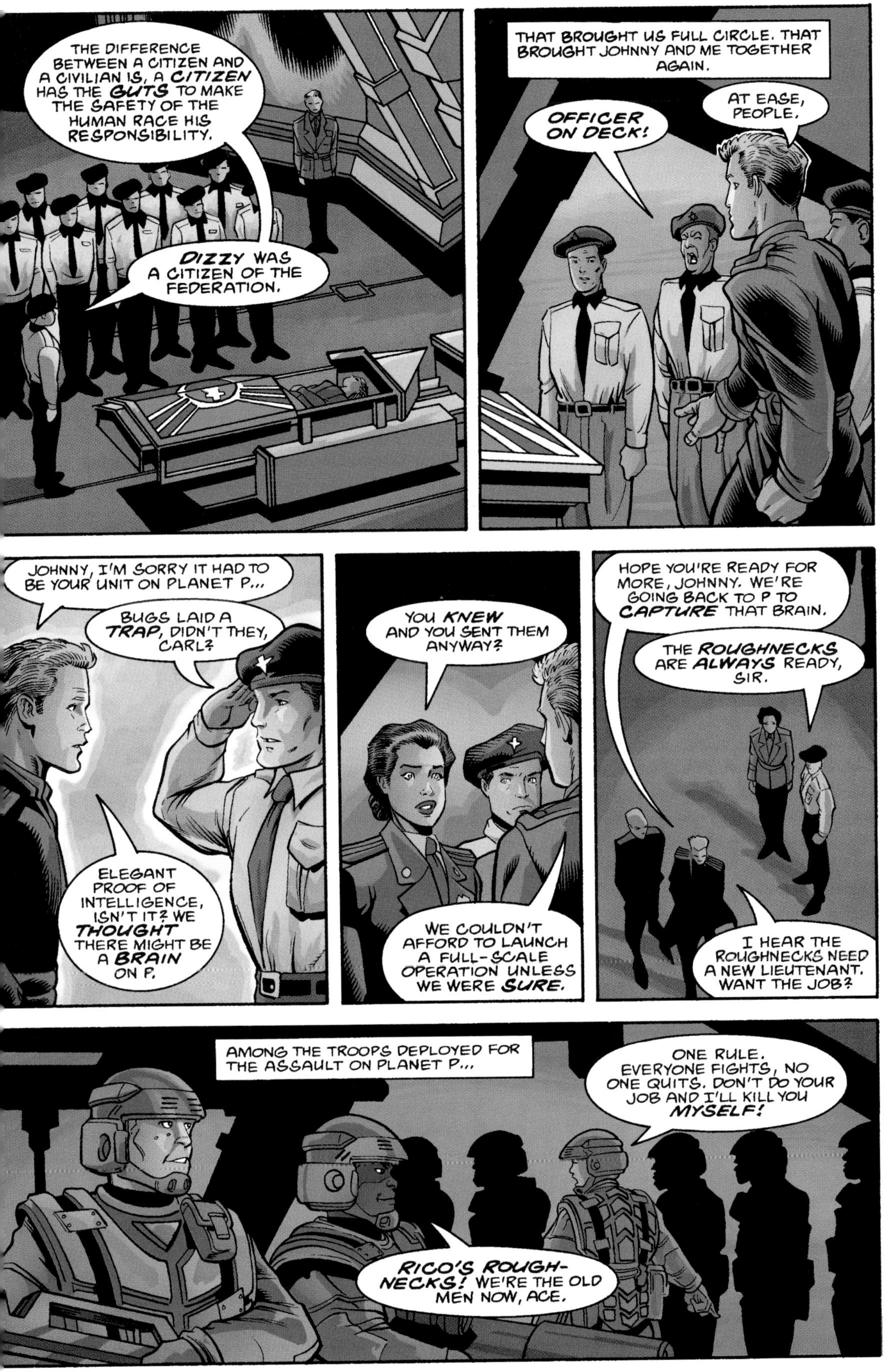
THE DIFFERENCE BETWEEN A CITIZEN AND A CIVILIAN IS, A CITIZEN HAS THE GUTS TO MAKE THE SAFETY OF THE HUMAN RACE HIS RESPONSIBILITY.
DIZZY WAS A CITIZEN OF THE FEDERATION.
THAT BROUGHT US FULL CIRCLE. THAT BROUGHT JOHNNY AND ME TOGETHER AGAIN.
OFFICER ON DECK!
AT EASE, PEOPLE.
JOHNNY, I'M SORRY IT HAD TO BE YOUR UNIT ON PLANET P...
BUGS LAID A TRAP, DIDN'T THEY, CARL?
ELEGANT PROOF OF INTELLIGENCE, ISN'T IT? WE THOUGHT THERE MIGHT BE A BRAIN ON P.
YOU KNEW AND YOU SENT THEM ANYWAY?
WE COULDN'T AFFORD TO LAUNCH A FULL-SCALE OPERATION UNLESS WE WERE SURE.
HOPE YOU'RE READY FOR MORE, JOHNNY. WE'RE GOING BACK TO P TO CAPTURE THAT BRAIN.
THE ROUGHNECKS ARE ALWAYS READY, SIR.
I HEAR THE ROUGHNECKS NEED A NEW LIEUTENANT. WANT THE JOB?
AMONG THE TROOPS DEPLOYED FOR THE ASSAULT ON PLANET P...
ONE RULE. EVERYONE FIGHTS, NO ONE QUITS. DON'T DO YOUR JOB AND I'LL KILL YOU MYSELF!
RICO'S ROUGH-NECKS! WE'RE THE OLD MEN NOW, ACE.

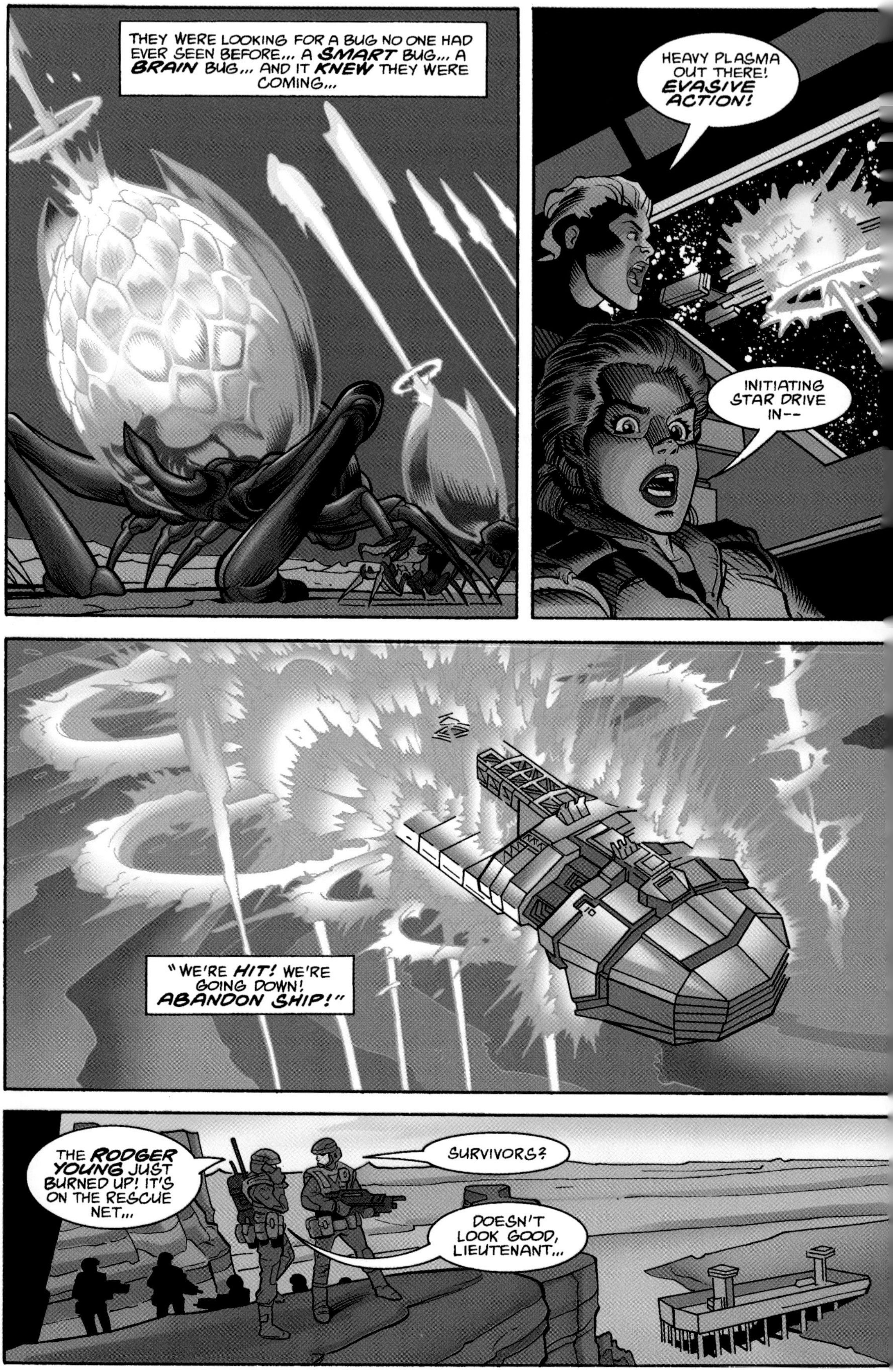
THEY WERE LOOKING FOR A BUG NO ONE HAD EVER SEEN BEFORE... A SMART BUG... A BRAIN BUG... AND IT KNEW THEY WERE COMING...
HEAVY PLASMA OUT THERE! EVASIVE ACTION!
INITIATING STAR DRIVE IN--
"WE'RE HIT! WE'RE GOING DOWN! ABANDON SHIP!"
THE RODGER YOUNG JUST BURNED UP! IT'S ON THE RESCUE NET...
SURVIVORS?
DOESN'T LOOK GOOD, LIEUTENANT...

AT LEAST TWO CREW MEMBERS MANAGED TO GET TO A LIFE POD-- CARMEN AND ZANDER.

CONTROL'S SLUGGISH! WE'RE HEADED IN!

"LIFE POD ROMEO YANKEE SIX THREE. IS ANYONE RECEIVING? ROMEO YANKEE SIX THREE *GOING IN!*"

WHAM!

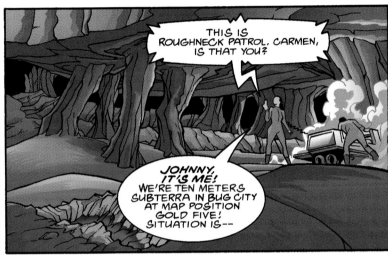

THIS IS ROUGHNECK PATROL, CARMEN, IS THAT YOU?

JOHNNY, IT'S ME! WE'RE TEN METERS SUBTERRA IN BUG CITY AT MAP POSITION GOLD FIVE! SITUATION IS--

--EMINENTLY HOSTILE!

B R A P

THREE CLICKS SOUTH BY SOUTHWEST... *THERE!*

I NEED VOLUNTEERS TO HELP PULL THEM OUT!

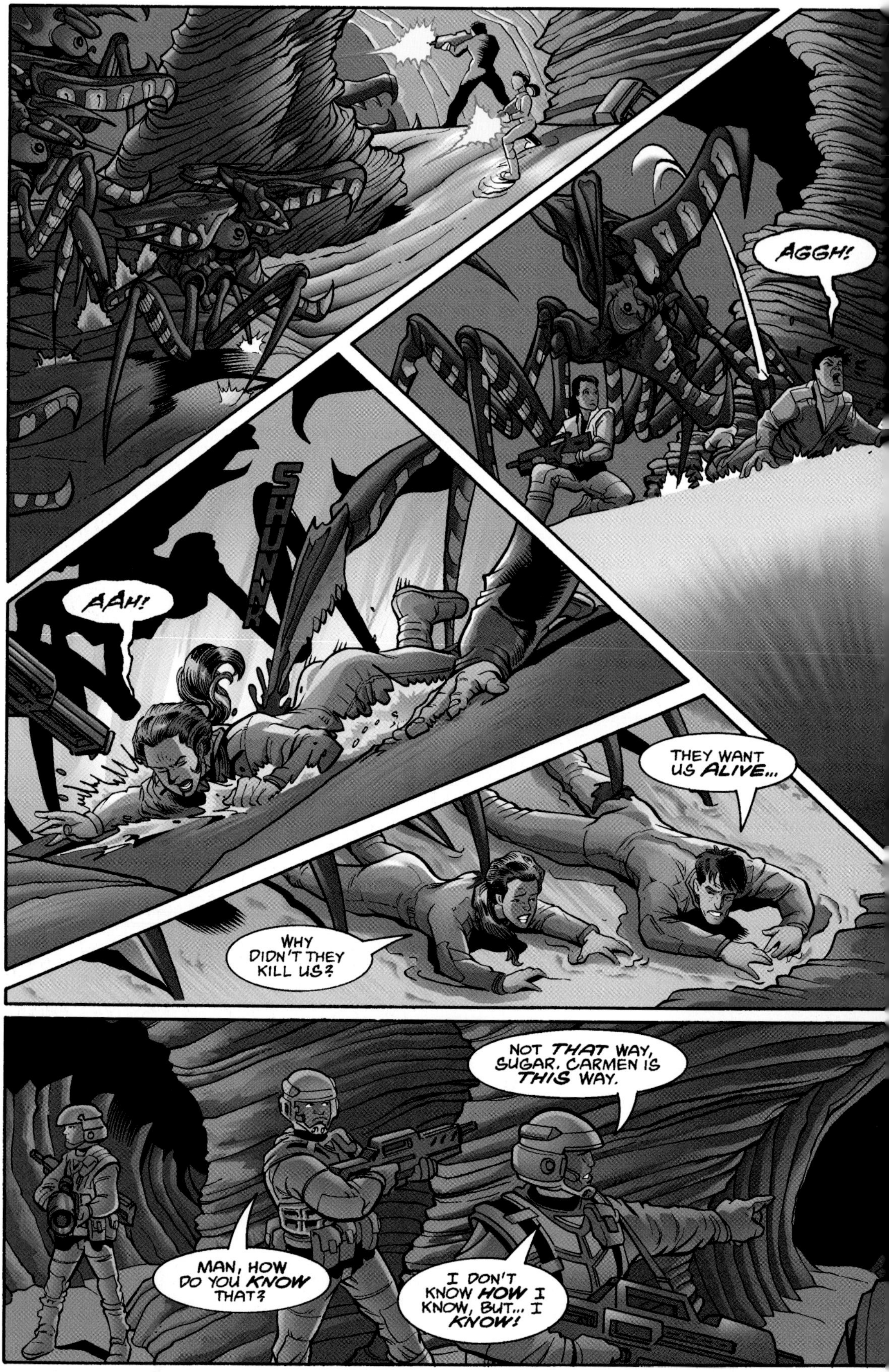
AGGH!
SHUNNK
AAH!
THEY WANT US ALIVE...
WHY DIDN'T THEY KILL US?
NOT THAT WAY, SUGAR. CARMEN IS THIS WAY.
MAN, HOW DO YOU KNOW THAT?
I DON'T KNOW HOW I KNOW, BUT... I KNOW!

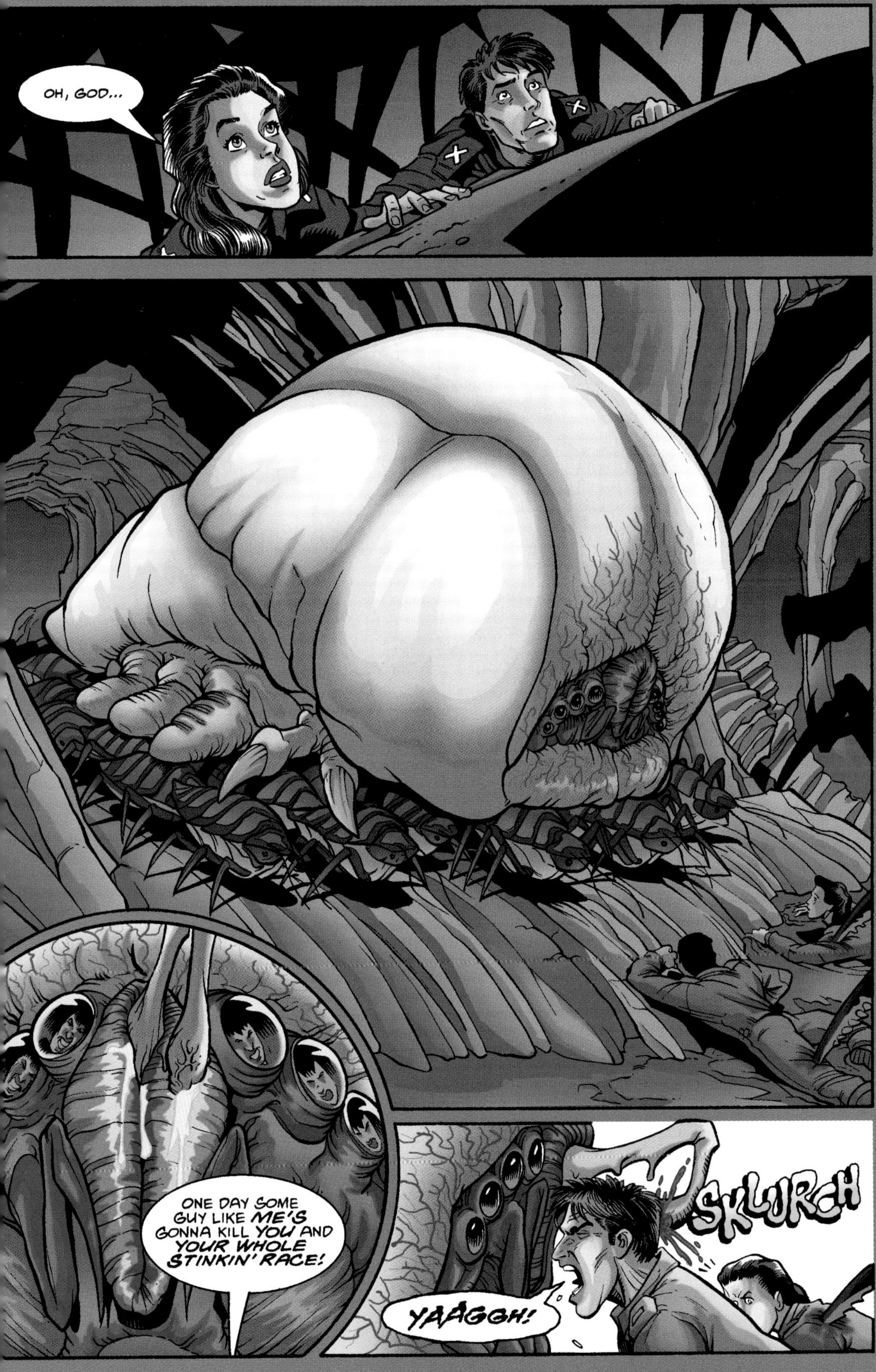
OH, GOD...
ONE DAY SOME GUY LIKE ME'S GONNA KILL YOU AND YOUR WHOLE STINKIN' RACE!
SKLURCH
YAAGGH!

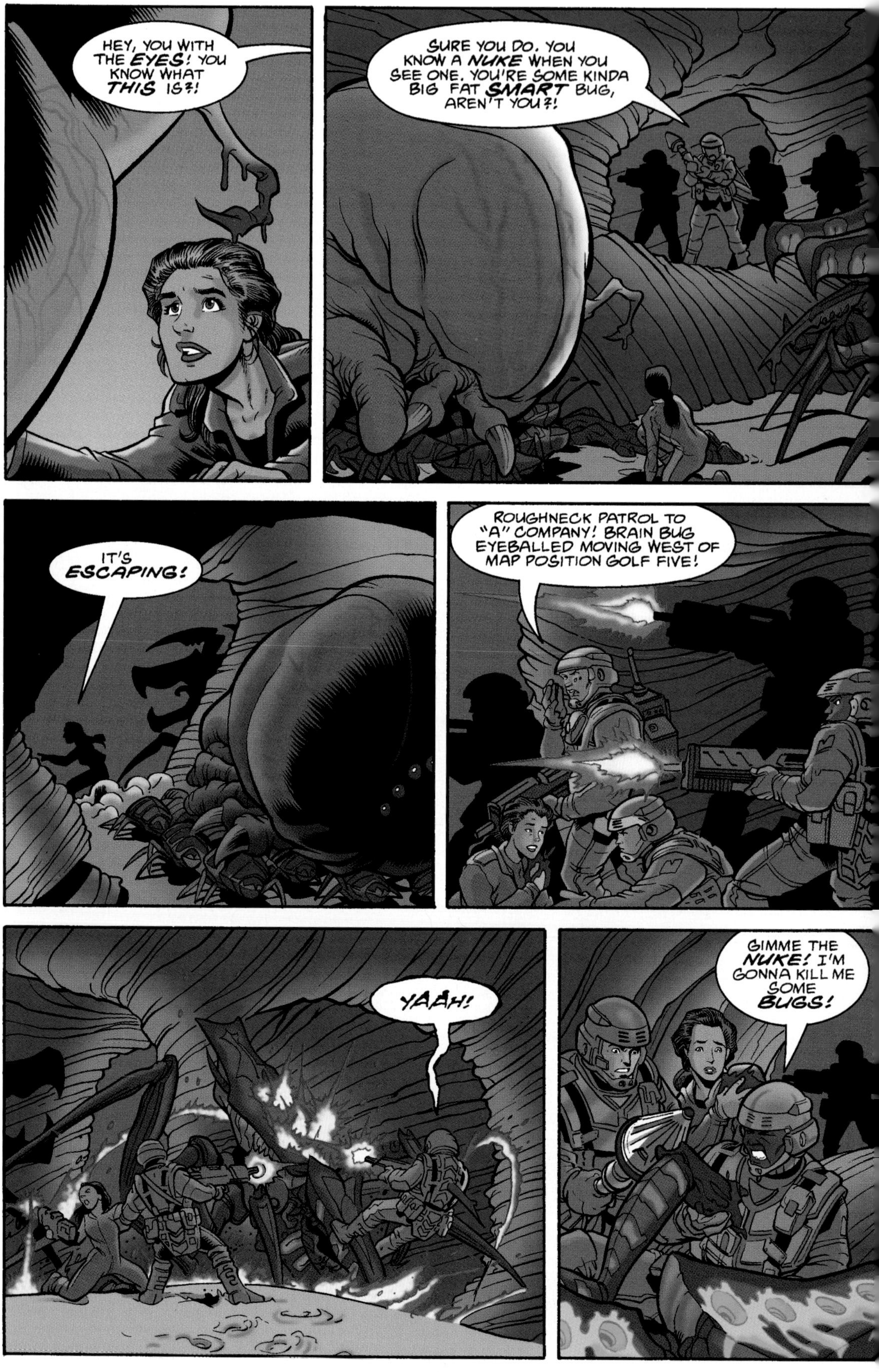
HEY, YOU WITH THE EYES! YOU KNOW WHAT THIS IS?!
SURE YOU DO. YOU KNOW A NUKE WHEN YOU SEE ONE. YOU'RE SOME KINDA BIG FAT SMART BUG, AREN'T YOU?!
IT'S ESCAPING!
ROUGHNECK PATROL TO "A" COMPANY! BRAIN BUG EYEBALLED MOVING WEST OF MAP POSITION GOLF FIVE!
YAAH!
GIMME THE NUKE! I'M GONNA KILL ME SOME BUGS!

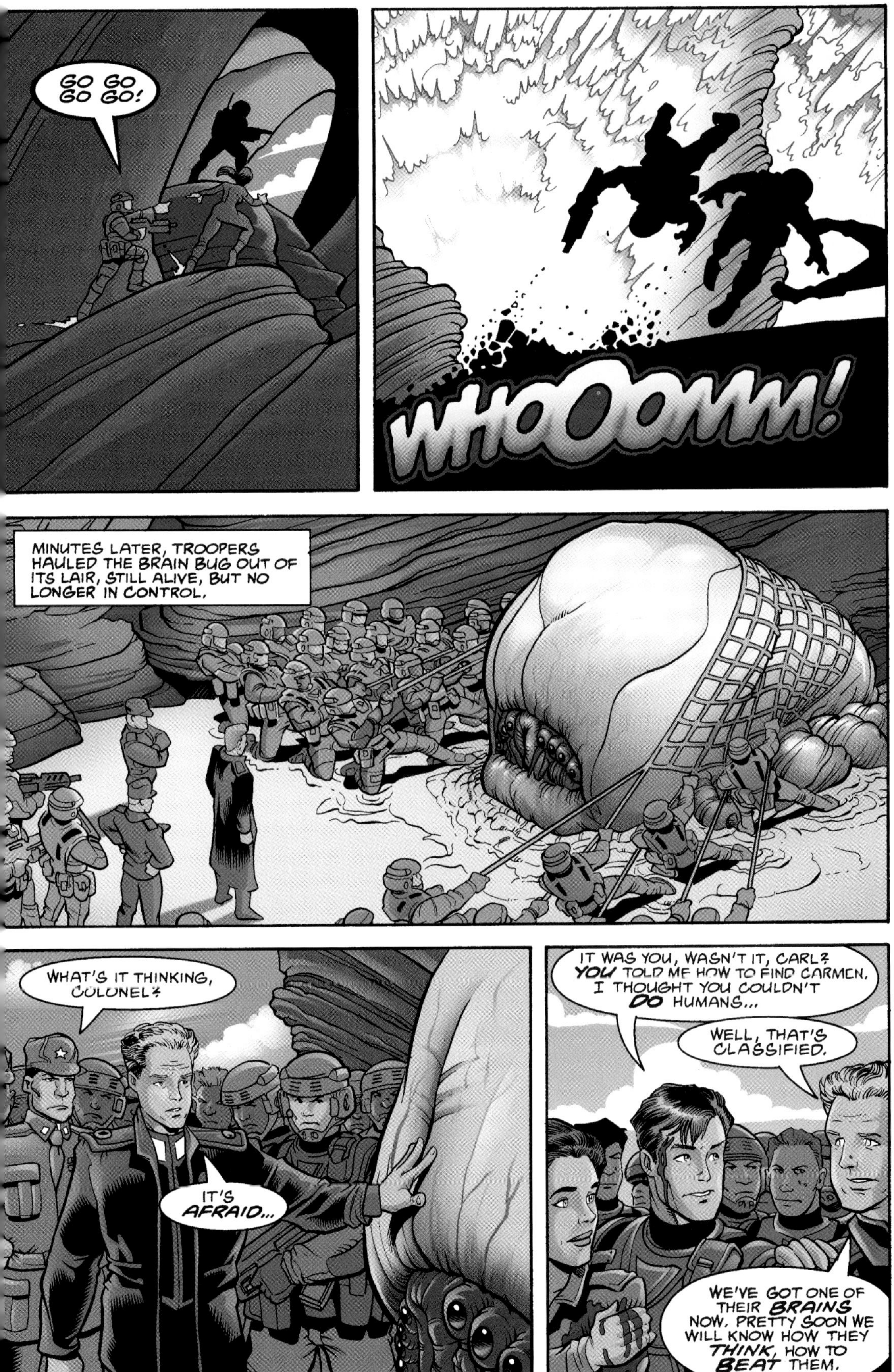
GO GO GO GO!
WHOOOMM!
MINUTES LATER, TROOPERS HAULED THE BRAIN BUG OUT OF ITS LAIR, STILL ALIVE, BUT NO LONGER IN CONTROL.
WHAT'S IT THINKING, COLONEL?
IT'S AFRAID...
IT WAS YOU, WASN'T IT, CARL? YOU TOLD ME HOW TO FIND CARMEN. I THOUGHT YOU COULDN'T DO HUMANS...
WELL, THAT'S CLASSIFIED.
WE'VE GOT ONE OF THEIR BRAINS NOW. PRETTY SOON WE WILL KNOW HOW THEY THINK, HOW TO BEAT THEM.

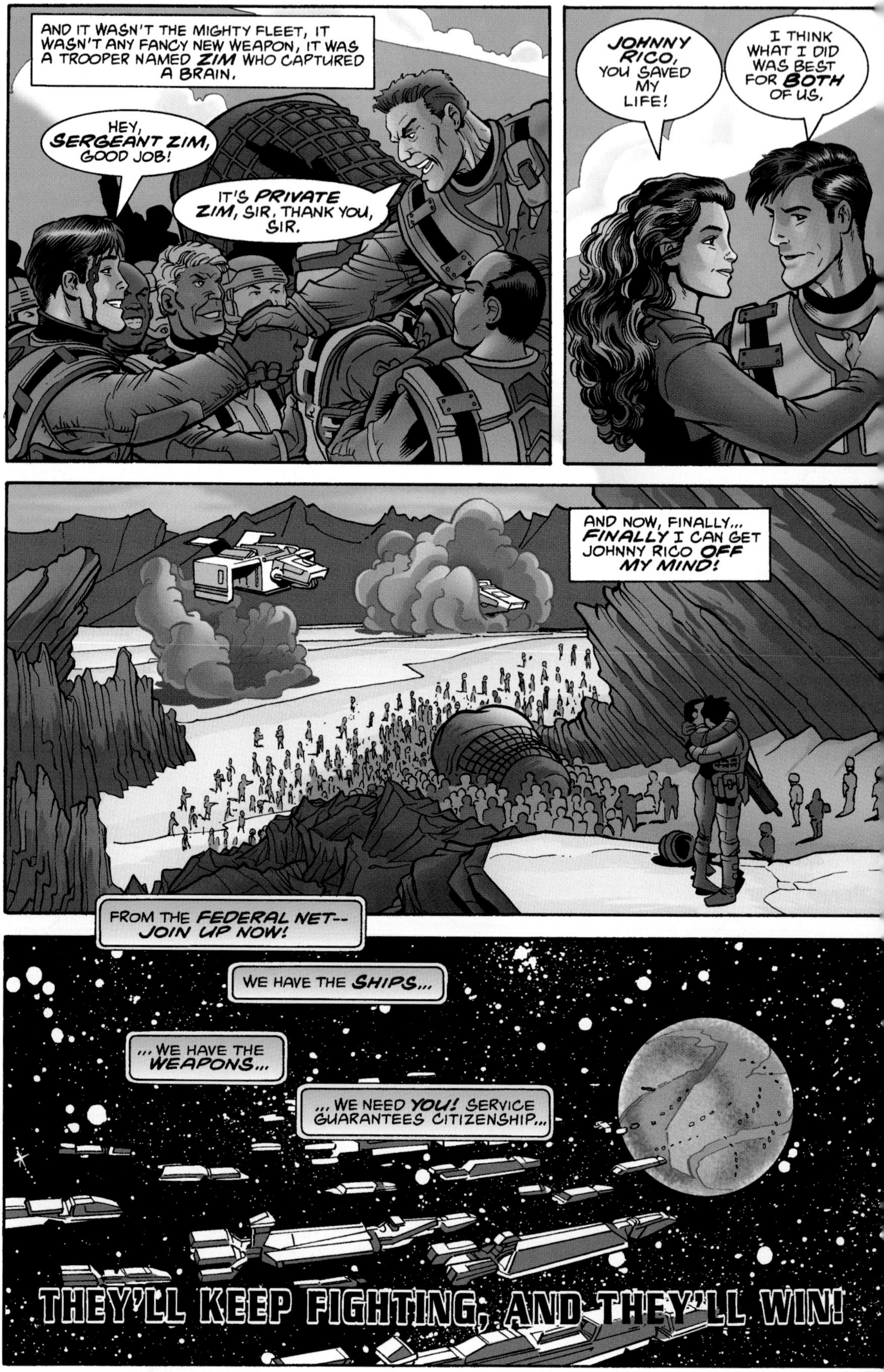
AND IT WASN'T THE MIGHTY FLEET, IT WASN'T ANY FANCY NEW WEAPON, IT WAS A TROOPER NAMED ZIM WHO CAPTURED A BRAIN.
HEY, SERGEANT ZIM, GOOD JOB!
IT'S PRIVATE ZIM, SIR. THANK YOU, SIR.
JOHNNY RICO, YOU SAVED MY LIFE!
I THINK WHAT I DID WAS BEST FOR BOTH OF US.
AND NOW, FINALLY... FINALLY I CAN GET JOHNNY RICO OFF MY MIND!
FROM THE FEDERAL NET-- JOIN UP NOW!
WE HAVE THE SHIPS...
...WE HAVE THE WEAPONS...
...WE NEED YOU! SERVICE GUARANTEES CITIZENSHIP...
THEY'LL KEEP FIGHTING, AND THEY'LL WIN!

Preliminary drawing for *Insect Touch*

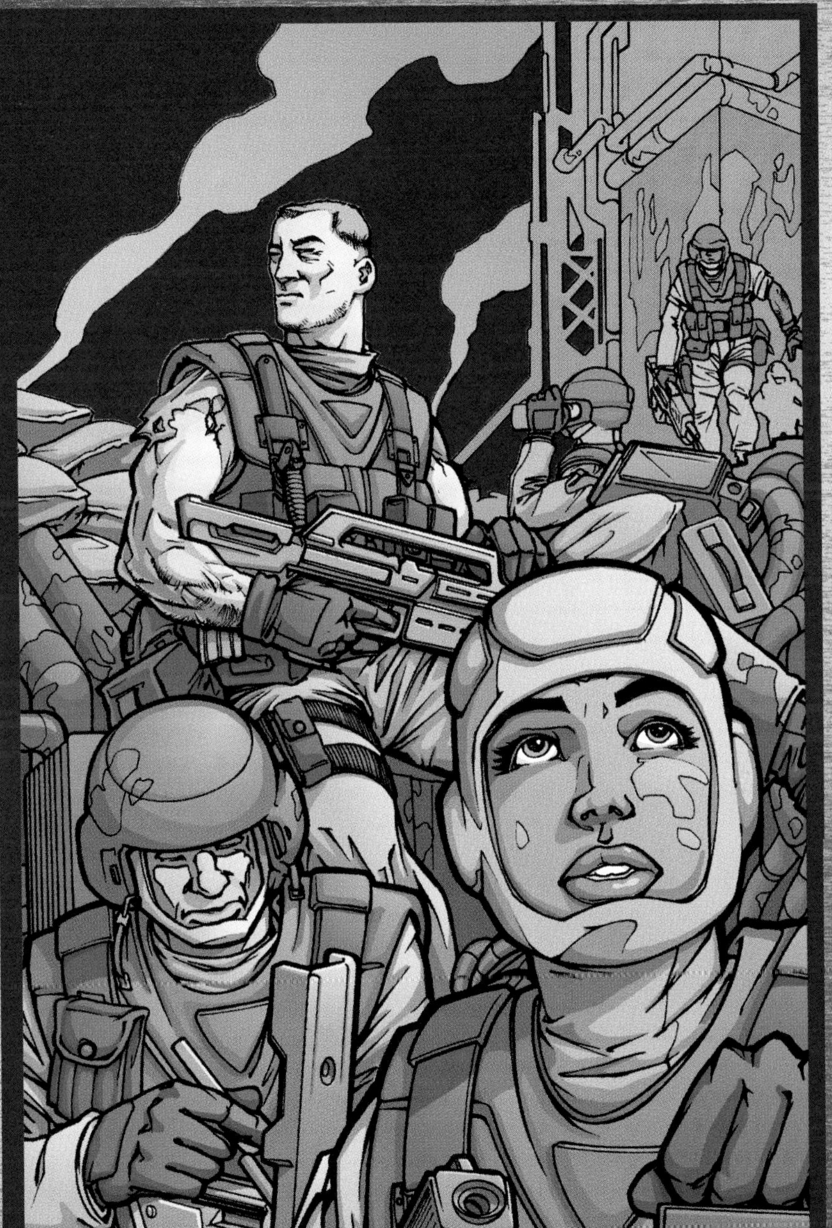

by Davide Fabbri and Paolo Parente

***Troopers* "color test."** This image was colored in several different styles, with this style winning out. The colorists have integrated contrasting colors and downplayed "airbrushing" to better allow the illustration and coloring work to complement one another.

This illustration shows the troopers carrying the weapons and wearing the uniform style from the *Starship Troopers* film — but colored in the Mars camouflage pattern used in *Insect Touch*.

Here are some of Davide Fabbri and Paolo Parente's preliminary drawings for the *Insect Touch* series.

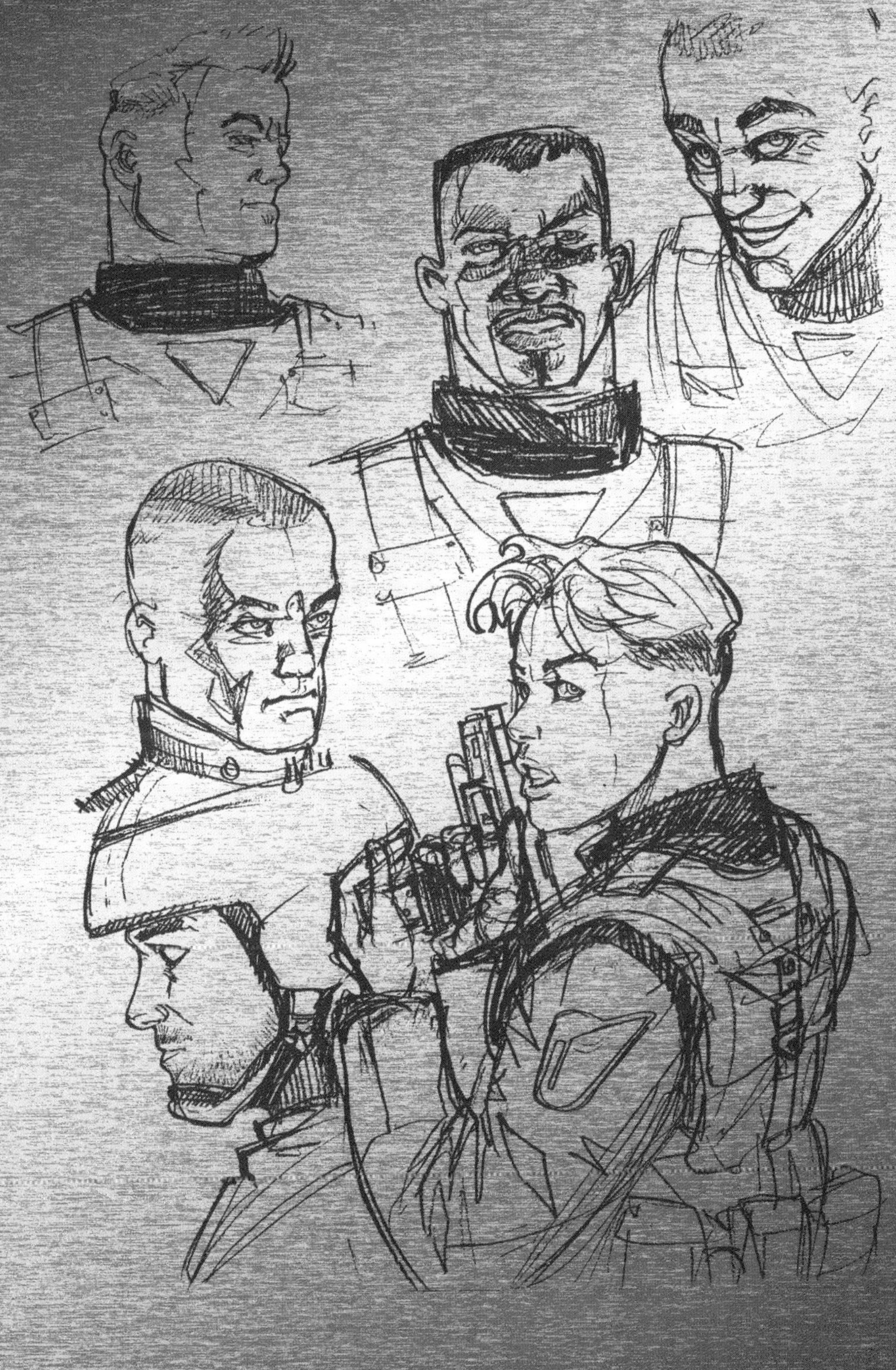

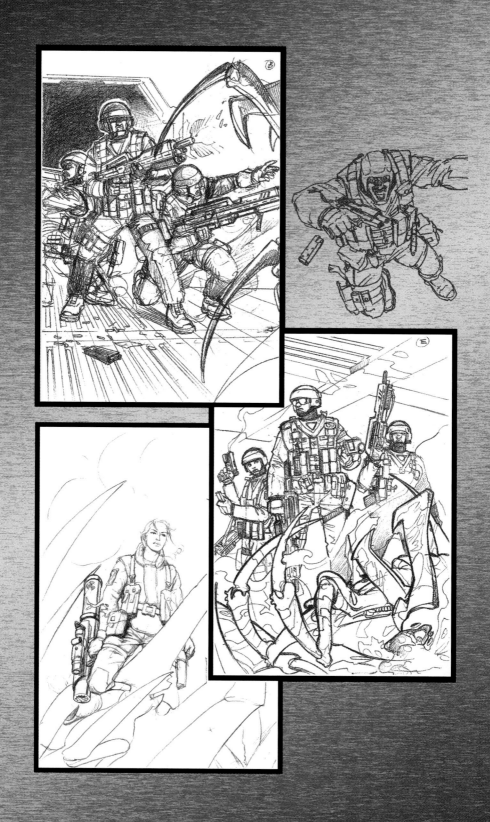

Sketches of weapons and issue one cover

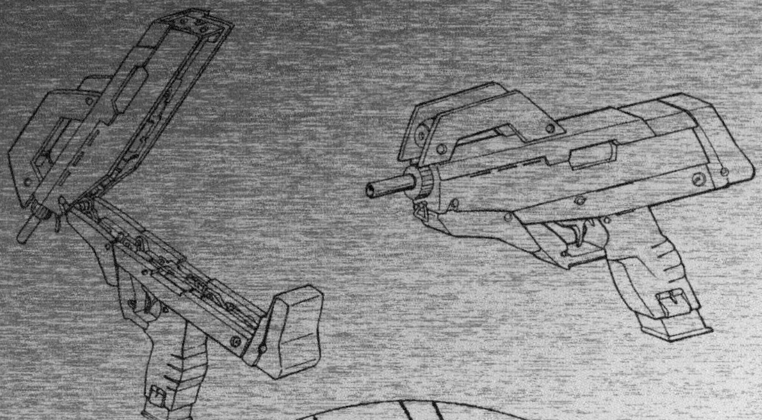

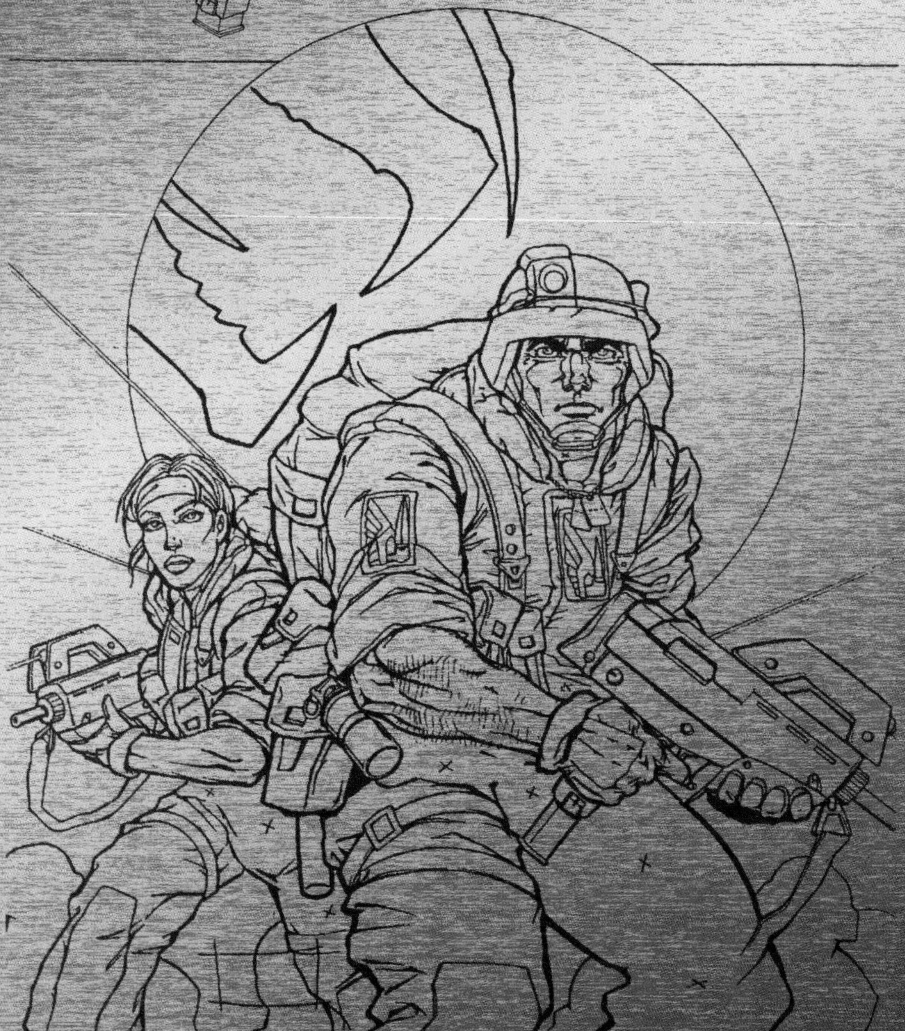

Troopers' Mars camouflage uniform and gun design

The trick here was to create a look for a time thirty years before the events in the *Starship Troopers* film — a "retro" look set in the far-flung future.

STARSHIP TROOPERS
THE MOVIE ™

THE FOLLOWING PAGES CONTAIN
PHOTOS FROM THE TRISTAR MOTION
PICTURE. IF YOU HAVEN'T SEEN IT,
GRAB A COPY AT YOUR LOCAL
VIDEO STORE AND PREPARE
TO BE INFILTRATED!